The Rule of Violence

D1561991

Over much of its rule, the regime of Hafez al-Asad and his successor Bashar al-Asad deployed violence on a massive scale to maintain its grip on political power. In this book, Salwa Ismail examines the rationalities and mechanisms of governing through violence. In a detailed and compelling account, Ismail shows how the political prison and the massacre, in particular, developed as apparatuses of government, shaping Syrians' political subjectivities, defining their understanding of the terms of rule and structuring their relations and interactions with the regime and with one another. Examining ordinary citizens' everyday life experiences and memories of violence across diverse sites, from the internment camp and the massacre to the family and school, *The Rule of Violence* demonstrates how practices of violence, both in their routine and spectacular forms, fashioned Syrians' affective life, inciting in them feelings of humiliation and abjection, and infusing their lived environment with dread and horror. This form of rule is revealed to be constraining of citizens' political engagement, while also demanding of their action.

Salwa Ismail is Professor of Politics with reference to the Middle East at the School of Oriental and African Studies, University of London. Her research focuses on everyday forms of government, urban governance and the politics of space. She has published on Islamist politics and on state–society relations in the Middle East and is the author of both *Rethinking Islamist Politics: Culture, the State and Islamism* (2003) and *Political Life in Cairo's New Quarters: Encountering the Everyday State* (2006). Her recent publications have appeared in *Comparative Studies in Society and History*, *Third World Quarterly*, *Social Research* and *Contemporary Islam*.

Cambridge Middle East Studies

Editorial Board

Charles Tripp (general editor)
Julia Clancy-Smith
F. Gregory Gause
Yezid Sayigh
Avi Shlaim
Judith E. Tucker

Cambridge Middle East Studies has been established to publish books on the nineteenth- to twenty-first-century Middle East and North Africa. The series offers new and original interpretations of aspects of Middle Eastern societies and their histories. To achieve disciplinary diversity, books are solicited from authors writing in a wide range of fields including history, sociology, anthropology, political science and political economy. The emphasis is on producing books affording an original approach along theoretical and empirical lines. The series is intended for students and academics, but the more accessible and wide-ranging studies will also appeal to the interested general reader.

Other titles in the series can be found after the Index.

The Rule of Violence

Subjectivity, Memory and Government in Syria

Salwa Ismail

University of London

CAMBRIDGE
UNIVERSITY PRESS

CAMBRIDGE
UNIVERSITY PRESS

University Printing House, Cambridge CB2 8BS, United Kingdom

One Liberty Plaza, 20th Floor, New York, NY 10006, USA

477 Williamstown Road, Port Melbourne, VIC 3207, Australia

314–321, 3rd Floor, Plot 3, Splendor Forum, Jasola District Centre, New Delhi – 110025, India

79 Anson Road, #06-04/06, Singapore 079906

Cambridge University Press is part of the University of Cambridge.

It furthers the University's mission by disseminating knowledge in the pursuit of education, learning and research at the highest international levels of excellence.

www.cambridge.org
Information on this title: www.cambridge.org/9781107032187
DOI: 10.1017/9781139424721

© Salwa Ismail 2018

This publication is in copyright. Subject to statutory exception and to the provisions of relevant collective licensing agreements, no reproduction of any part may take place without the written permission of Cambridge University Press.

First published 2018

Printed in the United Kingdom by TJ International Ltd. Padstow Cornwall

A catalogue record for this publication is available from the British Library.

Library of Congress Cataloging-in-Publication Data
Names: Ismail, Salwa, author.
Title: The rule of violence : subjectivity, memory and government in Syria / Salwa Ismail.
Description: New York: Cambridge University Press, 2018. |
Series: Cambridge Middle East studies
Identifiers: LCCN 2018007398| ISBN 9781107032187 (hardback) |
ISBN 9781107698604 (paperback)
Subjects: LCSH: Syria – Politics and government – 1971–2000. |
Syria – Politics and government – 2000 – | Political violence – Syria –
History – 20th century. | Political violence – Syria – History – 21st century. |
BISAC: POLITICAL SCIENCE / Government / International.
Classification: LCC DS98.4.I86 2018 | DDC 956.9104/22–dc23
LC record available at https://lccn.loc.gov/2018007398

ISBN 978-1-107-03218-7 Hardback
ISBN 978-1-107-69860-4 Paperback

Cambridge University Press has no responsibility for the persistence or accuracy of URLs for external or third-party internet websites referred to in this publication and does not guarantee that any content on such websites is, or will remain, accurate or appropriate.

Contents

Preface

This book undertakes a quest to understand how Syrians' experiences of political violence, both spectacular and routine, became formative of the Syrian polity over the decades of al-Asad rule (1970 onward). My interest in pursuing this quest formed during a period of fieldwork in Syria in 2005. The immediate political context, then, was marked by the suppression of the civil society movement that had emerged in 2000 and took organised expression in a number of discussion forums, in publications such as semi-independent cultural magazines and in artistic works. Although, at the time, the security services were arresting regime critics and silencing opponents, activists maintained hope and showed much personal courage in pressing for political change.

As an observer and participant in public cultural activities that took place in carefully circumscribed spaces of discussion and debate such as the al-Attasi Forum (closed in June 2005), the Journalists' Syndicate Club and the Institut Français du Proche Orient (IFPO), I both witnessed and experienced practices of silencing and of self-censorship. These practices drew the boundaries of what could and could not be said, establishing thresholds of the permissible in speech that were not to be crossed. Paradoxically, however, they gave rise to debate and disagreements among cultural activists and other engaged Syrians precisely about the contours of borders of public discourse and whether they should be observed. Yet many debates and discussions that inevitably veered towards the past, and proffered diagnostics of authoritarian rule to explain the country's political impasse, closed off pathways of memory and of reading the present in light of past experiences of violence, especially extreme violence.

In the course of interviews and conversations, a puzzle arose as much from my interlocutors' silences and ellipses as from their statements and declarations. In personal discussions with a number of politically engaged Syrians – activists in the civil society movement, dissident writers and former political prisoners – the authoritarian past and the dominance of the security services were commonly invoked themes. These themes prefaced the cultural and civil activists' analysis of the constraints on their action and the challenges they faced in their struggle for political opening and accountability. The name of Hafez al-Asad was uttered to invoke, in an almost mythical sense, a figure of dictatorship that pervaded all aspects of political, social and cultural life and stunted political growth. The silence about the Hama violence in my interlocutors' narratives of the not-too-distant political past was expressed in interrupted speech. In private or more intimate accounts of al-Asad's dictatorship, the atrocities committed by the regime in Hama remained largely unspoken – a seemingly absent sign and referent.

During several of the politically oriented cultural gatherings I attended in 2005, I observed the tendency to speak in broad terms about dictatorship and to avoid making reference to specific events and happenings. However, there also appeared to be forms of speech and signification that, while not allegorical, were suggestive of the silenced. This was at times achieved by juxtaposing certain images and narratives of the past and the present in a manner that underscores interruptions and ellipses. For example, one evening, at a gathering at the IFPO in Damascus, prominent filmmaker Nabil El-Malih screened, sequentially, two of his documentaries: one on the pre-Ba'th nationalist figure Fakhri al-Barudi and the other on the industrial pollution of the al-'Asi River during the Ba'th period. The two works, together, spoke to 'the then and the now' – to the then of national aspirations and to the current moment of destruction.

In some sense, the silence about Hama that I encountered in 2005 was made more puzzling by the fact that, at the time, a literary and artistic movement, preoccupied with the work of memory, had acquired some prominence in cultural circles in the country. This work journeyed to the past to retrieve prior selves and banished histories and to give account. In some of these early works of memory, the Hama violence figured in ellipses. Hama was a gap in narratives of the Syrian experience of life under the Hafez al-Asad dictatorship. The puzzle of silence on Hama crystallised for me one afternoon during a visit with a Syrian friend at her home in Damascus. Speaking about the progress of my research, I brought up the puzzle that this silence posed, saying: 'It is as if Hama was forgotten.' To this, she responded: 'We will never forget Hama.' Nothing more was said. My friend did not seek to elaborate. In turn, I refrained from pressing for an explanation, apprehending a closure in her brief response and immediate silence. The said and unsaid in conversations like this one and in the work of memory, led me to think that the Hama silence is infused with meanings and feelings that are powerfully present in Syrians' lives.

Looking back, I realise that I read, then, somewhat differently than I do now, the conversations and gestures that directed me to pose the question of the role of violence and memories of violence in shaping the Syrian polity. I recall that while I was in Damascus in early 2005, a friend from Aleppo, who was a civil rights activist and a former political prisoner, sent me, by email, a Word file of Manhal al-Sarraj's *Kama Yanbaghi li-Nahr*. I was conscious, then, of the risk he took in doing so (the novel was banned by the authorities). However, I was, perhaps, less conscious of the salience of the gesture he was making in enjoining me to read this novel about Hama.

Works of memory, which began to appear by the mid 2000s, gave a sense of what had been silenced or banished from public speech. These works brought forth ghosts of the past and showed that reckoning with it was urgent. In fictional writings, Syrian novelists sought to tell untold stories, to show that Hama was *nationalised*. Some, like Rosa Yassin Hassan, moved the account to the coastal region, telling a part of the story as it takes root in the unwritten histories of diverse communities. By the late 2000s, literary witnessing offered more untold stories from various regions of Syria. Although many of the writings were banned, they could be acquired in bookstores without much difficulty. Secrets of the past became open secrets.

In certain respects, this book is about an atmosphere, the weight of a particular history and hauntings that live on and inhabit the present. Enmeshed in Syrian narratives, it seeks to understand and assume a responsibility to tell a story, or part thereof – a story of the Syrian present as it has been shaped by a mode of government. Through the narratives of political prisoners, the memories of massacre survivors and the recollections of everyday life experiences of ordinary citizens, this book offers fragments of that story.

Acknowledgements

I undertook ethnographic research in Syria first in 2004–5 and then again in 2010–11. My conversations and interviews with Syrians as part of that work, and extending back to earlier visits commencing in 2002, shaped the approach and the terms of analysis orienting this book. These conversations and interviews opened to me ways of understanding Syrians' experiences of life under the Asad regime.

In the course of different phases of research for this book, I was helped by many Syrians to whom I feel greatly indebted. From the time of our first meeting in Damascus in early 2005, Samar Yazbek extended friendship and solidarity, for which I express my heartfelt thanks. I also thank her for suggesting interviewees and facilitating introductions. I appreciate, also, the conversations and exchanges that I had with Syrian journalists, writers, artists and political activists. In particular, I want to thank Sha'ban Abboud, 'Adnan Abd al-Razzaq, Muhammad Berro, Iyad 'Isa, Khaled Smaysam, Mohammad al-'Attar, Nabil Sliman, Mundhir Badr Hallum, Ossama Mohammed, the late Omar Amiralay, Yassin al-Haj Saleh, Selim Khayr Beyk, Anwar Badr, Ahmad al-Fawwaz, Subhi Hadidi, Samir Su'aifan, Khaled Khalifa, Mundhir Masry, Hassan Abbas, 'Imad Houriyya, Hala Mohammed, Bara' al-Sarraj, Rula Asad, 'Amer Matar, Karim al-Afnan, Nart Abd al-Karim, Shadi Abu Fakhr, 'Ola Ramadan, Fadi Fawwaz Haddad, Omar al-As'ad, Majd Sharbaji, Lina al-Shawaf and Mohamed Mahmoud (Hamoudy). I am indebted to Manhal al-Sarraj for generosity and openness during extended conversations with her about life in Hama in the 1970s and 1980s. I thank Khaled al-Khani for extending permission for my use, on the book cover, of an image of one of his extraordinary paintings.

There are many other Syrians who assisted me in various ways during my fieldwork in Syria and to whom I am very grateful. For reasons of safety, I am not able to name them. Some introduced me to their neighbourhoods in Damascus and others helped me gain an understanding of workshop production cycles and conventions of commerce in the *suq* of al-Hamidiyya. In 2011, while in Damascus,

I connected with a group of youth activists who were involved in the coordination of protests. Through them, I learnt much about trajectories of activism. More than that, however, I came to understand something about the courage and spirit of defiance that fueled the Uprising. In this respect, I owe a special debt of gratitude to 'Amer Matar. After I left Syria at the end of May 2011, I established further contacts with youth activists and had ongoing correspondence with some of them through to late 2011 and early 2012. I want to express my gratitude for their willingness to respond to my questions at a very difficult time. I am also thankful to the activists I interviewed in Beirut in 2015. I extend special thanks to the Syrian women in Shtura, Lebanon, for sharing with me stories of their past life in Syria. I am grateful to Samar Yazbek, Yazid Sayyigh, Jamil Mouawad and Jessy Nassar for their help with introductions to Syrians in Beirut, to Karim al-Afnan for assisting with contacts in Amman and to Jonas Skovrup Christensen for locating relevant research material.

I am indebted to colleagues at the School of Oriental and African Studies (SOAS), and elsewhere, for various forms of support during the writing of this book. Charles Tripp read the full manuscript and provided thoughtful and detailed comments and suggestions. I am very thankful for his probing questions about regime violence and its objectives. In the course of writing, I enjoyed and benefitted from conversations with Dina Khoury, Humeira Iqtidar, Banu Bargu and Hedi Viterbo. I am especially thankful to Hedi for his critical and helpful comments on several chapters of the manuscript. The manuscript benefitted immensely from the careful reading and thoughtful questions and suggestions of two anonymous readers at Cambridge University Press. I express my appreciation to SOAS colleagues Reem Abou-El-Fadl and Fiona Adamson for their collegiality and support. I have been fortunate to have worked with PhD students who share my interest in everyday practices of government and in political subjectivities, in particular, Hania Sobhy, Merve Kutuk and Veronica Ferreri. I am thankful to them for many thought-provoking conversations.

My thanks go to my friends Zuleikha Abu-Risha, Kamel Mahdi and Nelida Fuccaro for their help and camaraderie. I am grateful to Zuleikha for first introducing me to the city of Damascus and its cultural life. I recall with wonderment our walks through Suq al-Suf and al-Buzuriyyah, and our drives, in 2005, through villages of the coastal region.

I thank Raymond Hinnebusch, Marc Lynch, Jakob Skovgaard-Petersen, Helmut Krieger and Magda Seewald for their invitations to take part in events on Syria or to present on parts of this work at their respective institutions. I extend special thanks to Sindre Bongstad for his invitation to Oslo to present, in 2012, on various aspects of my work, including on the Uprising in Syria.

The field research for this book was made possible, in part, by two Economic and Social Research Council (ESRC) research awards (Res-000-27-0007 and Res-062-23-2283). During my two extended stays in Damascus, the Institut Français du Proche Orient (IFPO) hosted me as a research associate. I thank the staff at the Institut for their logistical support. I am grateful to Marigold Acland, former editor at Cambridge University Press, who expressed interest in the idea for this book. I also express my thanks to Maria Marsh, current editor, for her interest in the work and for all her efforts in seeing it through the publication process. I also appreciate Cassi Roberts' unfailing attentiveness to various aspects of the book production.

My deepest appreciation is for Brian Aboud who has contributed exceptionally and critically to the making of this book, closely reading and commenting on successive drafts. In so many respects, this work, from its inception, has been a collaborative undertaking with him. I owe its progress and completion to his unwavering support and commitment. Before the completion of this work, sadly, my mother passed away. I am profoundly grateful for the love and inspiration that she gave me throughout my research and writing, and for the anchoring she provided me. It is to her memory that I dedicate this work.

Introduction: The Government of Violence

Over much of its rule, the Syrian regime of Hafez al-Asad and his successor, Bashar al-Asad, used violence on a massive scale, deploying disproportionate physical and destructive force to silence its critics and opponents. Indeed, the regime, as constituted under the Asads, has as its nucleus not only the figures occupying the top rung of political office, but also the apparatuses of violence, in particular the security services and elite military units. This security regime (*al-nizam al-amni*) has consistently acted in ways that convey the message that violence is the primary and organising modality of action in dealing with domestic opposition. The extent and scope of killing and destruction mounted by the security and military forces over approximately forty years of the Asad regime has made manifest a politics of extermination and annihilation as integral to the form of rule in Syria. Rather than betraying an irrational approach to government, this violence is governmental, not in the sense of being merely repressive, but as productive and performative – as shaping regime–citizen relations and forming political subjectivities.

Long before the 2011 Uprising, Syrians lived in anticipation of regime-instigated and perpetrated massacres and of civil war. The fear of civil strife was lodged in their hearts and minds. When spoken about in public, this fear referenced civil wars elsewhere in the region, in particular in Lebanon and Iraq. However, it had other unstated frames of reference and arose out of ordinary Syrians' common understanding that a challenge to or confrontation with the regime would mutate into an internal war – one that would pit regime supporters and opponents against each other. Significantly, the dread and anxiety over an impending outbreak of civil strife found expression in artistic works featuring apocalyptic motifs and themes. Syrians' premonitions and anxieties that a challenge to the regime would result in mass killings and destruction emerged as shared affect and knowledge cultivated over the period of al-Asad rule and, especially, in and from the 'period of the events'. This was a period about which silence was imposed in public discourse, but was recalled in everyday routines of government. The 'period of the events' (*fatrat al-ahdath*), the years between 1976 and 1982, was framed by a duel between the Hafez al-Asad regime and an Islamist insurgent group with ambiguous and not fully determined ties to the Muslim Brotherhood organisation. In effect, the duel was one dimension of a broad confrontation between the regime and oppositional forces across the political spectrum. Cast as traitors and subversives, these forces were subject to either physical elimination or social and political expulsion through long-term imprisonment. During that period, events of spectacular violence, culminating in mass slaughter in Hama in 1982, and routinised violence of incarceration, disappearances and extra-judicial killings, established the pedagogy of governmental violence inscribed through embodied lessons and memories.

In this work, I approach political violence in Syria as a modality of government, ordering and structuring regime–citizen relations. The detention camp and the massacre were and continue to be the two main apparatuses of governmental violence. These apparatuses work not only to contain and neutralise opponents and dissidents, but also to establish conditions of rule and to order citizens' interpretative horizons and understandings of state/regime power.[1] The enactment of this political violence is grounded in the polarisation of the body politic and in the introduction and continual nurturing of a break running through it – the 'us' and 'them' divide. This polarisation should not be reduced to the tropes of sectarianism and religious conflict, although, as the expressions of social processes and socially constructed antagonisms, both would map onto the divisions that are created and nurtured by the apparatuses of political violence. This work is concerned, then, with apparatuses, mechanisms and practices of governmental violence, and the terms in which this violence has been constitutive of political life in Syria.

While in scholarly work on Syria the Hama violence of 1982 is recognised for its brutality and spectacular scale, its character, as constitutive of the body politic, has not been the object of detailed study and investigation. Yet the Hama violence is paradigmatic of the operation of one of the apparatuses of governmental violence, namely, the massacre. The Hama massacres belong to a particular pedagogy of rule that framed citizens' rituals of interaction with agents of the regime in Syria from the early 1980s onward. By virtue of its magnitude and its symbolic placement in the narrative of government and state – being

[1] The entwinement of state institutions and the Asad regime makes it analytically unviable to draw boundaries between the two. By virtue of the incorporation of the security apparatuses into the regime and the latter's control of all governmental institutions, the regime and the state became tightly intermeshed.

characterised as expressive of the logic of sovereignty conceived of as the power of death and life (Agamben 1998; Foucault 2003; Mbembe 2003) – Hama was elevated to the position of master signifier in the language of violence. As a defining element of the pedagogy of rule, Hama is instructive of the powers of the ruler. Hama's place in the imaginary – haunting and haunted – is the unsaid that elicits silences and contests. The spectre of Hama haunted Syrians in a myriad of ways. 'The events of Hama' (*ahdath Hama*), as the massacres and destruction of the city were euphemistically referred to, possess a spectral quality. While many Syrians who were not residents of Hama at the time remained uncertain about the actual scale of death and devastation the city experienced, they nonetheless lived with the knowledge that unspeakable horror had taken place. They also lived with the fear that this horror would recur and that the regime would 'do Hama again'. Indeed, other smaller-scale episodes of violence, such as the security forces' shooting and killing of a number of protesters in al-Suwayda in 2000, were dubbed 'the Hama experience'.[2] At the end of March 2011, when the Syrian security forces put Dar 'a under siege, Syrians feared a repeat of Hama. Hama was thus the prototype of an apparatus of government.

The memory of Hama remains a difficult cipher of the Syrian polity. When the 2011 Uprising broke out, recollections of the 1982 violence in Hama rose to the fore from the recesses of consciousness, defying their banishment from public speech during the previous thirty years. The imposed closure had rendered mute the significations invested in these memories. This does not mean that they were marginal to Syrians as subject-citizens. Indeed, the silencing and silence had their own signifying powers. Violence, as lived and remembered, extends the performances and performative acts of past violence into the present in the form of bodily inscriptions and cognitive and affective dispositions incited in acts of recall and in acts of omission, in the remembering and in the forgetting.

As a case of spectacular violence of rule, the Hama massacres and destruction have their specificity as well as their commonalities with other instances of mass annihilation and ruination. They are approached,

---

[2] The protests, which occurred in November 2000, were spurred on by a conflict between Bedouin sheep-herders and Druze farmers in al-Suwayda, in which a Druze youth was killed. However, they developed into a general confrontation with the security and military forces who fired on the protesters with live ammunition. One of my interviewees, a former resident of al-Suwayda, recalls the threats that were directed at al-Suwayda in statements to the effect that 'al-Suwayda was not dearer [to the regime] than Hama'. According to my interviewee, these threats were spoken about in the city municipality offices (interview, Paris, September 2015).

herein, to elucidate different facets of the massacre as an apparatus in the assemblage of practices of rule – an assemblage that includes the political prison as a space for the unmaking and remaking of political subjects. In approaching violence as a modality of government, I seek to bring into political studies an analytical vocabulary that would problematise the concept of violence, beyond conflict-centred perspectives, in terms of the techniques and rationalities of violence. In such a vocabulary and inventory of terms, I also seek to develop the analytics of horror as a framework through which to comprehend the cognitive, affective and symbolic work of violence.[3] In conjunction with developing 'horror' as an analytical construct for examining and understanding political violence, I draw on the psychoanalytic account of fear and bewilderment as advanced in Freudian analytics of the uncanny. I extend and recast the use of these concepts by means of an enquiry into their sociological grounding and their reconfiguration in and through governmental practices. My recourse to this vocabulary is guided by what I see as the necessity of examining extreme forms of violence as both emplotted and performative enactments that are generative of affectivity in the subjects drawn into the orbit of violent acts and performances as victims, witnesses and perpetrators. I extend this observation to assert that the affects generated through violence are the object of government and the terrain of making and unmaking political subjects.

The Place of Violence in Government

In the project of government promoted by the Ba'thist Asad regime, we find, in many respects, biopolitical objectives and rationalities expressive of the will to improve as discussed by Li (2007). As with other developmentalist and modernising regimes, a central objective of government was the management and improvement of the life of the population. Grand designs of modernisation, as exemplified by schemes such as the construction of the Euphrates Dam and the building of Thawra City, carried the stamp of such a project of the remake of subjects and nature. An early study by Raymond Hinnebusch (1989) outlined in great detail the contours of the modernisation enterprise in agriculture. Technicalisation, specialisation and rationalisation as the armatures of modern government were adopted as techniques and strategies for the actualisation of designs of improvement. The schemes of government entailed infrastructural build-up that comprised, among other things,

---

[3] As will be discussed below, I draw on Cavarero's (2011) exploration of the analytic uses of horror.

agricultural cooperatives, schools of agronomy and agricultural direction boards. Notwithstanding shortcomings and failures, the targets of abundance and welfare and the strategies deployed in their pursuit confirm and conform to a preoccupation with the fostering of life.

At the same time, this politics of life coexisted with a politics of killing, internment and incarceration on a mass scale. In fact, the entwinement of the two facets of political government and their merger was given a crude enactment and symbolisation in the coordination of events which combined such activities as the inauguration of dams or the distribution of seeds with mass rallies organised in support of the military assaults on Aleppo in 1980 and on Hama in 1982 (*al-Ba'th*, 19 March 1980; *Syria Today*, 21 February 1982). The merger of festivities of life and rallies of death, more than being mere expressions of sinister manipulation, conveyed the interconnections of governmental power and sovereign power. Alongside the school and the agricultural cooperative, the prison and the massacre arose as apparatuses of rule that instanced the state and regime. Within these apparatuses, the citizens' bodies were the sites on which the regime and state were produced. As noted for other political settings such as Ireland and Colombia, political messages are communicated through bodies traversed by violence (Feldman 1991, 8; Rojas and Tubb 2013; Uribe 2004a). In Syria, the tortured body of the prisoner, the mutilated body of the massacre victim and the humiliated body of the ordinary citizen bear, in interrelated ways, the imprints of governmental violence. At the same time, as Allen Feldman (1991, 7) observes, fashioned into a political artefact by violence, the subject, whose body is the object of such violence, is no less a political agent than the authors of that violence.

Neither the political prison nor the massacre existed on the margin of the polity in Syria. For instance, rather than being merely the negation of political life, the political prison/internment camp developed as a space for the undoing of the political subject and as a referent for the general population's understanding of the terms of rule. Structurally and operationally, the political prison is continuous with the polity: disciplining and remaking recalcitrant subjects while being a spectre for the purposes of instruction of the wider population.[4] Syrian dissident and former political prisoner Yassin al-Haj Saleh (2011a) rightly argues that the political

---

[4] In testimonies and diaries of Syrian political prisoners, representatives of the ruler/sovereign feature as violent torturers and interrogators engaged in committing brutalising acts on the body of the prisoner. For example, in a testimonial given by Reda Haddad, who was imprisoned between 1980 and 1995, two high-ranking military officers who tortured him are named. These were Hisham Bakhtiar and Ali Duba (Haddad 2004). Both Bakhtiar and Duba punched, kicked and whipped Haddad during an extended period of interrogation, in which electrocution was also administered to his body (Haddad 2004).

prisoner is not the exception but the general rule (*al-mi'yar al-'am*). Spatial arrangements of the edifice of coercive state agencies and acts of violence in the everyday also established the continuity between the space of the prison and its outside. The ubiquitous presence of security-service kiosks on city street corners, of military checkpoints throughout the Syrian landscape and the routine assaults by security services personnel on ordinary citizens going about their daily chores, blurred the boundaries demarcating the camp and the territory beyond it.

In tandem with the political prison, the massacres committed in Hama in 1982 came to represent a referential genre in the repertoire of horror managed by the regime. The discursive and symbolic coding of this horror, and the affective states and practices it patterned, have all been formative of Syrian political subjectivities. Consider, for example, that within silenced and interrupted narratives of the events of violence, narratives of certain enactments of violence came to represent emblematic memories of the horror that was visited upon Hama: narratives of mutilation linked to looting and particular stories about the severing of fingers, hands and ears to pry off jewellery from the dead bodies. Also emblematic are tales of atrocities that befell prominent community figures: the gouging out of the eyes of a number of city doctors, for instance. Although such narratives were hushed and muted, formalised accounts of the type that have emerged in human rights reports, cataloguing the destruction and killing, were known to Syrians of all generations who lived through the events.

Embodied transcripts of the Hama violence loomed large over the Syrian polity. Some youth activists of the 2011 Uprising reported that during the Uprising members of their families, for the first time, narrated details of the gruesome murder of close relatives during the massacres in 1982 (interviews with exiled activists in Montreal and Beirut, 2015). Parents and close relatives recalled silenced memories in a bid to dissuade the youth in their families from pressing on with their confrontation with the regime. Indeed, early on in the 2011 Uprising, novelist Manhal al-Sarraj (2011), the foremost Syrian literary witness to 'the Hama events', interrogated the ethic of sacrifice orienting the protesters' readiness to risk their lives and face certain death and destruction. The dread and anxiety experienced by al-Sarraj and by the families of youth activists are patterned in relation to the Hama experience. It may be argued that generational factors and related positionality from the events of past violence are factors in how memories of violence were brought to bear on activism during the Uprising. All the same, transcripts of historical horror and atrocities are not without their links with Syrians' experiences of regime practices of government in the everyday.

The type of violence mastered by the Syrian regime in conjunction or coincident with a governmental project aimed at the improvement of the life of the population is expressive of a puzzle of state power. This puzzle is similar, in some respects, to the paradox addressed by Michel Foucault in his analyses of the intersection, in modern times, of biopolitical power – a form of power that concerns itself with the fostering and management of life – with the old sovereign power to kill. In Foucault's account, the politics of mass killing in the modern period, as instanced in the cases of Nazi Germany and Stalinist Russia, finds its rationalisation in a racist discourse which operates by drawing binary divisions between those deemed worthy of life and those who are, by necessity, expendable. Foucault uses 'racism' to refer to the discursive articulations and processes through which political and ideological divisions are rendered into biological ones.[5] Notwithstanding the contentions regarding Foucault's unconventional usage of racism, what is of immediate concern is that a politics of mass killing is, perforce, calibrated through discursive and operational interventions that cleave into the body politic, creating interdependent zones of life and death. The questions that I raise in drawing on Foucault's analyses of the coexistence, in the modern period, of a politics of life and a politics of death, and of the convergence of one with the other, aim at getting a closer view of the politics of killing in Syria and the kind of political life it forges.

While Foucault poses the problem of the politics of killing (thanatopolitics) in the modern period as a paradox, Giorgio Agamben (1998) has countered that the subjugation of life to the powers of death has premodern foundations in the sovereign's power to create bare life – a form of life that is captured in the figure of *homo sacer*, the one who may be killed but not sacrificed.[6] This form of life, which is the product of abandonment and the spaces to which it is relegated, asserts sovereignty and is a precondition of sovereign power. In the modern period, sovereign powers of death materialise in the space of the internment camp, among other sites. Spaces of abandonment and exposure to death, exemplified

---

[5] Mbembe (2003, 17) notes that in the exercise of biopower, '[t]he function of racism is to regulate the distribution of death and to make possible the murderous functions of the state'.

[6] Mitchell Dean (2004) nuances Agamben's thesis on the sovereign power of life by pointing out that different concepts of life are at stake with different expressions of sovereign power. For instance, modern biopower subtends a specific concept of life, one in which it subjugates more aspects and spaces of life, bringing them into zones of indistinction and constituting them as bare life (see Dean for a reading of Agamben along these lines). In Dean's dialogue with both Foucault and Agamben, biopolitics, as a distinct phase of modern sovereignty, extends to capture bare life (*zoē*).

by the camp, emerge in this topography as components of projects of government where political life and bare life become indistinguishable.

Foucault's observations on the politics of killing in the modern period and Agamben's analysis of the production of bare life are relevant to my examination of the nature of political violence, its rationalities and modes of enactment in Syria. I draw insights from both Foucault and Agamben's discussions of the terms in which sovereign power and governmental power articulate, interconnect and merge at certain junctures and in particular spaces. However, I depart from both in interrogating the forms of political life of which governmental violence is productive. My interrogation is predicated on the premise that, in terms of its objects and in terms of its techniques and rationalities, political violence is formative of political subjects, and of terrains of action and resistance. In their analyses of the politics of death as the flipside of biopolitics, both Foucault and Agamben appear to place it outside the realm of political life. As noted by Johanna Oksala (2012, 100), thanatopolitics, for Foucault, is an excess of biopolitics that may be brought into check through liberal interventions.[7] Agamben, on the other hand, by positing that political life and bare life have become indistinguishable in the state of exception, projects a totalising vision of bare life and, as a consequence, negates the possibility of political life in which agency and resistance are understood to be possible. Rather than casting the politics of killing as an excess of biopolitical rationality, or as a negation of political life, I propose to approach political violence as governmental – underpinned by rationalities of rule and formative of terrains of subjectivation and political action.

In conceptualising as governmental the forms that regime violence in Syria takes, I shift the analysis to the affective and cognitive objects of this violence and to its role in fashioning political subjects. The affective and cognitive objects of physical violence appear to be marginal in Foucault's genealogies of disciplinary power and of biopolitics and in Agamben's analyses of the camp. Left out, also, are the social, normative and political terrains upon which techniques of body-centred violence and

---

[7] Mbembe (2003, 14) observes that Foucault's conception of biopolitics is not sufficient to take account of a form of sovereignty that has as its central project the '*generalized instrumentalization of human existence, and the material destruction of human bodies and populations*' (italics in the original). The centrality of destruction and killing to this project, Mbembe (2003, 27–30) proposes, represents a particular kind of politics – necropolitics. The forms of subjugation of life to the power of death include state siege, the generalisation of slaughter as the dominant form of war and the creation of zones of human capture that are dehumanising (Mbembe 2003, 40). In these worlds and spaces, Mbembe argues, the power of death rules over life.

emplotted acts of violence are administered and which they aim to alter. The technologies of violence centred on the body, as, for example, in the operations of the camp or the detention centre and the massacre, are no less constitutive of subjects than the modern prison, school, reformatory and psychiatric clinic. Behind the seemingly irrational quality of extreme violence, there are rationalities of rule that act through the subject's affect and cognition, thus revealing violence as a modality of governmental power.

The affect, as material and terrain for practices of government, remains at the margin of studies of governmentality. In a critique of the governmentality literature's tendency to leave out the affect in its theorisations of rationalities of rule, Elaine Campbell (2010) suggests that considerations of what she calls 'emotionalities of rule' would permit a more inclusive perspective on governmental technologies and apparatuses that 'propose and suppose particular ways of *feeling* about the world' (Campbell 2010, 39, italics in the original). Campbell points out that, in design, governmental strategies do not aim only at inculcating, in the subject, certain ways of thinking. Rather, governmental strategies aim, also, at engendering ways of feeling in the subject. I share Campbell's concern with the need to bring the affect into the investigation of rationalities of rule. Additionally, I share the view (Warwick 2004) that power works on the subject's psychic and affective capacities. It does not only bring them into effect.

Understanding violence as a form of governmental power underlines practices and strategies that have as their objective and outcome not only to harm the body, the mind and the affect but, also, to reconstruct, shape, discipline and normalise the subject of government. Practices of violence that generate the affects of humiliation, abjection and horror should not be dismissed as premodern or archaic, rather they should be examined in terms of rationalities aimed at making and unmaking political subjects. The operation of this governmental power unfolds on the basis of knowledge and assumptions about affect, emotions and cognition and about their sociality (i.e. their cultural embeddedness and their intersubjectively produced meanings). I illustrate the workings of these assumptions and practices by looking at body-centred violence that elicits feelings of fright and disgust and at emplotted performances of violence that are productive of cognitive uncertainty and uncanny experiences. As I will elaborate below, I use concepts of abjection and the uncanny to develop an understanding of the affective dimensions of governing through violence.[8]

---

[8] This examination of affective governance ties in with a semiotic analysis of violence

The analytics of affect guiding this investigation into Syrians' lived experience of violence draws on elements of varied theorisations that disclose different aspects of affective life and affectivity. In one of the pathways of these theorisations, affect is understood as 'the body's capacity to affect and be affected' (Anderson 2016, 9).[9] From this perspective, affect is a body's charge or emergent disposition that comes forth in encounters, contacts and interactions between and among subjects and between subjects and their lived environment. Affect is expressed in embodied feelings and emotions which are mediated by configurations of other forces that include, among other things, social histories, individual experiences, cultivated knowledge, memories and prior encounters (Anderson 2016). The attention to the social and historical mediation of affective experiences aligns with an understanding of affect as socially embedded, patterned and enacted in practice, as suggested by Margaret Wetherell (2012). Wetherell (2012, 78) proposes that it is in the course of situated social interaction that affect takes shape and is enacted in embodied practice. In this respect, affect lends itself to being approached in terms of patterned practice.[10] The patterning of affective practice occurs through repeated encounters and interaction, and is inflected by historical, social and cultural materialities (Wetherell 2012, 77–8, 89). By virtue of its social and historical imbrication and its processual emergence in interaction and encounters, affect is transpersonal and collective (Anderson 2016, 102). By the same token, affective charges are not solely or fully located in a subjective interiority, but are produced within and in relation to a given environment (Anderson 2016; Navaro-Yashin 2012, 21–7; Wetherell 2012, 78). As is the case with the affective force of encounters between subjects, the affective charge of the environment is sensed by the subjects in mediated terms. In its subjective and social manifestations, affective life constitutes a terrain of action and of governmental intervention.

---

as meaning-producing practices (meanings that emerge in relation to other signifying practices).

[9] This conceptualisation of affect is formulated in Gilles Deleuze's and Felix Guattari's work in conversation with Baruch Spinoza (Anderson 2016, 78).

[10] Wetherell's approach to the affect aligns with Ian Burkitt's (2014) analysis of emotions as patterned relations, expressive of socially embedded responses to the world. The terms of analysis that such an approach entails also resonate with earlier writings by sociologists and anthropologists of emotion. For example, Leavitt (1996) advanced a construct of emotions as socialised embodied feelings that are called forth in recurrent social experiences. Similarly, Abu Lughod and Lutz (1990) underscored that emotions are socially situated and hence are interpreted and appraised in relation to contextual factors.

These multiple dimensions of affect come into view in, while also illu-minating, aspects of Syrians' lived experiences as both subjects of vio-lence and of governmental practices that are constitutive elements of their affective life. At the level of subjectivity, a myriad of encounters with agents of the regime in various spheres of everyday life are gen-erative of a constellation of affects in the subject, for example, abjection and precarity. Further, mediating collectively shared affective practices and conditions are socio-political histories – histories that encompass events of spectacular violence such as the Hama massacres, as well as the routine violence that structures everyday interaction between the Syrian regime and ordinary citizens. This affectivity of rule through violence animates the environment and comes to be shared collectively, forming structures of feelings, organised in terms of abjection, precarity, dread, fear and horror.

Violence as Emplotted Horror: The Body and Affective Government

My interrogation of the affective structure of body-centred and performa-tive violence draws and builds on the analytics of horror.[11] Horror, as a construct, helps crystallise how performative and embodied dimensions of violence operate on and through the affect by calling forth aversive emotions and affects such as fear, disgust, humiliation and abjection in the subject to whose body violence is applied. Importantly, these affective dispositions and practices are also elicited in the subjects positioned as witnesses, spectators and bystanders. Forms of embodied violence exceed the body, extending, in their disciplining and reordering of the subject's world, to the affect and cognition.[12]

In theorisations of political violence, the concept of 'terror' is used to analyse both a style of government that rests on fear as well as the threat of violence or an action or activity aiming at inducing fear. Yet the

---

[11] Debrix and Barder (2012) argue that new forms of violence that exceed any calibrated calculus of life and death require an analytical move beyond biopolitics. They propose an approach that takes the concept of horror, as articulated by Adriana Cavarero (2011), as expressive of a new political ontology that defies rationalisation and representation. Although I deploy 'horror', also drawing on Cavarero, I do not subscribe to an analytics of horror that ultimately negates its governmental functions.

[12] In her seminal work *The Body in Pain*, Elaine Scarry (1985) advanced the view that body pain triggered by acts of body-centred violence, such as torture, unmakes the person. This unmaking is purposive, being the desired outcome of torture. Scarry sees the unmaking as conducive to the structures and objectives of interrogation. The softening of the subject through bodily torture aims to induce confession, surrender of self and subjugation. While, in interrogation, torture may be used in pursuit of superfluous infor-mation, its bodily effects – the wounding of flesh, the breaking of bones – are a prelude to the breaking of spirit and soul.

concept of 'horror' remains peripheral to these theorisations.[13] In one of the few works dedicated to exploring the politics of body-centred forms of violence, Adriana Cavarero introduced the concept of 'horror' as distinct from 'terror'. Cavarero draws the analytical distinction with reference to the affective and existential terrain of each. For instance, there are certain emotive dimensions of fear that are characteristic of horror. Among these, she points to disgust as a specific affective response to violence that offends the integrity of the body. Cavarero makes the point that part of the ontological human condition is the upholding of the dignity of the body through the preservation of its fundamental and necessary unity.[14] Dismemberment and other body-undoing acts of violence offend the ontological dignity of the body in its very being as a singular body (Cavarero 2011, 8). Horror is incited or called forth through the destruction of the figural unity of the body. Cavarero argues that death or the termination of life, in itself, does not offend the dignity of the body, as its figural unity is preserved until burial. However, in line with Freudian psychoanalytic explanations of certain ingrained human fears, Cavarero states: 'What is unwatchable above all, for the being that knows itself irremediably singular, is the spectacle of disfigurement, which the singular body cannot bear' (Cavarero 2011, 8).

The quality of excess in body-centred violence is often viewed as irrational and senseless. However, I argue that by considering the affective and cognitive states that horror generates in the subjects of rule, we can discern its rationalities and strategies of government. Acts involving intimately carried-out body destruction – as in the severing of a body part using a sword or knife with the perpetrator present – elicit a disorienting fear and a sentient horror in which the visual and intimate articulate. Intimacy could be considered as a defining feature of violence that falls into the category of horror. This is so because horror rests on a visual display of the repugnant and also on an imagining of the spectre of the repugnant and grotesque. Moreover, this is an imagining that threatens to engulf the self, positioned as an at-risk subject or spectator drawn into the conflict by virtue of being there, witnessing or watching.

---

[13] For an insightful discussion of the 'rhetorical functions' of horror in the writings of key liberal thinkers, see Anker (2014).

[14] There are resonances of Cavarero's propositions in the perspective on horror offered by Talal Asad (2007) in his exploration of western liberal responses to suicide bombing. Asad defines horror as a felt state of being incited by forms of body-centred violence that reveal and confront the subject with the precarity of human identity and of human ways of life (Asad 2007, 68–9). Asad's account is particularly centred on the sites and senses in which modern western subjects' sensibilities about identity have been invested.

Further, theatricality, staging, performance and the meanings articulated through them are all integral to the governmental practices of horror-type violence. Specifically, the generation and patterning of bewilderment, uncertainty and fear in the subjects of rule should be approached as a strategy for managing situated practices and relations in the context of violence.

To develop the analytics of horror in the study of political violence, I suggest that the interpretative codes of fictional horror furnish us with tools for illuminating the workings of real-life horror.[15] They do so in a number of respects that should not be conflated with the clichéd idea that reality imitates fiction, or the inverse. Real events of political violence, through staging and schemes of narrativisation, are enacted in a manner productive of horror. As argued by Feldman (1991, 14), 'political violence is a genre of "emplotted" action'. In their organisation and configuration, acts of violence unfold a narrative structure, open to interpretation and to further semiotic investment. Studies of horror fiction, in particular in the medium of film, offer schemes of reference for reading and interpreting real horror. For example, these studies draw attention to elements of the narrative structure that generate the feelings of fear and dread in the spectator, underscoring how particular film conventions introduce chaos and create disorientation in the viewer.[16] In a similar vein, emplotted acts of political violence pattern and order affects of horror (e.g. fear, disgust, dread and bewilderment).

---

[15] The cinematic genres of horror and film noir offer us a lens for consideration of the affective states that real-life horror elicits. Depending on spectatorship, horror – treated as a cinematic genre – is defined as the 'overwhelming dread-and-disgust that initially puts someone or something else at the centre of assault' (Nelson 2003, 84). As J. S. Nelson (2003, 84) puts it, 'horror happens at first to us as onlookers'. Explaining further, Nelson states: 'We see atrocities that mock any possibility of goodness, truth, or beauty to remain unmixed with monstrosity.' Later, we become cognisant that 'the source of perversion is turning to get us' (Nelson 2003, 84). At a symbolic level, generic horror works to create settings of the fantastic, monstrous and demonic, where conditions of intelligibility are negated (Nelson 2003, 85).

[16] Film noir conventions place darkness at the heart of the narrative and events. Indeed, techniques of photography, lighting, sequencing and flashback create disorientation in the viewer, introducing destabilisation with narratives of disorder and uncertainty, 'juxtaposing the bizarre and the fantastic' with 'realist snapshots' (Palmer 1997, 58). The eerie quality of film noir arises from the eruption of 'the disturbing' against 'the normal': 'an atmosphere of ultra-normal periodically ruptured by the weird, the violent and the disturbing' (Palmer 1997, 58). In the face of ambiguity, the spectator experiences film noir as 'anguish and insecurity, a genre of apprehension' (Palmer 1997, 58). It is relevant to note, here, that film noir presents a 'realist'-grounded horror to be distinguished from horror anchored in the fantastic.

The Political Uncanny

In approaching the affects and sensibilities of horror as objects of governmental violence, I draw further insights from psychoanalytic examination of uncanny experiences. The uncanny, in both psychoanalysis and in common usage, is a term that indexes a range of feelings brought forth by a particular event or encounter. These feelings, as well as their triggers, possess the quality of the unexplained. That which gives rise to the uncanny disturbs and unsettles the lines separating the real from the illusory, forcing the subject to question basic common grids of interpretation and explanation. In his essay on the uncanny, Sigmund Freud identifies a range of experiences that arouse in the subject feelings of fright and horror. A shared feature of these experiences is that they discharge a paradoxical sense of the familiar and strange as cohabiting and inhabiting one another. Freud defines the uncanny as 'that species of the frightening that goes back to what was once well known and had long been familiar' (Freud 2003 [1919], 124).[17] Lying at the heart of the uncanny and its frightening character is the encounter with strange objects and events that unaccountably give rise to recognition and familiarity. The uncanny – experienced when confronting the seemingly strange but disturbingly familiar – unsettles and frightens.

Uncertainty and doubt about the true nature of objects, events and others in one's surroundings permeate, as Freud (2003 [1919], 135) observes, the frightening experiences of the uncanny (e.g. 'doubt as to whether an apparently animate object is really alive and, conversely, whether a lifeless object might not perhaps be animate' (E. Jentsch cited in Freud)).[18] A sense of incongruity also arises in certain instantiations of the uncanny, suggesting that something is out of kilter but that the nature of the irregularity or incongruence is not graspable (Frosh 2013, 15). In most, if not all, experiences of the uncanny there is a sense of eeriness, haunting and disturbance in a given order, troubling because the possibility of gaining clarity is radically hampered and ambiguity predominates. In Freud's reflections, such experiences are accounted for with reference to a return of 'primitive beliefs' thought to have been surpassed (e.g. belief in the omnipotence of thought, the existence of ghosts, the return of the dead).[19] Judging the return of disavowed beliefs

---

[17] For an extensive treatment of the concept of the uncanny, see Royle (2003). See also Frosh (2013).

[18] In a related instantiation of the uncanny, Freud observes that it is experienced in relation to death and dead bodies (to the return of the dead, to spirits and ghosts) (see Freud 2003 [1919], 148).

[19] Freud specifies a second category of the uncanny linked to the return of repressed childhood complexes (for example, fear of castration).

as irrational, Freud (2003 [1919], 154) counsels that a simple reality check is all that is needed for the 'rational' subjects to rid themselves of the sense of disturbance and the feeling of being thrown off balance when confronted by objects and conditions that arouse feelings of the uncanny.

The 'reality-testing' formula recommended by Freud to banish uncanny feelings does not, however, accord weight to the social and historical grounds that materially and symbolically invest such feelings. In her exploration of uncanny feelings of hauntings, Avery F. Gordon (2008 [1997], 53) emphasises that hauntings are real, being the manifestations of silenced events and suppressed voices in a given social and material context. Gordon treats the sentiments of hauntings as being firmly situated in the material and social realm not to be exorcised by demonstrating that they are false, but rather, in the first instance, to be acknowledged as *real* and then to be understood in terms of the material and historical relations that make them intrude into 'the world of common reality'. Gordon (2008 [1997], 54) suggests that, ultimately, the uncanny is about the social world rather than the primitive or archaic. I take up Gordon's insights to examine the workings of the uncanny in structures of government and in modes of subjectivation in Syria. The psychic structure of the uncanny is not solely or necessarily that of the return of primitive beliefs or the return of the repressed. Rather, its structure is that of the material political and social world made uncertain by the conditions of horror for which a checking against reality is not possible, or is likely to affirm that the strange and radically implausible is, in fact, present and facing one head-on. Put differently, real horror, in its emplotment and narrative structure, arouses uncanny feelings. It solicits confirmation of the reality of the implausible and shocking, while preserving incongruity and incoherence so as to undermine conditions of intelligibility. I suggest that this out-of-kilter universe, with its interpretative codes and ambiguous and unresolved narratives, could be understood through the optic of the 'political uncanny'.

An example that I use to illustrate the workings of the uncanny in underpinning governance through violence is that of the death and return to life of a citizen, announced and confirmed dead and displayed as such – in the form of a dismembered corpse – and then declared, actually, to be alive. This is the story of Zaynab al-Hosni (to be discussed in greater detail in Chapter 5). The story unfolded over several weeks of late September and early October 2011, during the first year of the Syrian Uprising. Its circumstances were the object of much attention, discussion and debate within and between different forces in the Uprising and among observers worldwide. As this case illustrates, the feelings of ambiguity, uncertainty and fright associated with instances of the uncanny do not arise because primitive beliefs in the return of the dead are thought to find validation. Rather, the feelings come to the fore because of the social and political material reality: a person is announced dead, her corpse is delivered to her family, and then she appears alive once again. The occurrence arouses fear and fright at the secrets behind it and at the unknowability of the identity of the corpse and the unknowability of the corpse's relation to a supposed prior self/subject. The enigma and mystery of the occurrence, along with its featured gruesome violence, disorient and destabilise the subject positioned as spectator or witness. The uncanny feelings are invited by the terms in which violence is staged and performed.

Incited feelings of the uncanny are bound up with the subject's positioning in relation to events and objects on display in the spectacles of rule and violence. Such positioning impels the sense that the subject's vision can only produce awry or skewed views of the scene. Contrary to Slavoj Žižek's (1991) proposition that looking awry could, at times, be the only perspective affording clarity and comprehension – that is, a grasp of the Real – I use the notion of 'the awry' to draw attention to the state of bewilderment and disorientation into which the subject is drawn by virtue of the politics of horror and the structure of the uncanny and by his/her abject condition. The horror genre of governmental violence incites fears that may appear to resonate with the 'primitive uncanny' delineated by Freud and with the abjecting bodily horror described by Julia Kristeva (1982) (e.g. the feelings of disgust triggered in/by encountering bodily decay and death). However, these fears are not the primitive psychic fears of the reality-eluding subject, or of the ontologically abject, but of the subject, politically rendered abject, and of citizens positioned within a structure of rule in which, for those who rule, the uncanny is intrinsic to modes of maintaining a grip on the ruled's affect and cognition.

Violence and the Fashioning of Political Subjectivity

Following studies of subjectivity charted by governmentality scholars (e.g. Rose 1999 [1990]), I take the subject of violent authoritarian rule – rendered abject – as a problem for sociological and political enquiry. My analysis of the formation of political subjectivities in Syria seeks to account for the ways in which violence, as a modality of government, informs understandings of oneself and of others, furnishing an interpretative horizon and structuring modes of acting and interacting with government and with fellow citizens. This line of enquiry aligns with a quest for understanding the nature of governmental power – its reach, scope, agencies and agents – in nationalist authoritarian settings. The notion of political subjectivity builds on a conception of the subject as constructed through power practices and techniques of self-fashioning.[20] Further, as a construct, 'subjectivity' underscores the analytical element of how the individual relates to the world through socially and politically constructed and derived interpretative frames and through self-appraisals. The subject's understanding of herself/himself is mediated by social categories of classification, processes of normalisation and by techniques of individualisation and subjectivation. Political subjectivity, as a concept, is concerned with subject positioning and agency in relation to political government and apparatuses of rule. Political subjectivity is shaped through the subject's position or location in the socio-political order and, relatedly, by his or her experiences of interaction with government, namely the terms and style of being interpellated as a subject-citizen and the displays and discourses articulating and conveying the domain, reach and capacities of the power of the ruler (for example, through glory or acclamation). The political subject acquires understandings of her capacities and constraints in relation to prevailing practices of government.

One of the issues that I revisit in examining political subjectivities in Syria concerns the terms of the conceptualisation of the subject of authoritarian and 'totalitarian' polities. For example, typifications of subjectivities formed in these polities have long animated scholarship on Soviet politics. Indeed, scholars of Stalinist Russia speak of 'a Stalinist subject' (see Fitzpatrick 1999). Conceptions of subjectivity in 'totalitarian' polities, in particular in the Soviet Union under Stalin, were drawn around the idea of 'the Soviet man' as a particular kind of subject. This

---

[20] This understanding of subjectivity draws on Foucault's analyses of processes of subject formation. Foucault problematises the notion of the subject as ontologically 'prior' and 'self-founded' as developed in the history of western political thought (see Strozier 2002, 13). In contradistinction to the idea of the already existing subject, Foucault posits the subject as an effect of power relations that are dispersed across heterogeneous apparatuses, institutions and social fields. In other words, the subject comes into being as an effect of discourses and of practices of power and knowledge. In his genealogy of forms of power in the modern period, Foucault showed that disciplinary practices dispersed across prisons, mental asylums and schools are productive of modern subjectivities in western liberal societies. This perspective on subject formation has been critiqued on the grounds that it incorporates several kinds of omissions. Most notable is the charge that it negates the possibility that the subjects of power engage in resistance against their subjectivation. This critique, however, does not address an important aspect of subjectivation as articulated by Foucault, namely that it is through subjectivation that the subject emerges, not merely as a bundle of regulations and restrictions, but also as an embodied agent with capacities for being and acting. Scrutinising the implications of the processes of subjectivation (as discussed by Foucault) for conceptualising subversion of the subject's subordination, Judith Butler (1997) identifies the acting out of subjectivity, or the performativity of the subject, as a reiterative moment imbued with possibilities for enacting difference.

construct was formulated against the background of assumptions about liberal agency conceived as the expression of an autonomous self, acting independently of external constraints. The Stalinist subject emerged in this scholarship as the antithesis of the liberal subject and as its negation (the liberal subject being the true and worthy subject of modernity) (see Krylova 2000). The notion of the Stalinist subject has been critiqued for homogenising and abstracting forms of agency and subject formation. Recent studies have drawn portraits of other types of political subjects, ones that were neither indoctrinated nor followed the leader blindly (see Chatterjee and Petrone 2008; Edele 2007).

Extending this critical scholarship on practices of rule in authoritarian polities, and focusing on the study of the role of rhetoric in the Syrian system of rule, Lisa Wedeen (1999) sketches the Syrian political subject as a dissimulating subject, that is, a subject acting 'as if' he/she believed the ruler's proclamations. In Wedeen's account, the public spectacles of leader adulation along with the regime's rhetoric constituted a disciplinary discursive regime productive of the dissimulating subject. The subject's public practices of compliance, discussed by Wedeen, generated self-understandings and self-positioning in relation to the regime and fellow citizens. This performativity was undoubtedly elicited by the regime's use of state-directed and societally embedded surveillance entailing informing, reporting and watching. Dissimulation motivated by fear, distrust and ambiguity oriented subject performances. In this regard, there is a need to go beyond the spectacle and the public parades, studied by Wedeen, to investigate other governmental practices formative of the subject, including, as noted above, those that arise within violence as a modality of governance. To this end, I enquire into the practices and processes of subjectivation at work in the everyday in various sites such as the school and the family. The guiding question here is how have Syrians, and in particular the 'Ba'th generation', interpreted and related to life conditions, structures of authority and government in the everyday?

As interpellated subjects of the nationalist Ba'thist discourse, ordinary Syrians were called upon to enact political subjectivities also constructed in other postcolonial regimes: nationalist subjects, revolutionary agents and guardians of a threatened project. Internal threats, traitors, reactionaries or 'the enemy within' necessitated vigilance and surveillance on their part. Pre-Ba'th antecedents could be found in the revolutionary, nationalist mobilisation of a collective subject enthused by the anti-colonial liberation plan of industrialisation and self-sufficiency, as depicted in Omar Amiralay's film *Essay on the Euphrates Dam* (1970) and in other cultural productions in the 1960s and 1970s.

In a manner similar to that of the Stalinist regime, the Ba'thist regime and its leader created models of patriotic and heroic subjects. One such model, which will be discussed in Chapter 3, was Hamida al-Taher, a seventeen-year-old woman who undertook a suicide-bombing mission in 1986 in glorification of 'the Eternal Leader'. The regime's subjects did not necessarily remodel themselves in such heroic terms for cynicism and disenchantment mediated their reception of public rhetoric. Indeed, 'diminished' and 'attenuated', preoccupied with the pursuit of survival, compromising in or alienated by their public compliance, subjects did not reconcile themselves with the conduct that they felt compelled to enact. In many Syrians' recollections of everyday life under Hafez al-Asad, an abjected self is sketched out as a subject of lack and debasement, defiled, demeaned and flattened out. Yet, additionally, the discursive civilities of the everyday bring out a resourceful self in pursuit of material goods on the black market through smuggling. Also, at times, a defiant subject emerges through a resort to 'weapons of the weak' such as refusing to buy the national consumer items and, instead, purchasing smuggled goods. In this configuration of subjectivation and self-fashioning, there appears to be a coexistence of, on one hand, the nationalist subject of dreams and aspirations of nationhood with, on the other, the subject, rendered abject, pursuing scarce basic necessities such as a kilogram of rice, a tin of ghee or a box of facial tissues. In this respect, I pay attention to everyday life and mundane experiences, which enter into the making of political subjectivities. In Syrians' recollections of their everyday life experience, abjection, as both a process and a lived condition, emerges as an organising frame of meaning and as a cipher of the formation of political subjectivities under the dictatorship of Hafez al-Asad. It is relevant, now, to turn to a discussion of the interconnections between abjection and subjectivation.

Abjection and Subjectivation

My analysis of political subjectivities, formed and performed, underlines abjection both as a style of government and as a process that is formative of the subject of rule. Abjection is conventionally defined as the action of casting down or out and as the affective condition of being cast down or the state of being abject. As an analytic term, defining and understanding abjection has been significantly influenced by Julia Kristeva's work *Powers of Horror* (1982). In this work, Kristeva grounds a psychoanalytic explanation of abjection, locating it in the moment the child is expelled from the mother's womb. The drive to cast down and expel what is alien and to assert what is self and internal inhabits consciousness from birth. The expulsion is a work of purification of all that is unclean from the body and its surroundings. The source of disgust is paradoxically both internal and external.

Kristeva's conception illuminates the aversive affects felt towards that which is constituted as repulsive. Yet the ontological psychoanalytic character invested in the definition does not account for the social construction of 'the abject' or for the political processes of rendering a subject abject (see Tyler 2013). In her critique of Kristeva, drawing on Georges Bataille's essay on abjection, Imogen Tyler (2013, 19–21) offers a socially grounded understanding of abjection. In line with Bataille's conceptualisation, Tyler defines abjection as a process actualising the exclusionary forces of sovereign power – forces that strip people of their human dignity and produce them as dehumanised waste. Tyler situates the process of abjection in relation to neo-liberal government and to late-capitalist accumulation. My concern is to widen and embed abjection as a process structuring state–citizen relations, in particular, in authoritarian polities. Abjection, as a process in and of government, goes beyond asserting the sovereign power of exclusion, of casting down or rendering subjects abject. Rather, the process constructs political subjects whose agency and affect should be taken into account in order to explicate their forms of political action whether oppositional or co-opted and compliant. Indeed, as Tyler argues, rendering the subject abject positions her as an object of disgust for others (i.e. the 'normal' subjects). However, in the Syrian case, the processes through which subjects are rendered abject serve other purposes – a warning and a spectre, and a mechanism of undoing oppositional subjectivity. Disgusting and revolting subjectivity becomes a condition to be avoided. Embodied humiliation that casts down the subject threatens the integrity of oppositional subjectivity. While, in democratic polities, abjection feeds into practices of othering by articulating with categories of race, ethnicity, gender and sexuality, in authoritarian polities abjection is both a condition and a positionality that the subject inhabits in the course of engaging in oppositional politics and in the course of everyday life. Abjection, as a dynamic political process, is embedded in the political economy productive of socially and politically differentiated groups and in the materiality of the living conditions of groups and individuals struggling for the satisfaction of basic needs and necessities of life (see Fassin 2009; Giroux 2005; Mbembe 2003).

Abjection (*dhul*) and humiliation (*mahana*) are closely connected aversive affects, which are incited through socially embodied experiences of violence both physical and emotional. As a mechanism of government, abjection plays out not only through aversion, inciting disgust towards those cast down, excluded and rendered revolting, but also through the attack on the subject's integrity, her sense of self and self-esteem, thus destabilising her own borders and boundaries. In Syria, the starkest examples of processes of abjection that violate the subject's psychological and physical boundaries come from the experiences of detention in Tadmur Prison where subjects were rendered abject by violations of their bodily integrity and their sense of self-worth and dignity. Common practices in the repertoires of humiliation in Tadmur included forcing detainees to commit self-polluting acts – for example, being made to eat vermin or being forced to drink sewage water or to swallow a guard's spit – or by forcing humiliating conduct – for example, being made to kiss the guard's shoes or to clench shoes between one's teeth.

The practices of abjection noted in the space of the prison should be read in conjunction with ordinary Syrians' experiences of everyday dehumanisation and debasement in pursuit of basic necessities (food, for example), and of uncertainty in the carrying out of basic tasks like walking and crossing the street, getting on a bus, and so on. Such experiences were recounted by my Syrian interviewees to illustrate their having felt, endured and lived abjection – a condition conveyed in the expression 'ihna 'ishna al-dhul' ('we lived abjection'). Experiencing abjection and producing oneself as abject emerged in self-reflective narratives of everyday life under Hafez al-Asad. As a condition and a mode of subjectivation, abjection explained agency as both absent and recovered. It is in reference to defilement and contamination that some Syrians explained to me, in 2005, why it was not reasonable to contemplate the possibility of resistance against the regime. Yet the same conditions and experiences of abjection in 2011 were invoked by many supporters of the Uprising to assert that recovering one's agency to resist carried no risk as there was nothing left to lose. Indeed, the Uprising was framed as a rejection of abjection: 'death is preferable to abjection' (al-mawt wa la al-madhala) was a rallying cry in demonstrations across the country.

What should we make of the differing connections, drawn by my Syrian interviewees, between abjection, on one hand, and subjectivity and agency, on the other? Perhaps the context in which the socio-political meaning of abjection was rendered explains, in part, why inaction and loss of agency was claimed in 2005 and overturned in 2011. However, there are additional factors to consider: the visibility of regime violence, the extreme character of violations and a kernel of hope tended to by the historical moment of the Uprisings in Tunisia and Egypt. Out of Syrians' familiarity, if not intimacy, with regime violence, develops knowledge of its repertoires, and anticipation of frightening happenings. In 2011, participating in demonstrations and voicing their opposition to the regime publicly, many Syrians reclaimed agency by confronting horror and looking back. Facing the dangers that lurked was possibly intended to cut off the pathways of violence's grip on the mind and heart. Further, the conditions of visibility in 2011, it could be argued, provoked a sense of responsibility in the abjected subjects. Paradoxically, in the first phase of the Uprising the memories and the embodied lessons of Hama and of everyday encounters with security agents called forth fear and dread of regime violence, but also hope and courage to resist. In her study of the lived spaces of Northern Cyprus, Navaro-Yashin (2009, 6; 2012) contemplates what happens when the abject is domesticated and incorporated into the social order, suggesting that new subjectivities and a new political system are generated. In similar terms, I observe that within the narratives and arguments that Syrians use to interpret their agency and make it intelligible, abjection is appropriated as lived positionality, and not as an essence.

Social Memories of Violence and Regimes of Subjectivity

The role of violence in government and in structuring relations between ruler and ruled must be approached by examining not only experiences of violence in the present but also the lived social memories of past violence, be it spectacular or mundane and routine. Social memories of political violence develop intersubjectively in relation to events and experiences in the past. These memories are articulated in speech and in silences. If experiences of regime violence are formative of political subjects, so too are social memories of violence. In this regard, the terms in which violent events are remembered, recalled or silenced inform and shape the subject's positioning vis-à-vis political government and fellow citizens. In this sense, social memories of violence are components of interpretative horizons of the subject. Indeed, contending with a violent past and finding individual and collective terms of negotiating one's relations to it have been formative of Syrians as subject-citizens of the Asad regime.

The violence of the late 1970s and early 1980s was foundational to a new phase of Syrian politics and history. How the events of that period are recorded, suppressed and reconstructed structures relations and interactions among citizens and between them and the regime. In probing the social memories of violence, I seek to shed light on the place of the past in understandings of the present, in particular with reference to the formation of political subjectivities. The overriding question orienting this line of enquiry is that of the terms in which the past has been negotiated in the social and cultural production of memories of violence. Relatedly, how are the memories of violence lived and practised in the present? A dimension of my enquiry into social memories of violence is focused on how these memories are material to understanding conflict and contestation among Syrian political subjects and between them and government.[21]

In addressing the questions of the socially and politically formative role of memories of violence in Syria, I draw on sociological approaches to memory. Eschewing the individualist emphasis of earlier psychological perspectives on memory, these approaches have shifted the focus of analysis of memory to its social production. In critical engagement with Maurice Halbwachs's (1992) foundational work on 'collective memory', the concept of social memory is advanced to take account of the processual and relational nature of practices of recollection.[22] The sociality of memory rests on communication and transmission through which narratives of the past are intersubjectively constituted (Fentress and Wickham 1992). Further, the concept is predicated on the idea that acts of recollection and recall are undertaken in relation to socio-historical processes by differentially situated social actors (see Jelin 2003; Mistzal 2003; Poole 2008; Stern 2006). It follows that acts and practices of memory are framed by the power relations invested in the making of the permissible and the disallowed in discourses and practices that have a bearing on the body politic. By the same token, practices of memory are embedded in social relations and bear the inscriptions of social and political contests and struggles.

A salient dimension of my enquiry into the constitutive role of violence is to examine how social memories of regime violence have been lived by Syrians as political subjects. The practices of memory are, to varying degrees, shaped by the events and experiences of violence themselves (see Edkins 2003). As pointed out by Allen Feldman (2003) in

---

[21] Following recent scholarship on social memories, the conventional distinction between memory and history is problematised here. As noted by Olick and Robbins (1998, 110), social and cultural memory has become evidentiary material in historiography. Inversely, memory draws on and uses history. Further, history's claim to objectivity upon which it distinguishes itself from the subjective character of memory has been interrogated in assessments of the role of selection and interpretation of sources in historical work, which underscores the constructivist element in history's truths. Hence, the claims of objectivity in history writing should not, of necessity or by default, trump experiential and lived recollection. For an extensive consideration of the complex relations between memory and history, see Ricoeur (2004).

[22] Halbwachs' work emphasised the social component of memory. Yet, as critics have pointed out, his concept of 'collective memory' retained its static and essentialising character in treating groups as coherent entities and in privileging consensus and stability in recollections and frames of remembering developed by groups (see Connerton 1988, 37–40; McDougall 2010; Olick and Robbins 1998).

reference to violence in Northern Ireland, one of the objectives of violence is pedagogical – using markings on the body and the built environment to inscribe social memories into the political landscape. Through bodily and spatial inscriptions, subjects are instructed and reminded of interdictions against engaging in particular conduct. '[V]iolent acts on the body', Feldman (2003, 60) contends, 'constituted a material vehicle for constructing memory and embedding the self in social and institutional memory'. The learning process does not unfold in a uniform manner to produce homogenised subjects, but it is through living the lessons of violence that the subjects develop intimate understandings of the workings of power while also learning how to live their experiences of violence. Syrians have long recognised the pedagogy of violence, cultivating embodied modes of relating to one another and to the regime.

Driving my enquiry into the social memories of violence in Syria – specifically into how events are remembered and lived in the present – is the question of how the practices of memory have been formative and transformative of Syrians as political subjects. Frameworks for articulating memories are, by necessity, developed in reference to social arrangements and relations such as class, and communal and religious affiliation. In this respect, the question that arises is: What forms does social memory take? To answer, I probe, concretely, the memory work performed by subjects, by looking at 'the modes of retrospection' and the 'aesthetics of social remembering' as expressed in narratives of the events and experiences of violence.[23] I also examine the emblematic frameworks, which organise memories of everyday life under dictatorship and imbue them with meaning (Stern 2006).

The memory work performed by Syrians, as will be discussed in greater detail in Chapters 3 and 4, was constrained by the extensive censorship imposed on all forms of public communication and discourse and by the surveillance regime that extended into all societal spaces. In effect, ordinary Syrians' practices of memory have been, in part, patterned in relation to this censorship and surveillance. Understandings of the events and experiences of violence inhabit forms of speech and pervade silences in the everyday. Further, although transmission and communication of the memories of violence have been constrained, they are nonetheless communicated in everyday discursive civilities such as the injunction to silence, the conjuring of an interlocutor's subjectivity or the retrospective recall through which understandings of oneself and others are articulated (to be discussed at length in Chapters 2 and 3). In effect, the modes

---

[23] I take my cue here from Rivkin-Fish's (2009) approach to practices of memory in Russia.

of self-fashioning and the political subjectivities that Syrians enact are, to a large extent, shaped by their social memories of violence.

A Note on Methods and Sources

This study draws on multiple sources of data and research materials. One main source of primary data comprises 150 interviews that I carried out in Syria over an extended period of time, specifically between 2002 and 2011. Included in this period are two six-month fieldwork stays, the first between November 2004 and May 2005, and the second between December 2010 and May 2011. Additional interviews were carried out with different generations of Syrian exiles in Beirut, Amman, London, Paris and Montreal, most of which took place between 2011 and 2015.

The interviews pursued two interconnected lines of enquiry over the entire period of research. In the initial phase of the investigation, my open-ended questions were geared towards gathering data on the social and political transformation of Damascus under the rule of Hafez al-Asad and the Ba'th Party. To this end, I sought to trace urban reconfigurations tied to rural–urban migration and the associated emergence of new neighbourhoods on the expanding outskirts of Damascus. This strand of the enquiry was pursued through household-focused as well as workshop-centred interviews in the neighbourhoods of Qaboun, Barzeh and Mezzeh 86, and dealt with such issues as employment networks, patterns of social and cultural integration and social hierarchies. These issues were also the subjects of interviews with merchants in the *suqs* of Hamidiyya and Hariqa. The interviews for this thread of research took place mostly during the early period of fieldwork in 2005.

A second and connected thread of the enquiry dealt with memories of everyday life and, specifically, with what Syrians remembered of life under Hafez al-Asad. The narratives I collected for this thread draw, to a great degree, on recollections of civil-society activists, political dissidents and former political prisoners, as well as writers, filmmakers and other artists. The timeframe for this set of interviews stretches across my visits and stays in Syria between 2002 and 2011, and extends, subsequently, beyond 2011 to various locations where I met with and interviewed exiled Syrians. During the 2011 Uprising, and in its aftermath, I sought to gather data on trajectories of activism of young Syrian men and women in their twenties and thirties. The accounts of activism inevitably furnished recollections of everyday life and of growing up under Ba'th and Asad rule.

Along with the interviews, I maintained open conversations with many Syrian interlocutors. In Syria, some of them invited me into their networks of sociability in the artistic and cultural milieus and allowed me entry into discussion circles at informal gatherings. Despite the continued state-security surveillance of public events, the activities at various cultural venues were instructive of the cultural life of politically engaged Syrians. These venues included the Institut Français du Proche Orient, the Attasi Forum (closed in June 2005) and a number of bookshops where book launches and discussions took place. Beyond the Damascus-centred cultural space, I had meetings with civil-society actors and cultural workers, including ad hoc group discussions in Aleppo and Latakiyya.

There are limitations to the data gathered through the interviews that should be noted here. Interviews with civil-society actors and with youth activists, dissidents and engaged intellectuals were open and the exchanges less guarded than with other interviewees. For instance, interviews with ordinary citizens remained within implicit understandings of the boundaries of authorised speech. Particular topics were off limits in general. The Hama violence was the subject of silence more than of speech. I was able to interview only a very limited number of Hamawis (natives of Hama) in Syria. Most of the interviews about Hama were conducted with exiled Hamawis and took place following the Uprising. As a general principle, owing to the sensitivity of the subject matter covered in this study, I have maintained the anonymity of my interviewees.

A wide range of materials from the Syrian cultural and artistic scene, both local and diasporic, complements my interviews and observations including films, novels and memoirs and material from electronic media such as blog postings. Further, I reviewed government-controlled newspapers for coverage, in the 2000s, of Ba'th Party activities and for official, state narratives of events of that period. I also consulted issues of the Ba'th Party's official magazine, *al-Munadil*, for the 1980s and 1990s, and the publications of party auxiliaries (for example, the online reports of the Pioneers Organisation). The publications of Syrian and international human rights organisations are key sources of data on prisons. These complement prisoners' memoirs and fictionalised accounts of imprisonment in Syria. Official documentation, in the form of security service and police reports, manuals, regulations and the like, was not accessible at the time of research. If available, these would undoubtedly have constituted a rich source of information on the policies and practices of the agents of the regime.

At various points in this text, I use memoirs, diaries or novels as sources for understanding Syrians' experiences of both routine and spectacular violence. Given that the use of such material remains unconventional in social science studies, I will briefly highlight my approach to this material. For my investigation of the political prison/camp as an apparatus of governmental violence, prison memoirs and diaries and works of fiction all provide accounts of how acts of violence were experienced and felt. Other documentary material that would normally provide useful and important information – such as transcripts of trials of perpetrators, testimonies and reports of truth commissions, archival and public records from prisons and security directorates – was either non-existent or unavailable. Thus, the memoirs served as the most valuable resources for learning about practices of violence in the period of Syrian history under study. The memoirs and diaries of prison life have the quality of testimonial literature. They respond to the imperative of bearing witness and, in the current context, express an urgency to do so. They also testify to the impossibility of speech that can convey the lived suffering.

A drive to perform literary witnessing orients the fiction writings of Manhal al-Sarraj, Samar Yazbek, Khaled Khalifa, Mustafa Khalifa and Rosa Yassin Hassan, among others. The works of these novelists attempt to fill gaps in the historical narrative of events and life during the time of Hafez al-Asad, in particular during the period of extreme violence in the 1980s. For example, Mustafa Khalifa has stated during a television interview that he considers his prison novel to be a document and a testimony. In their narratives of ordinary lives and of how events were lived, the novels chart a route for grasping obscured times and lives. Al-Sarraj, as a writer of Hama, the city and its people, occupies a special place in writing against the erasure and denial of events and lives. In the mould of literary witnessing, her fiction is motivated by an ethical drive to recognise 'a searing memory'. The challenge of these works for the reader is not that of ascertaining the real and factual from the imagined and fictional but of sensing ways of doing and feeling at a particular time. The imaginary's role is that of speaking the unspeakable and of making sense of happenings, neither of which can be conveyed in and through standardised fact collection and reporting with their particular compositional structures and writing conventions geared to the expository and to facticity. As argued by Michael Richardson (2016, 9), fiction surmounts the limits of 'coherent narrative frameworks' of human rights reports.

Both fiction and memoirs offer terms for imagining and feeling experiences related in the narratives. For instance, the raw stories told by Aram Karabit in his prison memoir, and the fictionalised account of the 'assault of spit' in Mustafa Khalifa's prison novel, enable terms of comprehension that cannot be achieved with conventional documentary reports of prison conditions. Fiction and memoir animate the historical record with rich, layered and detailed narratives of people's lives, lived events and happenings. For instance, diary accounts of torture and humiliation in prison provide signposts for comprehending the rationality of violence inflicted on bodies. We see this sharply, for example, in Karabit's memoir, in the recorded moments of self-betrayal when succumbing to the orders of the guards, or when confronting the pressure to overturn and reverse oneself.

In Chapter 3, I make use of memoirs and testimonials of experiences of life under Hafez al-Asad. Syrians' memoirs and diaries about the quotidian and personal experiences of the everyday during that period are still limited in number. In this context, Maher Sharaf al-Din's memoir, and the testimonials collected by Mohammad Abi Samra, recover personal stories and speak the voices of those who are kept off the official record and formal accounts. In this respect, these writings have contributed to the expansion of subaltern accounts cast in the form of micro-level and detailed ethnographies of political subjectivities and the everyday. All translations from the memoirs, novels and other Arabic-language sources used in the book are my own.

Structure of the Book

This book examines the Syrian polity through the prism of governmental violence, which is understood to order regime–citizen relations in particular terms. It is concerned with both spectacular violence and routine violence and how they come to shape citizens' interpretative horizons and understandings of government and rule. The performative power of the extraordinary violence of Tadmur Prison and the Hama massacres extends beyond the subjects immediately affected by them. The atrocities at Tadmur and Hama have loomed large over the Syrian polity. Drawing on diaries and memoirs of former political prisoners, in Chapter 1 I sketch practices of subjectivation in everyday life in Tadmur. Through the reading of narratives and memoirs, it becomes evident that the objective of the seemingly irrational violence is to unmake political subjects. Indeed, the rationality at work does not aim to form subjects as much as to undo them, to get them to overturn themselves. Beyond the examination of the prison as an apparatus of government, the chapter advances the proposition that practices of violence were productive of a civil war regime. I trace the figurations of this regime through a revisiting of the events of massacres in Hama in 1982. The formations of violence that crystallised in the Hama massacres rest on the conditions of a latent permanent war between the rulers and ruled and between different components of society differentiated along multiple lines of division: sectarian, tribal, ethnic, regional, urban–rural and class. These divisions realign along an overarching political divide between loyalists and enemies/oppositionists.

Chapter 2 turns to another face of the Syrian regime – namely, its shadow structures and networks and their modes of operation. It analyses how a Syrian 'shadow state' articulates with authoritarian government working to enframe ordinary citizens' everyday activities. In particular, the chapter shows how regime-sponsored shadow networks and relations have interlinked with the politics of security in a manner that gives shape to 'regimes of subjectivities' in the everyday. The chapter sheds light on the identitarian dimensions of the constitution of the subject and of self-hood and situates this identitarian construction in relation to specific features of the political economy of the regime, which extends beyond the formal dimensions of the state to incorporate the 'shadow state'.

The exploration of processes of subject formation and the constitution of political subjectivities is pursued further in Chapter 3. Syrians' recollections of everyday life under Hafez al-Asad provide a point of entry into the processes formative of political subjectivities. In reflections on school and family life, we glimpse the experiences of growing up in Ba'thist Syria and the formation of the Ba'th generation. Individual memories aggregate to form a composite of the national experience and create emblematic frames of that experience. Relatedly, self-authoring accounts narrate how the national project shaped personal life trajectories of public intellectuals, artists and activists. These narratives bring to light the interconnections of the mundane events of life and those taking place on the national stage. They offer insights into how the national experience is woven into narratives of the self or self-authoring in a manner that gives account of the self and the factors that shape self-positioning.

In Chapter 4, I approach the politically formative role of Hama violence through the narratives of the events, exploring what memory practices tell us about Syrians' relation to the past. The accounts of the past are, by necessity, fragments of stories oriented towards different ends. Survivors' and witnesses' recollections and narratives of the events reveal how violence is lived and embodied and, therefore, the ways in which it is formative of political subjectivities.

Chapter 5 interrogates the performative structure of violence looking at an episode of a gruesome and mysterious killing during the first year of the Uprising and at three cases of massacre, which took place in the period that followed. Underscored in this interrogation is the contention that through staging, narrativisation and mimesis, enactments of violence create and leave unresolved the bewilderment and disturbance experienced by subject-citizens – a kind of political uncanny.

1   Violence as a Modality of Government in Syria

In 1970, during the coup d'état that brought Hafez al-Asad to power, key figures of the Ba'thist government, including the deposed president, Salah Jadid, his prime minister, Yusuf Zu'ayyin, and the then minister of industry, Marwan Habash, among many others, were arrested and incarcerated in the infamous al-Mezzeh prison near Damascus. Arrest and imprisonment of overthrown leaders is not unusual in such circumstances. In the Syrian context, where a degree of political turmoil had prevailed over the preceding two decades, al-Asad's military putsch was the expression of struggles within the Ba'th Party and the military. Purges in both the party and the military were carried out to eliminate threats to the vanquishing group led by al-Asad. Such tactics are common for the consolidation of contenders' political control. However, the new regime exercised the powers of exception that it conferred upon itself through emergency law, not only against its rivals, but also against wider segments of the political opposition. In time, these powers were used against all active groups and individuals in society. Indeed, incarceration, and both targeted and mass killing, became mechanisms of government.

How did the political prison and the massacre become apparatuses of rule in Syria? Conventionally, answers to questions such as this give explanatory focus to the challenge that the political opposition, in particular the Muslim Brotherhood, represented to the regime commencing in the late 1970s. From this perspective, the resort to violence by the group al-Tali'a al-Muqatila (regarded as an offshoot of the Brotherhood) is seen as the trigger and cause of regime violence. This optic on political violence under the Hafez al-Asad regime presents a simple causality that does not capture either the scope and techniques of violence, or the governmental objectives of violence. In counterpoint to this optic, then, it is relevant to note that prior to the conflict with the Brotherhood and the militant Islamist groups, the application of emergency law had resulted in the continual pursuit, arrest and imprisonment of political dissidents of all backgrounds. Indeed, diaries of communist political activists, dating from the early 1970s, chronicle the setting in of an atmosphere of surveillance and, also, a sense of siege felt by ordinary citizens ('Abbas 2006; Abu Nijm 2017; 'Issa 2016).

Commencing in the early 1970s, along with Islamist figures activists in communist and Marxist circles in Syria were being forcibly abducted from their homes and from public spaces. They would thenceforth disappear, often without word and without a trace. In response, much political activism of the period focused on the demand for bringing an end to emergency rule. Despite the expansion of surveillance by the security forces, mobilisation and agitation for change persisted among societal forces ranging from professional syndicates to shopfloor workers to students. The violent actions of the Tali'a provided a pretext to the regime to generalise and entrench governmental violence. The Tali'a campaign of assassinations against regime figures and affiliates, and its attacks on public infrastructure, set the scene for the expansion in the security forces' surveillance and repression activities throughout society.[1] The security services pursued a policy of internment on a mass scale, while regime-sponsored paramilitary units committed slaughter in villages and in city neighbourhoods where critics of the regime and opposition activists lived.

As noted in the Introduction, the political prison served as a template of rule and, as an institution, became continuous with the wider society. Indeed, the prison/detention camp became an apparatus through which government was effected by inciting feelings of humiliation and abjection in the subjects of rule. In this respect, I advance a primary argument to the effect that power treats the subject as a feeling as well as a thinking subject. Proceeding from this premise, torture and corporal punishment should be viewed as technologies for unmaking political subjects. The rationalities of these practices may be discerned from their objective of disciplining through the affect. As such, my account of these practices does not uphold the contrast between body-centred punishment and soul-oriented reform advanced in Foucault's genealogy of modern disciplinary power.

In addition to the detention camp, the massacre also served as an apparatus of governmental violence. Together, the detention camp and massacre were instrumental in establishing what may be termed 'a civil war regime', a condition wherein war came to be understood as a

---

[1] For an overview of the activities of the Tali'a group, see Abd al-Hakim (1991) and al-Sharbaji (ND). An early account of the regime's response, based on interviews with political insiders, is given by Seale (1988).

'permanent social relation', to use Foucault's terms.[2] The notion of war as a permanent social relation underlines the polarisation of the social body within a biopolitical frame, drawing divisions between those deemed worthy of life and those slated for eradication and death. A related argument, which will be elaborated in greater detail in Chapters 4 and 5, advances the contention that the performative acts of violence have a pedagogical intent: to instruct subject-citizens about the terms of rule and to orient their affective and cognitive states in relation to government.

I begin my discussion of the apparatuses of violence with an overview of the juridico-political frame of 'the state of exception' in the Syrian context. I advance the view that the power of the sovereign asserted in this juridico-political frame was deeply invested in a sacralised politics of leader deification and a kind of ideo-theology, akin to what some scholars of totalitarian rule (e.g. Gentile 2000) refer to as 'political religion'. Against this background, I proceed to tease out the terms of government effected through the political prison, looking at everyday life in Syrian detention camps as described and recounted in former prisoners' diaries and in fictionalised accounts of incarceration. Next, and finally, I enquire into the Hama massacre as a framework for the practices and strategies that established a civil war regime.

State of Exception, Sacralisation of Politics and the Civil War Regime

Emergency rule, in effect from 1963 until its nominal abolition in 2011, set the frame of political government and translated into the suspension of the law and the creation of a space outside the law.[3] During this period, the emergency law established a condition of 'a legal civil war' that, in Agamben's terms, 'allows for the physical elimination not only of political adversaries but of entire categories of citizens who for some reason cannot be integrated into the political system' (Agamben 2005, 2). Set out in Law 51, issued in 1962, emergency rule enables the suspension of citizens' civil rights and liberties. For example, Article 4 of the Law sanctions such measures as the prohibition of assembly, the imposition of restrictions on citizens' places of residence and limitations on their movement. The Law also invests the ruler or his deputy with the

---

[2] The term 'civil war regime' is used by Yassin al-Haj Saleh (2011b) to characterise the regime's deployment of practices reproductive of socio-cultural divisions that threaten to bring about violence. In this manner, there are similarities in our usage.

[3] The actual state of emergency was declared in Military Order 2 issued by the Military Revolutionary Council on 8 March 1963 when the Ba'thists took over political power through a coup d'état.

power to detain individuals suspected of representing a danger to public security and public order, and also to conduct searches at any time or place. Although, in principle, the powers of arrest should be confined in the hands of the ruler or his deputy, in practice they came to be invested widely in the numerous departments and branches of the security services. Article 4 also gives the ruler, or whomever he authorises, the right to confiscate property and impose trusteeships on businesses and companies. Further, it allows the authorities to monitor citizens' mail and communications, thus establishing provisions for the continuous surveillance of the population.

In tandem with the Emergency Law, the 'Law of Protecting the Revolution' (1965) criminalises whoever stands accused of opposing or resisting the principles of the Ba'thist Revolution (unity, freedom and socialism).[4] Punishment of individuals deemed 'resisters to the Revolution' includes life in prison and execution. Many political activists and dissidents were detained and brought to trial on charges of posing a threat to the Revolution.[5] The juridical dimension of the state of exception is theatrically staged in the state security and military courts.[6] Yet, additionally, many political activists and others who were randomly arrested were detained without trial for extended periods of time. It should be noted that the generalisation and normalisation of emergency law was achieved through a range of practices, including the securitisation of mundane undertakings and everyday activities, as will be discussed in Chapter 2.

Writing on 'the state of exception' as a form of rule, Agamben identifies two seemingly contradictory strategies at work: sovereign power creates and maintains a permanent state of war by nurturing a fracture in the social body, effected through 'us' and 'them' lines of division; and at

---

[4] Crimes specified under Article 6 of the Emergency Law were also named in the Penal Code, as, for example, 'crimes against state security and public safety' (Articles 263–311), 'crimes against public authorities' (Articles 369–387), 'crimes undermining the spirit of the nation and public confidence in the authorities' (Articles 427–459).

[5] In a further elaboration of the Law, legislative Decree No. 6, issued in January 1965, designated as 'criminal' those acts that violate the socialist order or legislative decrees of the socialist transformation. Actions or activities identified as crimes and as threats to the Revolution include: '[o]pposing the Unification of the Arab State or any of the aims of the Revolution or hindering their achievement, whether by way of demonstrations, assemblies, riots or by incitement to such, or by the publication of false news intended to create anxiety and to shake the confidence of the masses in the aims of the Revolution. The taking of money or any other benefit from a foreign state or from an organisation or individuals, whether Syrian or non-Syrian, or communication with a foreign agency, for the purpose of undertaking any action, verbal or physical, hostile to the aims of the Revolution' (cited in Amnesty International 1983, 10).

[6] These tribunals also have purview over crimes specified in the Penal Code, thereby normalising the state of exception.

the same time, this power puts into operation an apparatus – the political prison/internment camp – that has as its rationale the homogenisation of the people. How do we see these contrasting, yet interlinked, strategies at work in the context of emergency rule in Syria? The main target of intern-ment camps in Syria were dissident populations. In one influential char-acterisation from the 1980s, Rif'at al-Asad, the president's brother and leader of the Military Defence Companies, in a speech to the Ba'th Party Seventh Regional Congress in January 1980, referred to these dissident populations as 'the nationally diseased' (those with a defective sense of nationalism). This speech was made at the time of regime confrontation with a broad political opposition that included diverse Islamist forces as well as secular leftist groups. In the speech, Rif'at warned of an impending danger that would obliterate the Arab civilisation. He proposed to protect the nation and eliminate the threat through the isolation of 'the nation-ally diseased'. His recommendations to the Ba'th Congress included the establishment of labour camps. Deviant or errant subjects would be used to 'green the desert' while being subjected to re-education programmes. Rif'at proposed the issuing of a law of 'national purification' (al-tathir al-watani) for deviants 'who uphold destructive principles that threaten nationalist thought and national peace'. Following corrective educa-tion, 'the deviant in thought' would sit annual examinations to assess whether they had been cured. Those who were positively assessed would be issued 'national purification certificates'. This plan of correction and reform of deviant and errant subjects was never put into effect. Rather, the regime followed the path of abandonment in the terms discussed by Agamben (1998) whereby political detainees are made subjects of the sovereign's ban, that is, they are cast out and exposed to eradication. In the same logic, the massacre was the mechanism through which the enemy populations were to be eliminated.

How do we understand the political horizon within which there develops such practices and modes of organising and rendering pol-itical life? What were the discursive justifications and governmental rationalities behind these practices? Ideological postulates of nation-alism and developmentalism were structuring elements of the grand narratives of the Ba'thist regime. However, an important mechanism of government has been the sacralisation of politics. Many of the features discussed by Emilio Gentile (2000) to elucidate the processes of sacral-isation of politics in totalitarian movements and systems of government can be seen to be at work in Ba'thist rule. For example, in imagistic and discursive representations of Hafez al-Asad there are resonances of the Italian Fascists' adaptation of religious language to elevate and acclaim the leader (i.e. Mussolini). Further, as in totalitarian systems of rule, the Ba'thist regime began as a revolutionary movement espousing a project of radical societal transformation (which could be understood, in the terms used by Gentile (2000), as 'conquering society'). The project included the key precept that the Ba'th, as the single party, would be the sole leader in state and society (as stated in Article 8 of the Constitution). Societal transformation was to be achieved through the party and its auxiliary popular organisations in charge of mobilisation and collective indoctrination designed to instil the dogmas, beliefs, myths and commandments of the party in the minds of wide segments of the population (see Hinnebusch 1980 and 1990). The doctrinal identity of institutions and groups had to be assured (most importantly, the doctrinal identity of the army known as *al-jaysh al-'aqa'idi*, literally 'the doctrinal army').

An important aspect of the sacralisation of politics in Syria was the deification of Hafez al-Asad as a figure of national salvation. Al-Asad's deification should not be understood as his being regarded as a deity in the conventional sense, though the language of divinity was used. Rather, in regime rhetoric, as discussed by Lisa Wedeen (1999), al-Asad was gradually constructed as an omnipotent being in possession of exceptional qualities and attributes. He alone was capable of seeing regional dynamics and interests and grasping all the forces of struggle and dynamics of interaction. He alone could anticipate responses and see far enough ahead to know which plan would best preserve the nation's interest, stature and role. During the 2011 Uprising, pro-regime commentators reiterated these propositions tirelessly, this time in reference to Bashar al-Asad. In these statements, the idea was advanced that without Bashar al-Asad, the country would break into various statelets, there would be foreign occupation and countless disasters would befall the nation. These claims revive the persona of the saviour and the notion of eternality that were attached to Hafez al-Asad and that were given salience, in Orwellian fashion, through the teaching and memorisation in school of 'the Eternal Leader's' speeches. Furthermore, the project, mission and potentialities of the nation were wrapped up in the body and mind of the leader.

Hafez al-Asad's elevation to the status of a deity was not only projected by the official discourse but also by its subject-receivers. For instance, subjects gave credence and support to the ascription of a god-like status to the leader in the shouting of slogans such as '*ya Allah halak halak, yuqu'd Hafiz mahalik*' ('Hey God, move over and let Hafez take your place'), reportedly chanted at the time of the assault on Hama and again during the 2011 Uprising.[7] Further, evidence for the projection of Asad's deification can be found in the veneration accorded him by low-level soldiers and security service personnel who expressed disbelief that dissidents should harbour critical views of al-Asad. Faraj al-Biraqdar (2006), a Syrian poet and former political prisoner, recounts in his memoirs of imprisonment an instance when a guard, watching over a group of detainees being transported to a detention centre, scowled and asked, incredulously, what it was about the president that they did not like. Then he swore that the president's urine was a cure and that the place of his excrement should be a shrine. Besides this folkloric deity status, al-Asad, as deity, was central to the maintenance of the prevailing order in a 'metaphysical' sense – he, 'eternally', held the keys to the future and represented the mind and encompassed the thought unifying his followers.

Deviation from this quasi-religio-cognitive frame was an act akin to heresy. It was also diagnosed as a kind of mental deficiency that betrayed deviant thought processes and contamination with external and, therefore, diseased thought. The sacralisation of politics posits a hierarchy of modes of cognition and thought. As could be gleaned from al-Asad's speeches between 1979 and 1984, correct thinking is characterised as secular, scientific, modernist and nationalist. Ba'thists and their supporters represented the superior group or species. The ranking of others depended on where they stood in relation to Ba'thist tenets and in relation to the Ba'thist monopoly over political power. The deviant subjects confined in the internment camps were thus differentiated according to their doctrinal illnesses, with the Muslim Brothers – afflicted with an incurable illness – falling outside the possibility of correction. Hence, Law 49 of 1980 made membership of the group punishable by death. Large numbers of Muslim Brother prisoners were executed or killed en masse (as in the massacre in the Tadmur Military Prison in June 1980).[8] At that time, weekly executions of Muslim Brother prisoners were common. In some cases, military field courts issued death sentences after the execution took place. Additionally, countless others perished after being exposed to disease or being subjected to extreme violence.

---

[7] The ascription of divine status to Hafez al-Asad finds remarkable resonance in the deification of Mussolini. For instance, Mussolini was elevated to quasi-divine status in an oath, adopted from Christian prayers, in which the oath taker expressed belief in El Duce commensurate with belief in a deity (see Falasca-Zamponi 1997, 65).

[8] It is estimated that between 700 and 1000 prisoners, held on charges of membership of the Muslim Brotherhood, were killed in this massacre. The massacre is attributed to military units under the command of Rif'at al-Asad, and is understood to have been a retaliatory act for an attempted assassination of Hafez al-Asad.

Other political inmates and detainees – mostly leftists and communists – occupied a different place in the hierarchy of opponents. They belonged to a category of subjects targeted for the interruption of life or its suspension until further consideration.

During the war with the enemy population named 'the gang of the Muslim Brothers' (*'isabat al-Ikhwan al-Muslimin*) – but, in effect, encompassing all opponents of the regime – the leader's speeches named a caesura or break in which the nation/the Ba'thists/the nationalists stood aligned against the reactionaries and the agents of imperial powers. Indicative of the severity and depth of the break is al-Asad's repeated assertion that there would be no dialogue with 'murderers and reactionaries' (referring primarily to the Muslim Brothers) and that the only form of dialogue appropriate for dealing with this radically alien opponent was the kind conducted using bullets to kill (Asad 1980a, 1980b).

In Hafez al-Asad's and Rif'at al-Asad's speeches, and in their propaganda war, it is possible to discern the contours of a discourse that is akin to the racist discourse examined by Foucault. However, the break (the caesura) in the domain of the population, effected through this discourse, is ideational. Ba'thist discourse propagated the idea of 'a new man', possessing the 'correct' cognitive and moral capacities and abilities (*al-Munadil*, June 1985).[9] The discourse denounced the reactionaries in terms that echo the Stalinist idea of 'the objective enemy' noted by Hannah Arendt (1968), among others. In terms parallel to the language of Argentinean generals in the 1980s, in which they referred to the surgical removal of diseased elements or members, Rif'at al-Asad (1980) spoke of the necessity of performing excisions to the social body to cleanse it of the diseased elements (see Suarez-Orozco (2003) on the Argentinean discourse). The use of medical terminology, though in superficial and limited terms, was, in some sense, a means of introducing a 'biological' line of division – the mentally healthy who uphold correct Ba'thist thought as opposed to the mentally diseased who espouse oppositional views. It is noteworthy that the language of disease and medical cure – e.g. surgical excision – was deployed by Bashar al-Asad during the Uprising with respect to regime opponents and critics.

---

[9] For example, in an article on the training of party cadres from a 1985 issue of the party magazine *al-Munadil*, some of the ideal traits that should be possessed by partisan Ba'thists and ordinary citizens alike are presented: 'To achieve the Socialist Revolution, scientific thinking must occupy the right place in the mind and heart of each citizen' (*al-Munadil*, June 1985, 70–9).

The Prison Camp as an Apparatus of Government

From the late 1970s onward, tens of thousands of activists and dissidents of diverse political currents, such as Islamists and communists, as well as breakaway Ba'thists, were rounded up in successive waves of arrest. Members of groups such as the Communist Party-Political Bureau, the Communist Action Party, the pro-Iraq Ba'th Party, and the Kurdish Democratic Party were interned under emergency provisions. Both the leadership and the rank-and-file members of these groups were kept in prison for long periods of time and often without trial. In the early 1980s, the leader and most of the members of the Communist Party-Political Bureau were imprisoned. They were joined, shortly afterwards, by the leaders of the professional syndicates who, in their annual congresses, voiced critical and dissident views about the regime. The arrests continued throughout the 1980s and 1990s. Majed Hebo (2001), a writer and former political prisoner, put the total number of political prisoners in the country in 1984 at 14,000, representing a ratio of approximately one in every thousand Syrian citizens being in prison at the time. The number of prisoners had grown in the run-up to the Hama violence and continued to grow in the aftermath of the massacres, as security personnel conducted sweeps of all independent political groups, sometimes arresting the entirety of their membership. For example, by most counts up to 1000 members of the Communist Action Party were arrested and imprisoned in 1987. According to some estimates, the number of individuals subjected to arrest and interrogation for political reasons reached as high as 100,000 during the period of Hafez al-Asad's rule (Hebo 2001). The scale of internment gives credence to the contention that the regime's battle was not just with the Muslim Brothers, but also with any independent political grouping that espoused dissident political views. Further, the all-reaching practices of violence and control support the proposition made by one political commentator and dissident that the regime was at war with society (the statement is attributed to writer Abd al-Razzaq Eid). This generalised war produced 'at risk' subjects, as individuals could be arrested and detained at any time without charge and in the absence of any explicit justification. Any type of affiliation or encounter with members of dissident groups was deemed sufficient pretext for arrest. Many political prisoners spent years incarcerated as a result of a chance meeting or conversation with someone whom the security services were watching or tracking. Evidence for conviction on charges of political transgression or infraction could be as circumstantial as having in one's possession a copy of the Muslim Brotherhood publication *al-Nadhir* or the Communist Action Party's clandestine newspaper *al-Rayya*.[10] Further, arbitrary detention, combined with forced disappearance, enhanced the sense of threat felt by ordinary citizens and active members of opposition groups alike (see Ziadeh 2010).

Detainees were held in various types of internment institutions and facilities – either prisons or detention centres. Official civil prisons, established mainly for non-political crimes, comprised sections dedicated to the confinement of political detainees. Additionally, different branches of the security services controlled detention centres throughout the Syrian territory. A number of military prisons and detention cells, forming part of a network of prisons, were dedicated to political opponents. The most notable (and notorious) of these prisons were al-Mezzeh Military Prison near Damascus (closed in 2000) and Tadmur Military Prison in Palmyra, located in the Homs desert (reportedly closed in 2001 following a presidential amnesty for several hundred prisoners, and the transfer of remaining detainees to other prisons). Often, the security forces running detention facilities reported directly to the Martial Law Governor, as is the case with the General Intelligence Department (Amnesty International 1983, 13). In practice, and over time, many of the detention facilities became answerable to the generals who ran them.

Approaching the camp as an apparatus of government in Syria brings into view practices of violence that had as their objective the unmaking of certain political subjectivities, specifically dissident subjectivities that were construed as inherently threatening to the health of the body politic. The pursuit of this latter objective may be noted for other political settings where internment was used on a massive scale against dissidents and political opponents but also against anyone engaging in non-conformist behaviour. A range of violent practices often centred on the body were devised and applied to have the subject overturn herself in two senses: by renouncing her political convictions, and by forcing a reversion to a non-human being. I propose a further interpretation wherein these practices are viewed as operating on the detainee's sense of self with a view to negating her subjectivity. From this optic, I propose to integrate the affectivity of confinement and torture into the analysis of forms of biopolitical government. This is intended, in part, as a

---

[10] Arrested in Aleppo in 1980 at the age of 17, Muhammad Berro was convicted of the 'crime' of having in his possession a copy of *al-Nadhir*. He would subsequently spend thirteen years in prison, of which a substantial part was spent in Tadmur (Berro 2015). Nahid Badawiyya (2014), a former prisoner in Douma's Prison for Women, relates that her period of incarceration during the 1990s overlapped with the imprisonment of two teenage girls, one of whom was charged with 'disrespecting' the photo of the president in her civics coursebook.

corrective to the analytics of biopolitical government – as formulated by Foucault and extended by Agamben – which focuses on the life of bodies in a manner that privileges physicality.

The persistence of governmental violence in penal institutions in the present (as in Syria) sits in tension with Foucault's (1977) analysis of prisons as institutions of disciplinary power, where physical punishment and humiliation are done away with in the modern period. Indeed, Foucault presents both tactics – physical punishment and humiliation – as relics of a bygone era. It is the case that humiliation appears as an objective in Foucault's discussion of medieval forms of corporal punishment but, like pain, it does not perform a governmental function. As such, and for that reason, it was abandoned with the rise of modern disciplinary power (Foucault 2015). In Foucault's account, causing pain and the public display of pain, in premodern and early modern times, were, in and of themselves, the intended objectives. As neither humiliation nor pain was considered for its role in subject formation, they were cast as belonging to a different form of power that was superseded by disciplining surveillance and regimentation. Dissenting from Foucault's analysis of punishment in various western settings in early modern Europe, some social historians assert that humiliation, incited through physical and verbal assaults on 'the offender', was core to punishment until a much later date (see Nash and Kilday 2010, for example). The publicity and sociality of spectacles of humiliation accompanying punishments in the modern period support such contentions. Yet in these same nuanced histories of punishment, governmental work through the affect, accomplished by physical punishment and humiliation, is still absent as an object of analysis.

The continuation and expansion of torture in the modern period points us to a somewhat different conclusion with regard to its use and with regard to the purposes of physical punishment of the type administered to political dissidents and those deemed to be enemies of the state. Causing pain is not the ultimate objective of punishment (except, perhaps, for the outright sadistic guard who derives pleasure from inflicting cruelty). Rather, pain is the entry point for disciplining affective dispositions constitutive of the self. It is a negation of the care necessary for personhood, for the valuing of dignity and integrity. As power treats the population as being made up of thinking and feeling subjects with ideas and affect, it deploys torture and physical punishment with the objective of manipulating and altering the feelings and the thinking processes of the subject. Studies of torture present a near consensus that its main objective is to break the subject's agency and sense of self and personhood through the infliction of embodied pain (see Wisnewski 2010, 71). Feelings elicited through the experience of being tortured at the hands of another, in particular the feeling of humiliation, destabilise the integrity of the self and undermine the capacities required for agency. In this respect, torture and physical violence proceed on the basis of the type of assumptions about the subject, and about the means of controlling and directing individual conduct, that Foucault identified with the nexus of power and knowledge of the nineteenth and twentieth centuries. Torture manuals and the production of knowledge on effects, conditions and responses to torture in the field of psychology, and in other social and natural sciences, evidence this nexus.[11]

If, during the interrogation phase, torture is intended to extract information and to garner confession, at a later stage the purpose of torture is to discipline the subject and to fashion a humiliated subjectivity and thereby force the political prisoner to abandon and renounce his or her convictions. In this sense, torture and physical violence have a location in the political logic of government.

Humiliation and Subjectivation

In this discussion of the detention camp as an apparatus of government in Syria, I primarily focus on Tadmur Military Prison, as a paradigmatic case. Of the estimated 100,000 persons who were subject to arrest and interrogation throughout the country during the time of Hafez al-Asad's rule, about 20,000 went through Tadmur for varying durations (thousands of others were sent to other prisons and detention centres). Many endured a decade or more of incarceration there before being released or transferred to other prisons. Many others perished in Tadmur. While practices of torture and violence are documented for all Syrian prisons and detention sites, the case of Tadmur, as described in the memoirs and testimonials of detainees, serves best to illustrate

---

[11] As noted by Rejali (2007), much torture training is done through apprenticeship. The teaching of effective techniques of torture and expounding on Psychology's assumptions about them have been scrutinised with reference to the School of the Americas (SOA) curriculum and the CIA's training manuals (see Wisnewski 2010). This knowledge was shared and used in Latin American countries within the US sphere of influence, with the SOA training the likes of Noriega and Pinochet's military associates. Similarly, knowledge generated by the French military's practices of torture in Algeria was shared with the post-independence Algerian ruling military (Lazreg 2008). In the Syrian case, both training and apprenticeship in torture can be deduced from the practices of the torturers and the experience of torture as conveyed by the victims and survivors (see, among others, Berro 2015; Karabit 2010). Syrian political dissidents have addressed aspects of this question in their reflections on the production of 'the whip' or *sina'at al-jallad* (the production of the person who whips in order to discipline) (Berro 2015; Karabit 2010; 'Udwan 2003).

the enmeshment of practices of violence in processes of subjectivation. I examine memoirs, diaries and fictionalised accounts authored, variously, by Ratib Sha'bo (2015); Muhammad Salim Hammad (1998); Abdallah al-Naji (ND); Bara' al-Sarraj (2011); Mustafa Khalifa (2008); Yassin al-Haj Saleh (2003, 2012a); Faraj al-Biraqdar (2006); and Aram Karabit (2010), among others, to analyse practices of subjectivation structuring everyday life in the prison camp.[12] In their memoirs these former political prisoners detail practices of violence that are oriented to the undoing of human life. Ratib Sha'bo (2015), a former detainee, coined the term *istidmar* (combining *damar*, meaning destruction and ruination, and Tadmur) to describe the lived experience and being subject to the effects of the Tadmur regime of violence. For over two decades, Tadmur served as the exemplar site of internment where the body of the prisoner was a terrain of struggle between the sovereign, with his powers over life, and the detainees, for whom the preservation of human dignity and a sense of humanity was most at stake.

As a genre of testimonial writing, memoirs and fictionalised diaries of Tadmur tend to share some elements of narrative structure.[13] For instance, events are plotted from the time of arrest to the phase of interrogation and detention, and moving on to the journey through various prisons on the eventual road to Tadmur. Although the writings represent eclectic narrative styles – ranging from the documentary to the literary – they often, if not always, cover common experiences structuring life in Tadmur and revealing the relations between prisoners, on one hand, and guards, security service figures and prison authorities, on the other. There is a degree of systematisation of the prison experiences in the writings: descriptions of cells and wards; accounts of initiation rites upon arrival; chronicles of everyday rituals pertaining to morning inspections, food distribution and collection; and testimonial on the guards' overall and unremitting regulation and monitoring of the minutiae of living in the wards. Despite the commonalities, grids of interpretation of shared prison experiences are, for some writers, filtered through the lens of

---

[12] There are memoirs and testimonies of former political prisoners that cover experiences in other prisons. Some of these are by women prisoners. See, for example, Dabbagh (ND) and the testimonies in Hassan (2007). See Haugbolle (2008) for a discussion of prison literature in Syria as an emergent expression of an individual rights movement in the 2000s.

[13] In terms of writing style, the memoirs do not fall into a single genre. Some, like Salim Hammad's testimonial, are closer in form to documentary and eyewitness accounts. Others, such as Aram Karabit's and Ratib Sha'bo's chronicles, are deeply personal in their witnessing and their exposing of internal torments and suffering. Still others, like Biraqdar's and Mustafa Khalifa's, are literary, while Yassin al-Haj Saleh's (2012a) analytical essays on prison life tend more towards social science writing.

ideological affiliation. For example, detainees with Islamist affiliation invoked sectarianism to account for the brutality of the guards (Hammad 1998; al-Naji ND). Meanwhile, communist detainees analysed the sectarianisation of the prison resulting from the predominance of guards and security officers of Alawi background (Haddad 2004; Karabit 2010; Sha'bo 2015).

A Zone of Abandonment

In various respects, Tadmur localises a zone of abandonment in the Syrian polity. Located in the Homs desert, Tadmur was a military facility inherited from the French mandate administration. Following national independence, it became a space of banishment of political dissidents, alongside military personnel serving prison sentences in a separate compound. Isolated from inhabited areas and surrounded by military compounds, Tadmur prisoners were cut off from the outside in multiple respects. Prison memoirs depict spatial arrangements confirming conditions of abandonment. The facility is described as a large sprawling complex of buildings with individual holding cells and numerous collective wards, estimated to number thirty-nine in total, distributed around seven courtyards. In the memoirs, descriptions of Tadmur spaces emphasise the detainees' sense of isolation and desolation. This sense of isolation was intensified by the fact that visits were, on the whole, denied, although exceptions were noted and were made for prisoners whose families bribed the warden (al-Naji ND, 140). Newspapers, radio and other means of gaining connection with the outside world were forbidden. Prisoners spent twenty-three hours a day inside the wards, and were only allowed out to the courtyard nearest their ward for the one-hour breathing break (*tanafus*).

In his memoir of his years of incarceration, Bara' al-Sarraj describes the prison as exuding an atmosphere of horror that is sensed through characteristic sounds that played as a soundtrack to the day and night rhythms of life at Tadmur. All through the night, prisoners heard the sounds of the guards' boots thumping on the roofs above their cells. During the day, the pounding of prisoners' bare feet as they were made to run over the asphalt of the courtyard during *tanafus* exercises were overlaid with the shouts, insults and scolding of the security men. Their time in the cells and wards was punctuated by the hissing of whips, the piercing screams of the tortured coming through the high windows, the jangling of keys and the screeching of metal gates as they closed. In Bara' al-Sarraj's words (2011, 79) these sounds intermingled to compose a symphony of horror. Tadmur, Bara' al-Sarraj avers, possessed its own quality of fear – a type of fear that was synonymous with the place and that had no equivalent anywhere else.

In design, the compounds exposed the prisoners to the bitter desert cold as much as to the guards' constant surveillance from their positions on the roofs. Hammad (1998, 39) describes conditions and experiences of abandonment:

> The winter set in … the desert winter is merciless … in our ward we possess nothing but our tattered blankets, the windows and ceiling hatches are all open over our heads. Because of the cold and the damp climate and terrible nutrition, colds and rheumatism spread, and within a year tuberculosis reared its head. We only discovered it once it spread.

In the 1980s, prisoners experienced undernourishment as the food supply was meagre. Deprived of nutrition and left to battle the freezing cold of the Tadmur desert, many of the prisoners contracted tuberculosis and the rate of affliction reached an epidemic level. An entry in Hammad's memoir (1998, 39), dated June 1983, refers to a quarantine set up in Ward 35 for inmates diagnosed with tuberculosis. Having contracted the disease, Hammad was moved to Ward 35. Upon entering the ward, he found 'more than one hundred brothers consumed by disease' who 'were forced to sleep next to each other, exposing one another to contagion willing or not' (Hammad 1998, 61).

Prison conditions exposed the body to extreme hazards and threatened the physiological life of the detainees. Testimonials and memoirs of prisoners record the frequent outbreak of contagious diseases caused by the dire hygiene conditions of the detention cells and wards, the poor sanitary provisions and meagre food rations. Among the common afflictions were severe skin rashes and diarrhoea (al-Naji ND, 135; Hammad 1998, 46; Mustafa Khalifa 2008, 191–2). Al-Naji (ND, 135) reports that cases of dysentery and typhoid arose regularly for extended periods of time. Such conditions resulted in the death of an as yet undetermined number of detainees.

Pedagogical Violence: Ta'lim (Marking)

Recurrent themes in most of the prison memoirs pertain to the violent practices that were applied in a systematic fashion to political detainees. These practices are, in the first instance, inscriptions on the body, while also working on the subject's sense of self and on her/his sense of self-worth and dignity. The accounts show that conditions were akin to those characterising concentration camps, as noted by Agamben (1998, 135): the organisation of life 'with … meticulous regulations that do not spare any aspect of physiological life (not even the digestive function which is obsessively codified and publicized)'.

Typically, upon arrival at the prison, prisoners are inducted into the prison regime. Known as 'the reception party' (*haflat al-istiqbal*), the induction initiates new detainees into the practices of violence and humiliation. The reception ritual is designed to shatter the detainee's sense of personhood and to sap his or her dignity. In his fictionalised account of Tadmur, Mustafa Khalifa (2008, 46–8) records more than the ceremonial kicks and punches of the arrival ritual. In a scene of extreme degradation, one of the new detainees is ordered to drink from an open sewer in the prison courtyard. He resists and is subject to a vicious beating by prison guards that kills him. In the process, the guards make an example of him to elicit dispositions of compliance in other detainees.

The importance of the guards' bodily inscriptions during the reception ritual is heightened in the practice of *ta'lim*, which, in this context, means marking a prisoner for pedagogical punishment. In all collective cells, prison guards choose one or several prisoners upon their arrival to serve as an exemplum of punishment for the instruction of other inmates. The marked prisoner receives extra physical punishment, possibly leading to his death. The power of death is enacted in 'pedagogical killing' in the prison, but also in the wider social body through the massacre. *Ta'lim* is derived, in Arabic, from two different roots: that of *'ilm* ('learning') and that of *'alama* ('mark'). The practice denoted by *ta'lim* is marking, but to mark is also to teach. Marking is achieved by selecting a body for the exemplary inscription of biopower.

Ta'lim unfolds as a continuous practice and is intimately linked with overnight monitoring of the wards and morning inspection by the guards. For instance, especially during the evening hours guards, positioned on the roofs of the wards and surveilling the prisoners inside through hatches in the ward ceilings, would routinely call one or more prisoners for marking. Prisoners would be subject to marking during the night for making any slight movement or for waking up to use the urinal (Hammad 1998, 36; Bara' al-Sarraj 2011, 47; Sha'bo 2015, 264–5). Prisoners assigned to the role of ward supervisors were at greater risk as they stood guard below the hatch and were visible to the guards for longer periods. The marked prisoners were subjected to additional and extreme punishments. Every morning, two or three marked prisoners were taken out of the ward for punishment. Karabit (2010, 80) observes that this practice is a well-studied psychological operation intended to make fear and dread inhabit and consume the prisoner for the duration of the night. As explained by Karabit, the power of *ta'lim* derives from the fact that it is a delayed punishment. Often a guard would instruct a detainee to mark himself, but there were times when the ward supervisor was instructed to mark a fellow detainee.

Ta'lim also took place during breathing time (*tanafus*) when the prisoners were taken out to the courtyard to perform gruelling physical exercises selected for them by the guards. These exercises were interspersed by instructions to perform humiliating acts such as simulating animal sounds. *Tanafus* became an occasion to stage spectacles of debasement and ultimately to trigger a sense of worthlessness in the prisoners by implicating them as witnesses to the dehumanisation of fellow detainees or by making them objects of the spectacle. Episodes of *ta'lim* confront the prisoners with the dilemmas of being at the threshold of the human-non-human (to be discussed below).

Somatic Discipline: Breaking Bodies and Souls

The condition of being humiliated is accomplished, symbolically, if not literally, by 'fracturing the eye' (*kasr al-'ayn*) so that the subject is rendered unable to look the guard in the eye. Indeed, the required body posture upon arrival at Tadmur was to keep the head down and never lift it to look at the face of a guard or an officer. Failure to maintain this posture led to beatings. In the evening, prisoners were required to cover their eyes with blindfolds (referred to as *tamasha*, literally a blinder) (Karabit 2010, 65). *Kasr al-'ayn* is also practised outside the prison to fashion a non-contesting subject, as will be examined when we turn to the political subjectivities formed in relation to dictatorial government.

The regulation of all aspects of physiological life puts natural life at the centre of practices of punishment. Thus, the period allocated to 'breathing' (*tanafus*) – that is, getting out of the cell into a courtyard – is also the time selected for intensified punishment (see Amnesty International 2001; Hammad 1998). As a consequence, 'breathing' is turned into the most dreaded and hated activity. A time assigned to the most basic bodily function exposes the body to the conditions of bare life. Writing about 'the breather regime', Hammad (1998, 31) notes the enforced posture and movement:

After breakfast, we remain still, awaiting an hour of torture ... at some point, the guards call us for breathing. We go out to the courtyard, our heads down, each one of us grasping the waist of the brother in front of him ... the cables and batons that beat down upon us lead us to where [the guards] want.

The regulation of breathing includes the banning of speech and movement and the requirement of standing, without moving, facing the wall (Hammad 1998, 31).

As with breathing, other basic bodily functions involved exposure to punishment. Trips to the bathroom and to the showers were pretexts for lashings and beatings before and after the performances of bodily functions and cleanliness rituals (Hammad 1998, 19). Physical punishment reserved for bathroom trips were also recorded by Begoña Aretxaga (1995) in her work on Irish Republican Army (IRA) prisoners. Other body-care practices were marked with physical violence. For example, shaving of the head and face was done by prison barbers using dull razors that caused cuts to the scalp and deep wounds to the face (Hammad 1998, 31–2; Karabit 2010, 25).

Aretxaga (1995) refers to these techniques of punishment as a breakdown of rationalisation and as the excess in the exercises of punishment, whereby power indulges in its own theatrical staging. I would suggest, however, that these exercises contain their own rationalisation, wherein humiliation and producing a humiliated state of being are the objectives. Torture works on affect and its objective is not only to cause physical pain but, also, to bring about the degradation and diminishment of the subject's sense of human self, heightening the experience of being demeaned, soiled, dirty and violated. These dimensions of torture are clear in the use of methods that involve the penetration of body orifices and in sexual aggression. For example, among the methods of torture reported by those who had been detained in Syrian prisons is making prisoners sit on a bottle with its mouth penetrating the anus. Apparatuses such as *al-dulab* (the tire), *bisat al-rih* (the flying carpet) and *al-kursi al-almani* (the German chair) force the body to be bent and moulded in ways intended to inflict damage and cause disability.[14] While these devices tend to be used during the interrogation phase, the assault on the body persists with daily beatings, whippings and battering. Punishments for misdemeanours include slapping the face and banging the inmate's skull against the wall or the metal bars of the cell. The acts of physical violence that guards in Syrian prisons carried out, as a matter of routine, have been documented for political prisons and camps in other countries.[15]

[14] *Al-dulab* is a large rubber tire that a prisoner has to slide under his or her neck, placing it under the arms then forcing the rest of the body within the remaining circle, leaving the lower extremities hanging upward from it. *Bisat al-rih* is a plank of wood to which the prisoner is strapped then strung up to hang while receiving punishments. *Al-kursi al-almani* is a metal chair to which the hands and feet of the prisoner are tied. The chair's back is moveable and lifts in a manoeuvre that hyperextends the spine, placing intense pressure on the neck and limbs.

[15] There are striking similarities between the punishments involving intense physical violence and extremely demeaning acts detailed in Syrian prisoners' memoirs and testimonies and those documented for the concentration camps in Nazi Germany, the gulag in Stalinist Russia, the political prison in Greece under the dictatorship, and in South American states under the rule of the military generals in the 1970s and 1980s (Cesereaunu 2006).

In his discussion of torture in Argentina, Marcelo M. Suarez-Orozco (2003, 385) argues that we must explain the very action of torture as well as the specific form that the torture takes. He underscores the expressive symbolism of torture, pointing to the signification of certain acts of torture, such as the electrocution of men's genitals, a practice common to many torture settings in South America and the Arab world. This practice, it has been argued, could be read as a castration metaphor. In accounts of detention and interrogation, techniques of torture that target genitalia figure repeatedly – for example, the crushing of testicles at the hands of the torturers and punches and kicks to the genital area often resulting in damage leading to the excision of the testicles. According to Suarez-Orozco (2003, 385), the encounter between torturer and victim is enacted as a face-off between 'the macho army' and 'dangerous subversives' targeted for emasculation.

The sexual language of torture and its iterative performance recalls and re-inscribes mythic gods with powers of retribution over the body. In the cosmology of the Eternal Leader – the omnipotent and omnipresent – sexualised torture is a kind of retribution visited on the wicked. In a macabre scene from Mustafa Khalifa's (2008, 227) novel-cum-memoir of life in Tadmur Prison, *Al-Qawqa'ah* (*The Shell*), the narrator describes an attack by an assistant guard on a political prisoner. While executing the acts of punishment, the attacker, nicknamed *Wahsh* (beast), demands to know from his victim and the other detained dissidents what it is that they do not like about the leader (Hafez al-Asad). He then bellows that the leader will fuck them and will fuck their mothers and their sisters. The image that develops in the guard's verbal attack is a figuration of the body of the leader with his sexual organ conjured as the largest (Mustafa Khalifa 2008, 227). The guard then breaks into the slogan 'long live the president'. Mythology and folkloric tales are integrated into the technologies of domination.

Breaking Borders and the Human-Non-Human Threshold

A catalogue of practices of humiliation is compiled in the growing number of Syrian memoirs of detention and imprisonment. Repertoires of humiliation include the forced eating of insects and vermin, the drinking of urine and the kissing of a guard's boots (see Hammad 1998, 35).[16] The

---

[16] Such practices of torture are comparable to those applied to Kurds imprisoned in the Diarbakir prison in Turkey. There, they function as 'softening' strategies designed to break the prisoners and get them to shout slogans of allegiance to the Turkish state (Zeydanlıoğlu 2009).

cruelty and debasement intended by these punishments are a variation on practices noted for more 'humane' and 'civilised' detention centres. Aretxaga (1995) also recorded that IRA prisoners were given food that was soiled with urine or had insects in it. Defilement and contamination are designed to soil the body and the person beyond the possibility of ever becoming clean again. Hammad (1998) writes in his testimonial of life in Tadmur that it was routine for guards to force prisoners to lick soiled matter, including spit, off the ground. In *Al-Qawqa'ah* (*The Shell*), the narrator/prisoner describes a scene of repulsive invasion of the body when the guard spits inside his mouth and forces him to swallow the spit (Mustafa Khalifa 2008, 101–2). As a result, he feels his insides soiled to the point that they can never be clean again. In his words, the spit is stuck to the wall of his stomach. The subject's sense that it would not be possible to be cleansed again captures the tear or rupture in the self.[17] The taint and defilement reside within the walls of the stomach, nurtured and kept alive in the memory of being tainted.

Defilement and contamination of the body are precisely the type of threats and dangers that, in their actualisation, create the state of abjection, negating the subject's personhood. To this end, prison guards inflicted punishments devised to provoke self-repulsion and the feeling of abjection. One of the commonly recounted incidents in detainees' narratives is that of the prisoner made to eat a dead mouse. Hammad (1998, 76–7), Mustafa Khalifa (2008) and al-Biraqdar (2006, 51–3) recount such stories in much detail. The forced repulsive act, in their narratives, leaves the prisoner shattered and broken. What such accounts point to is that the underlying purpose of forced self-debasement and humiliation is to destabilise the subject's sense of selfhood.

The destabilisation of bodily borders is a technique of overturning the subject against herself (see Kristeva (1982) on borders). Karabit (2010, 89) gives a troubling account of the forced breaking of borders between his bodily fluids and those of a fellow inmate:

They [guards] knocked on the door and shouted, 'Get out for the wedding.' We rolled into the court like terrorised bird formations. 'Get naked …' Not long after, the Whips came out … their cables burnt our skin … They went about torturing us in a systematic way. Shouting: 'On the ground. Crawl on your elbows and knees.' We proceeded to do as instructed. We did so until we were bleeding. One of [the guards] shouted at me: 'Ward superintendent [Karabit's assignment].'

---

[17] This manner of soiling and contaminating the prisoner was also used in exemplar camps such as the Russian gulag where guards dropped urine on the bodies or into the mouths of the inmates (Cesereaunu 2006).

I saluted him and stood guard. 'Go there and stand by the one at the corner.' When I stood face-to-face with the person there, he ordered: 'Spit on him, spit on the old man, the man with white hair.' I stood in shock, not knowing what to do. I said, 'Sergeant, he is an old man.' He shouted: 'Spit on him.' I said: 'He is old, he is like my father.' I spoke while my face was down. Lifting your face in Tadmur is a crime. He said: 'You son of a whore, mark yourself (*'alim nafsak*). Here there is no "my father". You are all scum' … He repeated: 'Spit on him' … Silence fell on the place. The guards were waiting for the farce to climax … I was face-to-face with Abu Nijm [the old man]. His eyes in my eyes, the saliva in his throat in my mouth, and mine in his, each spitting on the other. I spit at myself, at my destiny and his, and at the destiny of our countries, my misery, his misery and the misery of our countries.

The narrative of the assault of bodily fluids, also noted for other camps, conveys the kind of battering directed at the human spirit. The assault triggers responses at the level of the affect such as humiliation and estrangement with respect to one's body seen as being stained beyond cleaning. Karabit's testimony illustrates the disjunction within the self that Ratib Sha'bo (2015, 363) diagnoses as resulting from the subject's human self being assaulted or from standing as a silent witness to someone else's torture and suffering. In his words, the witness's feeling of relief for not being the object of torture, even momentarily, and his forced silence kill within him his self-pride and any spirit of rebellion. Reflecting on the practice of positioning prisoners as witnesses of dehumanising suffering, Sha'bo describes the quandary they face, the fears and the internal rupture that can never be healed:

They take one of the members of the ward to torture, not far from his mates, rather in front of the entire ward and within earshot of everyone. You are forced to accept this. Any rejection is a form of suicide, or worse than suicide: disfigurement and disability. When you accept this, something inside you is broken forever. It will be registered that you were not the man you ought to be. You did not act with the courage worthy of such situations. (Sha'bo 2015, 363)

Thus, the fashioning of the 'unheroic' subject and the engendering of memories of cowardice appear to be at the heart of the duel between the 'petty sovereigns' and the recalcitrant subject.[18]

These affective responses to another's suffering emerge precisely at the threshold of the human and non-human. In his prison diaries, Ratib Sha'bo (2015, 244) reflects on the lines/borders between the human and the animal, expressing his anguish that, in Tadmur, the limits are absent and the borders are open. He ponders the possibility that the mind that

---

[18] Lawrence Langer (1991) coined the term 'unheroic memory' as a category of Holocaust testimonial recollections.

designed this prison would seek to bring about a human's reversion to a state of animality: 'I could not protect myself from the fear that the designers of these tortures and the innovators of counter-humanity would deprive the human of his sense of physiological humanity.' In a bleak vision of further debasement, Sha'bo conjures a circumstance where a prisoner was chained to a pole and rendered immobile. Unable to move, he would be forced to meet his physiological needs of expelling bodily waste (urination and defecation) at the spot where he was chained. The question for him is 'when confronted with the unrestrained imagination of liquidation and not just debasement and humiliation, which is more extreme, liquidation or reversion to animality?' The anxieties and fears viscerally conveyed through these reflections reference the menace of self-debasement leading to nullifying the human self.

Arts of Human Dying and of Human Living

The practices of humiliation, punishment and violence to which prisoners were subjected should not be considered in isolation of the prisoners' own practices that aimed to claim and affirm a worthy human life and negate the objectives of the camp. Indeed, the accounts and memoirs of Syrian detainees point to how the interned instrumentalised their bodies, turning them into sites of resistance and not just sites of the inscription of coercive and disciplinary power. In this context, and as pointed out by Aretxaga, the body is invested in the intersubjective relations with other prisoners and with the guards. For example, prisoners strove to counter the effects of physical assaults by the guards, which, in some instances, accompanied daily routine occurrences such as the collection of food containers delivered to the front of the cell. As such, they devised tactics to alleviate the risks that these practices posed to the life of the elderly or the ill among them. Thus, volunteers, usually from among the younger prisoners, put themselves forward as food collectors (Hammad 1998, 36; Mustafa Khalifa 2008, 63–4). These men, who exposed their bodies to punishment to spare the more vulnerable detainees, were called the *fida'yyin* (literally 'those who sacrifice' – a term used in reference to front-line soldiers running reconnaissance missions). These acts, intensifying the body's experience of humiliation and pain, permitted the reintroduction of virtuous subjectivities back into the prisoners' world – a world of degradation and bare life.

In Tadmur, executions of Muslim Brotherhood detainees were common during most of the 1980s. In the face of routine hangings on a weekly basis, detainees improvised life-affirming practices. For instance, those condemned to death would give away their clothes and other belongings as they prepared for execution. They often did this in association with making wills that included requests for a message to be communicated to their families or friends, asking for forgiveness and bestowing their few material possessions to fellow detainees. The rituals surrounding death in the wards sought to safeguard the humanity of the persons and resist the reversion to the non-human state. Resistance to dehumanisation took the form of such rituals as the preparation for burial of the bodies of 'martyrs', the administration of burial rites and rituals – such as reading the Quran and praying – and speaking of and remembering the martyrs after their execution or their death by other means (Hammad 1998; Mustafa Khalifa 2008, 134). In the same vein, practices of memorisation were common and signal a striving to keep alive a hope that there will be time, in the future, for remembering. Bara' al-Sarraj (2011) writes of memorisation practices that helped the prisoners in preserving the memory of events and of the space of the camp (see also al-Biraqdar 2006). Memorisation appears as a technique of self that is used against the practices aimed at unmaking the subject. Through repetition exercises, detainees committed to memory chapters of the Quran, entire passages from books, names of dead prisoners, specific events and entire days in the prison (al-Naji ND, 130; Bara' al-Sarraj 2011, 23; al-Biraqdar 2006; Mustafa Khalifa 2008, 76–7).

Along with the arts of human dying which the prisoners strove to enact, arts of human living were cultivated in the struggle to meet simple everyday needs and to improve living conditions in the wards. Detainees learnt, through trial and error, how to make various items out of the nylon wraps of the daily bread rations (Bara' al-Sarraj 2011, 44). Ratib Sha'bo (2015, 245–9) describes the wonderment that the communist prisoners felt upon settling into their wards in Tadmur at the time they were transferred there in the mid 1990s as a punishment for refusing to renounce their party affiliations and their political views. Sha'bo remarks that they marvelled at the nylon nets that the previous detainees left behind on the walls of the ward. The nets were suitable for hanging washed clothes, and were used as such. Through trial and error, the new detainees discovered how to manufacture nylon thread for mending clothes. The needles for mending were made out of the bones that could sometimes be fished out of the food they were given. Creating these primitive implements and resources were essential to fortifying the self and maintaining human living at the threshold of the human-non-human life conditions of the prison.

In highlighting these practices and viewing them as arts of dying humanly and of living humanly, it is not my purpose to romanticise the struggle for survival and for life in the camp. Rather, I want to underscore that these arts were possibly the only means by which prisoners could conduct resistance. The forms of power exercised through the body of the prisoners precluded particular acts of outright resistance or, at best, made them obsolete. It would not have been effective, for example, for the Tadmur prisoners to go on hunger strikes to protest, or to seek to change or draw public attention to their conditions. As a politics of death was at the heart of incarceration practices at Tadmur, a hunger strike to the death would likely be managed by hastening the strikers' death in the context of isolation and abandonment. Thus, unlike other jurisdictions where such tactics were adopted (e.g. Ireland, Turkey) as ways of mobilising support externally or altering conditions internally, they were of no possible utility in Tadmur.[19]

Overturning Oneself: A Polity at Ransom

The practices of torture documented in Tadmur, and other Syrian prisons, had as their purpose the undoing of the prisoners as political subjects, and their reconstitution in a way that is devoid of dignity and that is incapable of dissenting. Most telling about this objective is the periodic 'negotiation' or *musawama* (literally 'bargaining', in the words of former prisoners) sessions that political prisoners were called to attend.[20] In these sessions, the exchange or bargain was generally offered to members of secular parties detained in sites less severe than Tadmur (for example in 'Adra Prison or in the Sheikh Hassan detention facility, both in Damascus). In their memoirs and testimonies, political prisoners recount incidents of bargaining wherein, at different intervals of their incarceration, they were hauled in front of military committees composed of high-ranking officers who reviewed their cases individually and demanded that they renounce their political affiliation and dissociate themselves from their leaders and comrades in return for release from prison.[21] In exchange for personal liberty, the prisoners had to declare their allegiance to the president. Both renunciations and declarations had to be signed by the detainees (Hebo 2001; Karabit 2010, 37; Sha'bo 2015, 174). In his memoir, Karabit (2010, 38) recalls that following the refusal by a number of detainees from the Communist Party-Political Bureau to agree to the bargain

---

[19] See Bargu (2014) for the Turkish case.

[20] Yassin al-Haj Saleh (2011a) characterises the practice of *musawama* as a requirement for the dissident to overturn himself or herself.

[21] Bara' al-Sarraj (2011, 66, 68) recounts being summoned to several meetings by these committees, including one that took place in October 1995, and was presided over by General Hassan Khalil and Commander Hisham Bakhtiar.

and to sign off on the statements and declarations, an army colonel met with one of the group's leaders to try to enlist him in the conversion task. The exchange or bargain at times involved the condition that the prisoner sign a statement of self-critique denouncing her/his previous views and promising to cooperate with the security services. In their efforts to secure this bargain, the security services and prison officers often drafted close family members to put pressure on the prisoners to agree to the exchange. Refusal to accept the bargain often resulted in an escalation of punishment and transfer to Tadmur Prison (as in the cases of Majed Hebo, Ratib Sha'bo, Aram Karabit and Yassin al-Haj Saleh, to name a few).

The effects of the internment camp are not limited to the political detainees, but extend throughout society. In fact, the detention system aimed at society at large and not only at the dissidents. As in the disappearances in Argentina (Robben 2000, 95), detention stoked feelings of anguish among relatives, colleagues and friends about the fate of the detainees and the kind of suffering they were likely to be enduring. Additionally, accounts of punishment in prison reached the families and social circles of detainees. Family members, up to fourth-degree relatives, were screened out of public employment and faced restrictions on movement and travel. They were also subject to enhanced surveillance and monitoring, being cast as members of a risky population. Further, family members were, at times, summoned by the security forces to bring about the public surrender of political convictions on the part of the prisoner. For instance, in his prison testimony Majed Hebo (2001), a Communist Action Party activist, recounts that his father tried to convince him to renounce his political views and declare allegiance to Hafez al-Asad in return for his release. Hebo's refusal to do so led to a break-up of family relations, a common outcome for political prisoners who rejected the deals offered by the security services. Through a wide range of practices, imprisonment and conditions of detention interconnected with everyday life outside the prison. Arrest, interrogation and detention came to be seen as hazards of everyday living that could arise in encounters with the security officers ubiquitously present on the streets, or that could result from entrapment by informants working as taxi drivers and vendors at street-corner kiosks.

The Politics of the Massacre in the Civil War Regime

Alongside the detention camp, war served as a technique of population government by the Asad regime. The massacres committed in the drive to uproot the Islamist insurgency of the late 1970s and early 1980s, and then again to crush the Uprising in 2011, unfolded as part of a war against a population deemed recalcitrant. In this section, I want to explore the massacres as a manifestation of a 'civil war regime'. This is a regime that corresponds, in some of its features and styles of operation, to Foucault's analysis of politics as 'permanent war' which, Foucault (2003, 50) suggests, is an originary or primary condition of politics – it founds the state and the law.[22] In the Syrian civil war regime, as in the permanent war discussed by Foucault, drawing binary lines through the social body is core to the logic of population government.

To approach the massacres in Syria as expressions of the civil war regime, I draw attention to the rationalities behind them, their specific forms and their intended objectives. Through a constellation of practices and techniques, a division of the population into 'us' and 'them' was enacted. The 'us' part of this division should be read to include supporters of the regime, while the 'them' side is comprised of opponents or the political opposition. This latter – the opponents – are constituted as expendable. What can be discerned, in this regard, is the same eradicationist or liquidationist logic found in fascist regimes that presided over civil wars, of which Francoist Spain is a telling example. I use the 1982 mass killings in Hama as an illustrative case of the practices and techniques of the civil war regime in Syria.

---

[22] In his account of war as foundational of relations of power, Foucault identifies the emergence, in post-medieval Europe, of a historico-political discourse on society in which war is understood as a permanent social relationship and, as such, the basis of social relations (Foucault 2003, 49–50). The discourse, in its first birth, was used as a tool of organisation for social struggles by different social forces: the aristocracy in both England and France, the bourgeoisie in England, and the popular forces in both countries. Importantly, this historical discourse was a declaration of the rights of 'peoples' and of 'races' against their lords and, ultimately, against their subjugators. It was out of the wars and battles in these struggles and in the massacres committed in them that the law was born. Foucault cautions that this does not mean that the birth of law meant the end of war or served as an armistice establishing peace. Instead, 'beneath the law, war continues to rage in all the mechanisms of power, even in the most regular. War is the motor behind institutions and order. In the smallest of its cogs, peace is waging a secret war' (Foucault 2003, 50). Foucault contends that the historico-political discourse of war had a second birth in which the idea of a perpetual or uninterrupted war takes the form of 'race war' whereby society or the social body is divided, in a binary mode, into two races (Foucault 2003, 59–60). Racism, as a technology of government, develops in tandem with the emerging modern rationality of government holding that the state's objective is to tend to the health and welfare of the population. In other words, racism is fundamentally entwined with biopolitical government – government that has as its object the life of the population.

The Will to Kill: Identifying the Enemy Population

The official objective of the assault on Hama was the elimination of the Islamist opposition. This objective was, however, framed in relation to a grand mission. Rif'at al-Asad, who is thought to have been the strategist of the ground attack, conceived of the regime's response to the challenge of opposing groups within the frame of grand undertakings or great works that require spectacular sacrifice. In his speech to the Ba'th Party Seventh Regional Congress in 1980, less than two years prior to the Hama massacre, he invoked Stalin's vision for a great Soviet state, which necessitated that large numbers of people be eliminated. Extolling chauvinism in support of national ideologies, he exhorted his listeners to embrace chauvinism, citing, as exemplar, Stalin's actions for the sake of the Revolution: 'Stalin, O Comrades, liquidated ten million humans for the sake of the Communist revolution, taking into account only one matter and that is chauvinism for his party and for the party's perspective.' Rif'at cites the example of other nations and groups that showed chauvinism in their national ideologies and that were, as a result, models of achievement. He concludes that chauvinism in favour of the Ba'thist idea is a historical necessity that requires large-scale sacrifices.

In a number of speeches, Hafez al-Asad (1980b, 1982) explicated the necessity and rationale for the liquidation of the Muslim Brothers. Such announcements, as noted by Jacques Sémelin (2003, 198), belong to the discursive repertoires of massacre politics. The will to kill, articulated in the speeches of Hafez al-Asad and Rif'at al-Asad, was also communicated in announcements and declarations attributed to army generals and governors, in statements asserting willingness and readiness to kill thousands (e.g. General Ghazi Kan'an declaring a willingness to 'plant a thousand flowers' in the Homs desert). The idea of revolutionary violence as an imperative was propagated in the media during Hafez al-Asad's presidency (*al-Ba'th*, 18 March 1980) as it was under his successor.

Rhetoric about conspiracies and foreign plots organised the public discourses of the leaders and loyalists. One of the dominant motifs of this rhetoric was the charge that the Muslim Brothers worked in conjunction with President Sadat in Egypt to facilitate the implementation of the Camp David Accords and, hence, the betrayal of the Arab and Palestinian goals of liberation (*al-Ba'th*, 18 March 1980). Reactionary agents of imperialism and plotters against the Arab nation, the Muslim Brothers and, by extension, any opponent of the regime were enemies of the people (*a'da' al-sha'b*). The sole appropriate response to this enemy was liquidation.

Thus, in public discourse, the regime constructed a category of dispensable subjects, namely the Muslim Brothers. Their status as dispensable subjects was confirmed in Law 49 issued in 1980, which made membership of the group punishable by death. Similarly, the recalcitrant populations of Hama were subsumed under this category of subjects slated for elimination. In some sense, the label 'Muslim Brothers' became shorthand for populations that opposed the ruling regime and that, as a result, were rendered dispensable. As elaborated in the discussion of the sacralisation of politics and its articulation with the civil war regime, the massacres in Syria were supported by a murderous discourse (a discourse authorising or sanctioning murder). The murderous discourse of the Syrian regime projected the existence of an enemy population of traitors and murderers – nationally diseased and ill in their patriotism who had to be excised from the body politic. The war was waged as a cultural war and a civilisational war and, above all, as a war of ideas. The old sovereign power to kill must take a cosmic form and assume a transcendental horizon – a quasi-religious order framing war between orthodoxy and heresy or deviance. The cleavage introduced into the population takes the form of a civilisational and a cultural division, thus fracturing the social field in ideological terms, with the line of fracture being that between correct thinking, on one side, and diseased thinking, on the other. Suarez-Orozco (2003) characterises state-sponsored violence in Latin America in the 1970s and 1980s in words that aptly describe the state of war unleashed by the Syrian regime against the enemy population:

[T]orture and death of 'subversives' was the magical treatment against the spread of an infectious way of life. To simplify their thinking and to focus energy, the armed left, the democratic left, intellectuals, artists, psychiatrists, psychologists, sociologists, children, pregnant women and other deviants were bunched together as representatives, or potential representatives, or sympathisers with an international assault penetrating the fatherland from the outside, growing, spreading within. (Suarez-Orozco 2003, 386)

A Politics of Annihilation and Ruination

The scale of the Islamist insurgency in Syria in the late 1970s and early 1980s remains undetermined. As estimated by observers and as can be gleaned from accounts provided by the protagonists, the number of Islamist insurgents was relatively small. According to Syrian human rights organisations, there were 300 armed Islamists in Hama belonging, predominately, to the militant group al-Tali'a al-Muqatila ('The Combatant Vanguard'). Other observers, and some Hama residents, put the number between 300 and 1000 (interviews with former Hama residents, London

2011, Stockholm 2011). An estimate of 300 active Islamist militants is given for Aleppo in 1980 prior to the army's mobilisation and crushing of their bases in that city.[23] The challenge that the insurgency represented, it could be argued, arose in relation to its tactics rather than its numerical strength or military capabilities. During this period, the Tali'a launched a bombing campaign, targeting military buildings, Ba'th Party offices and state cooperatives (Seale 1988; see also the memoir of Ayman al-Sharbaji (ND), a Tali'a activist). It also carried out a series of assassinations of high-profile figures associated with the regime. The Tali'a was additionally responsible for the massacre, committed in 1979 by Colonel Ibrahim al-Yusuf, of seventy-nine Alawi cadets at the Aleppo Artillery Academy. In response, the various security branches intensified their surveillance and arrest of youth in activist milieus. Thousands of Muslim Brothers, and dissidents belonging to oppositional leftist groupings, were rounded up and imprisoned. Also, the military and security forces were mobilised to crush opposition in Aleppo and Idlib and, in the process, committed a number of massacres in 1980 and 1981. In this respect, the regime deployed the military option early on in the confrontation with the Islamists and other opponents.

Against this background, the immediate catalyst for the assault on Hama was the continued activism of the Tali'a group in the city as well as incidents of attack on Ba'th Party cadres and on a security post. In light of the estimated number of armed insurgents, the extraordinary violence unleashed on the city does not find rationalisation simply in the rules of armed engagement, whereby the mobilised force should be proportionate to the numbers and capabilities of the opposing camp. However, principles of military rationalisation do not apply to this armed onslaught on the Hama population. The massacres in Hama were part of a war against the enemy population, codenamed the Muslim Brothers. Yet, in effect, the war extended beyond them to all opponents of the regime as well as all civilians who harboured some sympathy for the opposition. At the same time, the Islamist insurgency used terrorist methods and articulated a mirror image of the regime's polarising discourse (al-Sharbaji ND).

The assault on Hama was led and carried out by two paramilitary units, namely the Defence Companies, whose commander was Rif'at al-Asad, and the Special Units under the leadership of Ali Haydar, and was supported by army divisions, most importantly the Third Division under General Shafiq Fayyad. In the early hours of 3 February 1982, armoured

---

[23] A number of massacres were committed during the military campaign in Aleppo in 1980.

tanks surrounded the city, while forces positioned at the Mahrda barracks nearby shelled homes and neighbourhoods, combined with aerial bombardment. To create a state of siege, water, electricity and telephone lines were cut off. Once the siege was complete and Hama's isolation secured, the military men dispersed throughout the city carrying out their mission of killing, looting and destruction.

The military forces proceeded to round up residents from their homes and to congregate them in schools, stadiums and sports centres and cemeteries. Documentary material and accounts of the massacres point to a policy of systematic killing of males above fifteen years of age. Groups of women and children were also killed (SHRC 2001). People were amassed into groups and shot collectively. In a number of massacres, entire families and residents of whole streets were brought out into open space and shot. In a report of one of the massacres, named the Sirhin massacre, a survivor testified that people were driven in eleven buses from various neighbourhoods in the city of Hama to the village of Sirhin where they were ordered to disembark and were later shot and thrown into mass graves that were already filled with bodies of those killed in other massacres (SHRC 2001).

Mass killings and detention in makeshift detention camps were a daily occurrence for a four-week period. The Hama massacre, in effect, is a chain of massacres committed in various neighbourhoods of the city. Executions of small and large groups of people took place in private dwellings, in alleyways, in grocery stores, in workshops and factories, thus inscribing the experience of horror throughout a multitude of city spaces. During this period, and in its aftermath, Hama became a spectacle of death. It served as an exemplum of the ruler's power over life and his right to kill with impunity in a manner that recalls the conduct of the sovereign described by Achille Mbembe (2003) as necropolitics: a form of politics concerned with the subjugation of life to the powers of death.

In the course of the shelling and bombardment, entire buildings, historical quarters and markets were razed to the ground (Amnesty International 1983; SHRC 2001). Neighbourhoods such as al-Kilaniyya, home to great architectural works of earlier historical periods, became rubble. Adopting counter-insurgency tactics, snipers were positioned on the roofs of public buildings in the vicinity of old city quarters. Snipers gave cover to army units as they bulldozed their way into the narrow streets of neighbourhoods such as Suq al-Shajra. These operations were also opportunities for looting of shops in neighbourhood markets.

The military operations and the mass killing were part of a policy of pacification by eradication that extended beyond the rebels to the entire city. The obliteration of entire neighbourhoods and mass slaughter is expressive of a form of sovereignty whose primary objective, to borrow Mbembe's words, is '*the generalized instrumentalization of human existence and the material destruction of human bodies and populations*' (Mbembe 2003, 14; italics in the original). The attainment of this objective is poignantly expressed in the words of Hama residents to the effect that, in the aftermath of this ruination, 'the city became lifeless' ('*asbahat al-madina hamida*) – life was sapped out or sucked out (interview with Manhal al-Sarraj, 2011). Hama represents a case where war, instead of being on the margin of the state, is conducted throughout the whole of the social body. War has been a tool of political organisation supported by the militarisation of many aspects of Syrian society. In a speech given at the time of the massacres, Hafez al-Asad (1980b) asserted that it was not possible to end the state of emergency, as demanded by the dissidents, because the country was in a state of war – reference being here to the war with Israel. The declared state of war with the external enemy had the home front as its rearguard. Yet, contrary to the official discourse, the home front was always the primary battlefield. In this sense, Hama was an exemplary site of home-front battlefields where war is conducted against the enemy within.

Formations of Civil War

The civil war regime, as the framework of ruler–ruled relations, draws energy from the lines of friction drawn between loyalists and enemies – between 'us' and 'them'. In his first documentary film titled *Step by Step* (1979), filmmaker Ossama Mohammed sought to gain insight into the structural foundations of governmental violence. Mohammed follows the everyday life of an ordinary peasant family in one of the villages of the Sahel. Living in poverty and relying on harsh farm work that brings meagre income and crop yields, one of the young men in the family opts to join the military as a non-commissioned officer. Following a period of training, he returns to his village in his uniform, now feeling more confident and secure in his future. Mohammed asks him probing questions about the obligations to which a post in the military may give rise, and the nature of loyalty it invites. In response, the young man assertively and unhesitatingly replies in the affirmative that he is willing and ready to kill whomever the leader identifies as an enemy, including his own siblings. The absolute and unquestioning obedience expressed by Mohammed's subject may reflect, in part, a certain idealism of youth, but is also undoubtedly the result of a training and indoctrination regime. This loyalty and ideological alignment are, however, produced through myriad ways in which conviction, as much as opportunism, is a motivating factor.

The division of society into 'us' and 'them' was entrenched through the militarisation of civilian forces and their enlistment in the war against the enemy population. For example, the security services armed Ba'th Party cadres and youth adherents in the Revolutionary Youth Federation, or 'Shabiba', and the National Union of Students. At the emergency congress meeting of the National Union of Students in March 1980 – held to declare allegiance to the leader – the union president, Hassan Hamed, announced the plan to form armed units from among committed university students (*al-Ba'th*, 18 March 1980). The role of youth organisations in this war was acknowledged by Hafez al-Asad, in his speeches, as a testament to their valiant patriotism and nationalism. Further, the Popular Army (*al-Jaysh al-sha'bi*) was reactivated with the arming of party members and recruits from party auxiliary organisations. According to local observers of developments of the period, the peasants' armed detachments comprised more than 30,000 members (Batatu 1999, 255). In accounts of the security services' strategy, some party cadres confirm that they received directives from generals in various security directorates and from members of the Party National Executive to recruit party members and affiliates from among criminal gangs and thugs for the purpose of unleashing them in an unrestrained manner, at the appropriate time, against political opponents (see al-Doghaym 2005). In a short memoir of the period, Mahmud al-Sayyid al-Doghaym (2005), a member of the Ba'th Party's Executive Branch in Ma'arat al-Nu'man, a town in the Idlib Governorate, recounts being summoned by higher-ranking party officials to the city of Idlib to be given directives on how to implement this particular tactic of the civil war regime.

In the context of the 2011 Uprising and ongoing conflict, both anti-regime activists and regime loyalists provided new information on the role of Ba'thist branch members in suppressing the Islamist insurgency in 1982 and afterwards, and in crushing the Muslim Brothers. Although their accounts are cast in terms that align with their current political positions, there is agreement that Ba'thist branch members collaborated with military security, in places like the Idlib towns of Binnish, Taftanaz and Sarmada, in conducting the regime's war against the Muslim Brothers. The figure of Khaled Ghazala, a teacher, and a Ba'th Party branch member for Idlib city, emerges as a hero for some and a villain for others. Ghazala, in conjunction with his brother who was a military officer at the time, organised a 'special task force' charged with the liquidation of the Muslim Brothers. Residents of the towns where this 'task force' operated would later come forward and accuse Ghazala of having masterminded the killing of entire local families (Kuluna Shurka' fi al-Watan 2012a).

Writing under a pseudonym during the Hama period (early 1980s), Michel Seurat referred to the regime as having formed 'fascist-like pha-langes' to which peasants, workers and youth were recruited (Michaud 1982, 30). This underscores a structural feature of the regime: the gang-like formations operating as a force against other social groups and cre-ating civil war-like conditions whereby some formations can act as death squads. The formations to which Seurat refers could be seen in operation in the violence that erupted in the town of Jisr al-Shughur in March 1980 and culminated in the massacre of 200 anti-regime civilians. In one of the earlier instances of massacres during the period, the Special Units (*al-Wahadat al-Khasa*) – a paramilitary formation run by Major-General Ali Haydar – killed protesters who had occupied the headquarters of the Popular Army (*al-Jaysh al-Sha'bi*) in the town. The constellation of actors in this bloody confrontation captures the civil war-like conditions that were established through the arming of civilians and the formation of militia attached to key regime figures. As in Jisr al-Shughur, the town of Saraqib (also in the Idlib Governorate) experienced, during the same period, some of the first clashes between citizens and regime forces and affiliated militia.[24] One chronicle refers to continued spontaneous mobil-isation that became known as the 'uprising of Saraqib' (Shilash ND). In response to protests by diverse political groups and increased youth activism, the security forces mounted a campaign of arrests. A cursory look at the list of detainees and disappeared persons in the 1980s maintained by Syrian human rights organisations would reveal a sub-stantial proportion having issued from various towns and villages of the Idlib Governorate as well as from Idlib city (SHRC ND).

The co-optation of civilian forces into the generalised war against all regime opponents served to reinforce the lines of division, bringing popular forces into the orbit of rule and thereby creating the veneer of popularity. The regime recruited heads of clans and tribes as relay points with the security services and the Ba'th. This was done with a view to reproducing their authority and delivering their constituencies to gov-ernment. Notably, the regime armed a number of clans in rural Idlib and Aleppo, in places like Saramein, Sarmada and Ma'arat al-Nu'man.[25] Other accounts indicate that tribes in the Badiya were called upon to

[24] These events became known, later, as the 'Electricity Generator Events' (*ahdath muhawlat al-kahraba'*) (see Shilash ND).
[25] Interviews with former residents of Idlib and with journalists who were observers of these developments at the time (Damascus, April 2011, Amman 2012).

monitor the territories around Hama and Aleppo and to act as watchers and informants for the security services (Rae cited in Chatty 2010). Note, for instance, the comments of Diyab al-Mashi in Omar Amiralay's 2003 documentary *Flood in the Country of the Ba'th*. In the interview, al-Mashi, a Member of the Syrian Parliament and the shaykh of al-Mashi clan and of the eponymous village, situated south of Manbij in Aleppo Governorate, affirmed his role in mobilising against the militants and other opponents of Hafez al-Asad (Amiralay 2003). He further recounts that he was rewarded by Hafez al-Asad, who granted him the gift of a new vehicle for his private use. Members of al-Mashi's clan, including his son, would later engage in the suppression of protests at the beginning of the 2011 Uprising (Tawfiq 2016). Other tribal leaders, besides al-Mashi, enlisted their followers to oversee the flow of arms across the border from Iraq (Rae cited in Chatty 2010). Mahmud Sadeq (1992, 80) notes that Bedouin tribes in Hama and Homs were armed by Rif'at al-Asad and equipped with tanks and artillery (this armament was later used by the same tribes to settle internal conflicts as was the case in the confrontation between the al-Hasna and al-Fawa'ira tribes). As Sadeq (1992, 80) points out, such conditions are intended to blackmail society and create a fear of massacre as armed groups are used to terrorise populations and threaten the slaughter of regime opponents.

Conclusion

In response to the March 2011 Uprising, the Syrian regime unleashed its war machine against the population. The immediate use of violence to crush the protests in Dar 'a and, subsequently, to lay siege to cities, towns and villages across the territory brought war to the surface. The social relationship of war at the foundation of the state/regime became visible once again. Regime–society relations in Syria should be understood in terms of violence as a modality of government in which the detention camp and the massacre were technologies of power applied to the population. Governmental violence nurtured binary divisions in the body politic, polarising society into 'us' and 'them'. This fracture is entwined with the sacralisation of rule in the person of the leader – a deification of sorts – and is grounded in a juridico-political frame of the state of exception.

The political prison was not merely a site of banishing the political opponents of the regime. It developed as an apparatus for the negation of the dissidents' will and resolve to hold independent views and act upon them. The practices of subjectivation, documented in prison memoirs, aimed to destabilise the dissidents' sense of self through the incitement of feelings of humiliation, degradation and abjection. Most telling about this governmental rationality is that a national security panel periodically visited prisons to meet with political detainees and assess whether they abandoned their dissident views and were ready to cooperate with the regime as informants. That a signed renunciation of one's views was required for release after completion of a prison sentence indicates the importance the regime accorded to the objective of having the dissidents overturn themselves.

Alongside the project of long-term rehabilitation of dissidents, the regime mounted large-scale operations of mass killing against 'insurgent' populations. In this respect, the Hama massacres were a cornerstone of the civil war regime, setting a template of rule through violence. Tracing the contours of this violence, I outlined key elements of the civil war regime that arose through practices of polarisation and mobilisation around the 'us' and 'them' divisions.

The analytical lines developed in this chapter highlight a form of politics that framed citizens' everyday interaction with government and that, through its sites and events, became constitutive of citizen subjectivities. In Chapter 2, I examine the subjectivities formed in relation to practices of government and rule that articulate with violence. The chapter turns to the materiality of the cleavages running through society, looking at the political economy of the 'us' and 'them' divisions.

2   Authoritarian Government, the Shadow State and Political Subjectivities

In one of its faces – the face that is made visible when we examine its use of violence – the Syrian state can simply be labelled as a murderous state, which commits powerful destructive acts. This face – that of the state of exception – should not, however, occlude other faces and, for the purposes of this chapter, I draw attention to the features that make the Syrian state a 'shadow state'.[1] I also draw attention to the role that illegality plays in structuring the polity and, more specifically, in forming political subjects. Of particular relevance here is to examine how the regime's control of resources and its sponsorship and management of illicit economic activities supported a system of patronage that is integrated into practices of government and rule. The Syrian shadow state articulates with authoritarian government working to enframe ordinary citizens' everyday activities. In this form of government, a key feature is the securitisation of most aspects of life with the aim of maintaining regime power. This chapter examines how such practices of government and rule in Syria have shaped the constitution of 'regimes of subjectivities'. Following Mbembe and Roitman (1995), 'regimes of subjectivities' refers to the processes that give rise to social imaginaries structuring individuals' and groups' modes of relating to themselves and to others.

The analysis of political subjectivities presented in this chapter underscores the relationship between, on one hand, the form and nature of the state and its mechanisms of rule and, on the other, the subjects that are formed and performed. An important dimension of this enquiry

---

[1] My use of the term 'shadow state' retains elements of its original formulation by William Reno (2008 [1995]). In Reno's definition, the shadow state, exemplified notably by the case of Sierra Leone, refers to a system wherein the ruler maintains authority by virtue of control of resources and commerce used to service patronage networks. This substantive aspect of the definition of the shadow state is preserved in my use of the term to identify practices of government based on informal arrangements for the control of resources and on illicit economic activities on the part of actors in the ruler's patronage networks. However, my aim here is not to postulate on the presumed weakness or strength of the Syrian state. Rather, my concern is to examine aspects of the political economy that shape regime–citizen relations.

into political subjectivities is to analyse practices of government and how they give shape to the subject's modes of interaction with government agents and agencies and with fellow citizens. A second and equally important dimension is the examination of contextual variables, both micro and macro, that anchor and provide ground for the constitution and performance of political subjectivities. Interrelated variables such as socio-economic location, individual and group social histories, and social and symbolic capital invest the subject with a materiality and history. Such variables are the stuff of the lifeworld in which subjectivities are enacted, come to life and become productive of sense and sensibilities.

My analysis situates the construction of Syrian political subjectivities in relation to state mechanisms of government, and to particular socio-economic transformations, which unfolded over five decades following the advent of Ba'thist rule. I want to shed light on the identitarian dimensions of the constitution of the subject and of selfhood and to situate this identitarian construction in relation to specific features of the political economy of the regime, which extends beyond the formal dimensions of the state to incorporate the shadow state. This exploration is situated against the backdrop of state-building processes represented in the expansion of the bureaucracy and of the army and the security forces alongside state nationalisation of industrial enterprises and the expropriation of large rural estates. With much public resources devoted to the military and with the adoption of developmentalist policies that favoured industrial investment, major societal reconfigurations unfolded. Central to these reconfigurations was a large-scale rural–urban migration that brought about a rapid demographic transformation in major cities, including the capital. The patterns of socio-spatial settlement of rural migrants in these cities and the dynamics of their incorporation into the lower echelons of the state – especially the apparatuses of coercion – constitute key variables in understanding the subjectivities that emerged in this period.

Analytically, the chapter deploys social categories that ordinary citizens use in their everyday interaction and exchanges. These categories help us understand the social imaginary and discursive frames orienting their positioning, relations and self-understandings (self-apprehension). 'Wanted citizen', '*zalamat al-amn*', '*mahsub 'ala*', '*mad'um*' and '*shabih*' are categories designating the subjectivities constituted, assumed and conjured up in conversations, social exchanges and everyday dealings. The constitution of these subjectivities is closely connected to the working out of social and political norms of interaction. Integral to the formation and performance of these subjectivities are discursive civilities structuring everyday communication and exchange. In the Syrian context, these civilities include secretiveness, the deployment of rumours, and the use of mental maps to locate one's interlocutors in the web of power and control and as a means of filtering out information and interpreting utterances. As noted, modes of interaction with the state shape the formation of political subjectivities. A key argument presented here is that political subjectivities are anchored in the materiality of state–society and regime–society relations and interaction, both of which are marked by generalised corruption, securitisation and clientalisation. Thus, in this discussion, I highlight clientalisation and *istizlam* (making someone a hireling or a lackey) as mechanisms of control that are demeaning, degrading and uprooting of the subject. Such mechanisms are at work in the constitution of the subject as *mahsub 'ala* (belonging to x's coterie), *mad'um* (propped by the powerful and recipient of their support) and *min jama'at fulan* (from the group of x). Similarly, the practices of illegality and corruption that permeate state–citizen interaction are the grounds for the constitution of 'wanted citizen' (*muwwatin taht al-talab*). Within such conditions and constraints, subjects are compelled to transgress and become wanted citizens by evading the law and, as a consequence, they exist in fear of being caught or found out (Tizzini 2002). He/she is a compromised subject who pays the price in silence or in complicity. In this respect, my analysis hones in on the terms in which citizens become entangled in the webs of power and control.

In what follows, the first section begins by sketching relevant features of state/regime practices of control and government and by drawing out the processes through which political subjectivities are fashioned. Towards this end, attention will be given to the Ba'thist regime's practices of enframing, and modes of subjectivation and incorporation. Then the discussion moves to situate the constitution of political subjectivities in relation to the political economy of the shadow state. The last section underscores the identitarian dimensions of subject formation. The chapter concludes by briefly noting that the articulation of authoritarian government with the shadow state/shadow regime effects a slide from homogenised subjects to precarious and exposed subjects.

Authoritarian Governmentality

Enframing Citizens, Forming Subjects

Having developed in the mould of populist revolutionary regimes, one of the defining features of the system of rule in Syria has been the enframing of citizens within 'the popular organisations' (*al-munazamat al-sha'biyya*) directed by the Ba'th Party. From its rise to power, the party came to occupy a central position in coordinating diverse social and political organisations in Syria – regimenting, disciplining and orienting citizens' actions and relations. As discussed by Raymond Hinnebusch (2001, 46–51), the Ba'th Party, under its radical wing, was remodelled in the 1960s after Leninist-type parties and restructured in a hierarchical and pyramidal fashion with units operating at all levels of society. It is worth recalling here the party's form of organisation so as to better grasp the degree and intensity of its penetration of societal spaces. The basic party unit, known as the group (*firqa*), is found in schools, factories, public firms, villages and neighbourhoods (Hinnebusch 2001, 76–8). At a higher rung, the section (*shu'ba*) comprises a minimum of two groups and, above it, at governorate level, is the branch (*far'*) to which representatives of lower-level units are elected. Available data on party membership indicate that a massive expansion took place from the 1970s to the 1990s (Batatu 1999; Van Dam 1996).[2] By the early 2000s, the party claimed over 800,000 active members (*'udw 'amil*) and one million supporters (*nasir*) (the total representing over 10 per cent of the Syrian population in that period) (Hamidi 2005).[3]

It is commonly stated that nowadays the party is a hollowed shell – a claim that is borne out by the doctrinal impoverishment it suffered over the last four decades and by the abandonment, in practice, of the revolutionary objectives of socialism and popular democratic government. However, the hollowing-out of the party does not mean that it became irrelevant as a governmental apparatus. The governmental work of the party should be examined in terms of its role in socialisation and education, and in terms of how its rituals and rhetoric inform an institutionalised imaginary. Through its various organisational units and auxiliaries, such as the Workers' Federation and the Women's Federation, the party engages in extensive work of socialisation and indoctrination, propagating the regime's 'ideo-theology' and teaching correct Ba'thist citizenship. With the setting up of the Partisan Training School in 1968 (*Madrasat al-i'dad al-hizbi*), the party formalised the training of cadres. Educational activities at the School cover both doctrinal and military

---

[2] For an analysis of party membership in the 1980s, taking account of the distribution of members by governorate, see Van Dam (1996, 125–9).

[3] In his speeches, Hafez al-Asad addressed issues of recruitment into the Ba'th and advised on matters of indoctrination. Expounding his vision on these matters he stated in one instance: '[W]hen we say recruit one thousand citizens in the Tartous Branch, [this] means expend efforts day and night to educate this thousand people … teach them and debate them' (Speech to the Party Seventh Regional Congress dated 4 January 1980). Similarly, he is reported to have pronounced to party cadres: 'I want that one hour be dedicated on a daily basis to partisan work' (cited in *al-Munadil*, January 1980, 129).

training. In writings on the principles and objectives of the training, it is stated that the success of partisan formation rests on instilling 'a unified political orientation and unity in political thinking' (*al-Munadil*, June 1985, 72). In 1987, and pursuant to directives issued at the party's Eighth National Congress, twelve new School branches were established, graduating 5,259 cadres in that year (*al-Munadil*, July–August 1989, 76–7). Among other things, the School organises partisan education campaigns such as the workshops for 'consciousness raising' in villages (e.g. the 2003 campaigns in Homs villages aimed at countering 'passivity').

Many Syrians and Syria analysts concur that the party became a façade of rule behind which the actual rulers – namely the president, the security services and senior military officers – managed political affairs in the country. Yet the continuation of party activities, on a large scale and on a regular basis, points to the importance and centrality of the work that it performs. Throughout the Syrian territory, party units hold annual, quarterly and monthly meetings. Alongside auxiliaries such as the Shabiba (the Revolutionary Youth Federation), these units convene not only to express their ritual allegiance to the Ba'th Party and its leader, but also to review and monitor a wide range of affairs. For example, it is conventional for meetings of Shabiba branches in the governorates to be attended by the head of the party branch, by the governor, by the branch secretary, the head of the police department and many other senior party members at the level of the governorate. In such meetings, reports on cultural, technical and economic activities are presented and discussed. At regularly convened meetings attended by upper-echelon party officials, cadres from the group and section make specific recommendations and demands on behalf of their areas, such as, for example, asking that a new school be built, additional teachers be appointed, and so on. Briefings on educational or employment conditions are made at these meetings and serve to articulate grievances and to promote sectional interests. A review of Syrian media reports on the subjects discussed and recommendations made at the annual and periodic meetings of party sections and branches between 2000 and 2010, shows that such matters as the construction of schools, the performance of pupils and teaching staff and the paving of roads are conventionally addressed. Individuals holding the post of party group secretary or head of party section are commonly credited with securing the setting up of schools, or channelling employment investments into their villages and towns (drawing on Syrian newspaper reports of section and branch meetings in *al-Ba'th* and *Tishrin* newspapers between 2000 and 2010). In a study of tribal co-optation into the Ba'th, Sulayman Khalaf (1987) notes that

Ba'thist cadres – whom he dubs 'village comrade type' – were able, by virtue of their party networks, to secure utility services and other benefits for their villages. In other accounts, Ba'thist cadres were identified as informants to the security forces in their towns and as collaborators implicated in repressive policies. At the lowest rung, the group secretary enjoyed influence in matters relating to the appointment of teachers. He or she exercised authority to interrogate unit members and to determine whether they were 'positive citizens' and 'friends of the state'. In some towns and villages, the approval of group secretary was needed to open a store or process other types of licensing papers. Notably, group and section executive committee members were credited for bringing public services to their areas.

In his study of the Revolutionary Youth Federation (*Shabibat al-Thawra* or 'Shabiba') in the 1970s, Raymond Hinnebusch (1980) noted that careerism and ideological commitment were among the motivating factors for joining and becoming active within these mobilisational institutions. These drivers of membership and involvement persisted into the 1990s and 2000s and figure both in self-criticism and in critiques of these institutions as well as in the declarations of present-day adherents and supporters. Nonetheless, the careerist drive for membership in Ba'thist organisations was encouraged through a system of reward and sanction. Importantly, upward mobility in the party was linked to privileges and employment opportunities. A review of the profile of upwardly mobile party members shows a typical trajectory for those who rise to positions in the command bureaus at both governorate and national level. A common path for membership of these bureaus runs through the Shabiba and the National Union of Students. Very often, members of the branch and regional command offices were actively engaged in the Shabiba at group and then at branch level and held positions in the National Union of Students or in the Workers' and Peasants' Unions. In these organisations, the cadres build partisan networks and gain access to resources for themselves and their clients.[4]

---

[4] Partisan networks can be traced in the profiles of Ba'thists who rose through the ranks of the party to occupy positions in the central committee and the regional command (e.g. Salam Sanqar from Homs, Riyad Hijab from Deir al-Zour and others in the regional command, or Ibrahim al-Sa'ati and Zohayr Ramadan who are party bosses of sorts, the latter in the Ministry of Culture, the former as the National Union of Students president for many years). The trajectory of these figures demonstrates sustained engagement with the Ba'th from an early age, initially through the Revolutionary Youth Federation (Shabiba), and then through the assumption of positions in the committees of the group, section and branch levels of the party.

The frequency and regularity with which the meetings, conferences and workshops of the party units are held underscore the value that the party and the rulers have placed on the symbolic performance of a popular mobilisational organisation. However, beyond the symbolism, and despite the consistent exhortation of the senior members that the regular meetings of group and branch units should be attended by all members (suggesting a high degree of absenteeism), the activities should not be explained away as being nothing but a charade. Instead, we should consider that they contribute to the cultivation of certain forms of allegiance and adherence among members which, then, are incorporated into other performances and directed actions. The empty and formulaic slogans reiterated at these gatherings naturalise the language of adherents. In the process, they become well versed in the arguments and narratives that authorise some citizens as patriots who then denounce others as agents of foreign and enemy powers. Further, through particular performances the rituals implicate the participants individually and collectively. Illustrative of the kind of intimate implication that participation in these activities entails is the signing, in blood, of an oath of allegiance to the president (reported for meetings of Shabiba branches of the governorate of Deir al-Zour in 2005). Party activities have been essential for the performance of dominance and legitimacy and for enlisting cadres as supporters and adherents who are not only beneficiaries but, also, relays or connectors of the president and the party. As will be argued in Chapter 3, the emotional and normative investment nurtured through engagement in Ba'th activities during the 1980s could no longer be commanded of all citizens. New imaginative resources would develop among citizens, contributing to the breaking down of the Ba'thist hold over the frames of identification and selfhood.

Party offices at both local and national levels oversee the work of auxiliary organisations such as the Shabiba and Tala'i'. The formation of subjects begins at an early stage through the work of the Vanguard Organisation (Tala'i').[5] The Tala'i' initiates the political socialisation of children in primary educational institutions. The stated objective of the organisation is to fashion vanguardist children who are inculcated with nationalist and anti-imperialist values and who are loyal to the ideological principles of the party. As will be elaborated upon in Chapter 3, the recollections of many Syrians of their time in school and of their

---

[5] According to many Syrian observers, the idea of establishing the Tala'i' was formulated by Hafez al-Asad following a visit to North Korea in 1974 where, along the route from the airport, he was greeted by thousands of cheering youngsters from the Young Pioneers Organisation.

enlistment in Ba'thist youth organisations reveal a sense of dissonance and self-distancing from the activities in which they partook. The dissociation that is effected in these recollections does not, however, negate the role that these organisations play in enframing citizens and shaping their institutionalised imaginary by disseminating the regime's narratives. With the aim of achieving full co-optation of the young, the work of the Tala'i' extends from running weekly meetings in schools and annual competitions in the arts and sciences, to the setting up of cultural festivals and summer camps. By many contemporary accounts, the ideological material promoted at these events and activities stultified many years ago, and would later be rejected by many. Yet in various respects, the Tala'i', as well as other youth organisations, were formative of subjectivities (as will be discussed below and, subsequently, in Chapter 3, when we consider recollections of everyday life under dictatorship).

Tala'i' programmes contribute to the propagation of the Ba'thist ideology to which students are exposed in their civics and *futuwwa* (physical training) classes at primary level. In these classes, the teachings of the president are the subject of study and memorisation – memorisation practices aiming to etch his words and image in their minds. The president's many figurations embodying his exceptional stature, skills, wisdom and authority are imparted to the students at an early age. Omar Amiralay's (2003) documentary *Flood in the Country of the Ba'th* captures one instance of the process of indoctrination. The film's classroom scenes illuminate aspects of ideological propagation focused on the cultivation of such dispositions as obedience to authority and acquiescence to the prevailing order.

The work of the Tala'i' continues in later stages of organisational membership: in the Revolutionary Youth Organisation (*Shabibat al-Thawra*) or Shabiba at both preparatory and high-school levels, and then in the National Union of Students. A primary objective behind the sustained efforts to incorporate the youth into the Ba'th is to make them unavailable for any contending force and to curtail the possibility of an alternative political force emerging. In the rhetoric of the Shabiba and the National Union of Students, the youth are to be fashioned as bulwarks against reactionary powers and counter-revolutionary forces. Towards fashioning the youth as protectors of the regime, patriotism and allegiance to the regime are articulated as indivisible principles. Ba'thist discourse dwells on these general principles of youth interpellation. Beyond the foundational goals of Arab unity and independence, it does not offer a dynamic and developing programme. Rather, it is around the notions and sayings of the president – considered as axiomatic but now turned into clichés – that the interpellation of the youth takes place. As with all party literature and publications, these sayings frame the content of the educational and training material produced by both the Shabiba and the Tala'i'.

In the 1970s, to ensure a core of loyal and active youth supporters, the regime introduced recruitment into specialised regiments. Thus, in addition to the military training received at school, some students enlisted into the parachutist classes, attracted by the advantages and privileges associated with completing training in such military subjects (e.g. extra marks on high school transcripts and improved chances of admission into elite university faculties, in particular the medical school). An indication of the privileged place of these specialised youth regiments is that the president gave an annual address to the graduates of the parachute training courses. More importantly, the parachutists were called upon to enforce conformity during the period of the Islamist insurgency in the 1970s and 1980s, as when female parachutists forcibly removed the headscarves from the heads of pious women in Damascus and elsewhere. The passage of Ba'thist youth into a military role is facilitated through their incorporation into armed units such as the Popular Army (*al-Jaysh al-Sha'bi*).[6] In this sense, the youth organisations perform coercive functions and not simply ideological ones whereby cadres would be called upon to intimidate opposition and to act as counter-revolutionary forces when needed. A kind of fervent vigilantism appears to have been cultivated and reproduced over a long period. Whenever the regime is challenged, Ba'thist youth are mobilised to silence critical voices. In his testimonial on youth vigilantism during a 2005 protest against the continuation of emergency rule, Yassin al-Haj Saleh (2005a) notes the terms in which patriotic slogans and vows of allegiance to the leader were formulated and deployed to intimidate and discredit the protesters.

The Politics of Security

The centrality of the politics of security and of securitisation in government has undoubtedly played a determining role in the constitution of political subjects. Syrian analysts and commentators have highlighted 'fear' as a powerful emotion guiding citizens' relation to government and to fellow citizens. Writing in *al-Quds al-Arabi* in 2000, Riyad al-Turk, a leading political activist and former political prisoner, wrote that fear had become generalised and permeated social relations both among citizens and between them and the authorities. He asserted that fear governed a wide range of interaction: between students and their teachers and

[6] A formation of a similar type was created under the name of Ba'th militia (*kata'ib al-Ba'th*) during the Uprising in 2011.

among friends, government employees and Ba'th cadres.[7] Further, in an influential essay, Abd al-Razzaq Eid (2005) discussed the culture of fear maintained by the security apparatuses. However, Eid located the origins of this culture in Arab and Islamic tradition, rather than in the workings of the security services, thus perpetuating an essentialist and culturalist understanding of the mechanisms of control. Pace Eid, fear, as used here, is understood as an emotion cultivated in practices of discipline and is not an ingrained character trait that is specific to particular cultures and personality types. The idea of fear as a cultivated disposition is captured in the words of a dissident and former political prisoner who, in conversation with me, spoke of 'fear that instructs' (*al-khawf al-mu'alim*), or what may be termed 'the pedagogy of fear'.[8]

The pedagogy of fear develops through practices of monitoring, surveillance and discipline of citizens. The infrastructure of this pedagogy comprises detention centres, prisons and interrogation chambers, populating the Syrian landscape. The intelligence and security forces reportedly ran thirty prisons in Damascus and Aleppo alone (Human Rights Watch 1991). As pointed out by Subhi Hadidi in 2000, the intelligence services managed facilities for the interrogation of 1000 people at any one time in Damascus.[9] These capabilities would be enhanced during the 2011 Uprising when schools and public buildings were converted into detention centres holding tens of thousands of activists and suspected dissidents. The regime's cultivation of fear among the subjects is also pursued through the extensive use of watchers, informants and report writers, who are essential to creating the atmosphere of suspicion, as will be discussed below.

Employing large numbers of watchers, informants and report writers, the security services infiltrate intimate and private areas of social life, and not just the public domain. For instance, until May 2005 citizens were required to obtain security clearances for sixty-seven activities, some of which were routine, everyday activities such as babysitting, operating a bakery, working as an ambulant photographer and posting an obituary in public.[10] Engaging in any of these activities made ordinary citizens

---

[7] See *Middle East Mirror*, 14/145, 31 July 2000.
[8] Interview with Ahmad al-Fawwaz (Damascus, 17 March 2005). The theme of 'the pedagogy of fear' at work in government is poignantly captured in Syrian author Zakariyya Tamer's short story *Tigers on the Tenth Day* (2002 [1974]). An allegorical tale, it traces a tiger's journey from freedom to complete submission in captivity. The tiger's trainer implements a set of measures that bring about the animal's transformation from a roaring beast to a meowing, docile cat content with eating grass.
[9] See *Middle East Monitor*, 24 November 2000, 22.
[10] The list was published in the daily newspaper *al-Thawra* on 25 May 2005.

the subject of management and regulation by the security services and, in the process, exposed them to techniques of ensnarement, i.e. being recruited as an informant and watcher. As in other securitising regimes, surveillance work is contracted out or farmed out to individuals in certain occupations such as kiosk operators, taxi drivers and real-estate agents. Such individuals were identified by my Syrian interviewees as performing relay activities of surveillance and reporting. By virtue of legal requirement, individuals in these occupations must report to the security services and are assigned a contact person who collates and processes the information. At a very rudimentary level, many of the security-related services require citizens to submit details of personal information that can be used to track them (for example, a personal identity card is required to get a mobile telephone line or internet connection while other mundane transactions require the taking of fingerprints).

Through a proliferating security apparatus that comprises four directorates and fifteen departments – including Political Security, National Security, General Security, External Security, Military Security and Air Force Security – oversight is exercised over a wide range of activities, ensuring that all public institutions are under state security control. The diverse security and military departments have branches throughout Syria, including small towns and villages. The spatial distribution of these departments and their infrastructural build-up ensured the securitisation and militarisation of the Syrian territory. Military posts, units and institutions were implanted in strategic locations and often blurred the lines between civilian and military spaces, in effect militarising social spaces and relations among ordinary citizens. In Damascus, which was classified as a border area (*mantiqa hududiya*) because of its 'frontline' positioning in the war with Israel, the urban and suburban landscape became populated with military installations and units stationed to protect the regime and the capital as much from local resistance as from external threat. A number of military constellations were implanted by Rif'at al-Asad in the 1970s. Prominent among these was Unit 586 whose non-commissioned officers built an informal neighbourhood in the Mezzeh Mountain. Now known as Mezzeh 86, the neighbourhood derives its name from the military section whose members settled there. Another of Rif'at's divisions was set up in Ish al-Warwar, a zone of the town of Barzeh, on land expropriated from its original inhabitants. Barzeh is located in an agricultural area on the northern edge of Damascus. The military appropriation of Barzeh land expanded with the infrastructural build-up that included a military hospital and various other military installations. In nearby Qaboun the barracks of the Special Units (later renamed the Special Forces) came to occupy a strategic location, controlling the roads to the suburb of Tishrin and, further, to the town of Tal in the north. Military personnel from these units set up informal housing next to their barracks. The military encirclement of Damascus was further consolidated with the formation of the Fourth Armoured Division in the 1990s, which took over much of the land of Mu'adamiyya in the Western Ghuta.[11] The Republican Guard and the Fourth Division occupy positions of dominance spatially. Expanding from the Mezzeh military airport – also built on Mu'adamiyya land – the families of the Fourth Division are housed in new compounds in Hay al-Mashru'. Military units and housing quarters were also incorporated into new housing projects. This is the case, for instance, with the Dummar Project, where the neighbourhood of al-'Arin and the Presidential Guard Headquarters are perched over the residential islands housing segments of the professional middle classes.

This pattern of appropriation of land for military purposes and for housing military personnel is evidenced, also, in the governorate of rural Damascus. There, areas identified as frontline or borderline territory became sites for housing settlements for military divisions stationed in their vicinity. Most notable is the area of Qatana (in the eastern section of Jabal al-Shaykh), where the First Armoured Division was set up and, in connection with this military presence, two neighbourhoods sprung up, namely Al-Basil neighbourhood, and the neighbourhood formed out of the Military Housing Compound (*al-Iskan al-'Askari*).

Political Subjectivities and Everyday Discursive Civilities

In this section, my purpose is to sketch out the political subjectivities that are formed in everyday interaction among ordinary people in a context defined by governmental practices of enframing and securitisation of societal spaces. Subsequently, I will turn to the political economy that furnishes the material anchoring of the political subjectivities under discussion. My account of political subjectivities draws on my interviews with Syrian political activists and dissidents, ordinary citizens and former political personalities and on informal discussion and observations during fieldwork visits to Syria. As noted above, integral to these subjectivities is the cultivation of discursive civilities informed by relations and interaction with institutions of government. Discursive civilities refer to a kind of politically and socially informed communicative competence

---

[11] The Fourth Division evolved out of the Defence Companies that were under Rif'at al-Asad's control in the 1980s.

that individuals cultivate to guide their conversations with others in the everyday.

Owing to the securitisation of vast areas of social life and to the sense of exposure to surveillance that permeates mundane exchanges, subjects develop competencies to locate an interlocutor's proximity to governmental power and her/his relation to the security apparatus. They are then able to better decipher speech and filter it in order to arrive at a clearer understanding of the intended message and to judge the risk of entrapment or of becoming implicated in a potentially transgressive utterance. These communicative manoeuvres enter into the production of a particular kind of subject that we may qualify as 'anticipated' – one who may not be present during an interaction or instance of conversation, but whose eventual arrival or presence is conjured up, expected or seen to be highly probable, if not inevitable. This is the subject referred to as *zalamat al-amn* or agent of the security forces. This political subjectivity is salient in Syrian political life, not only for the services the subject renders to the state/regime, but also for the role he/she plays as a present or absent/anticipated speaker or listener in a wide range of actual and possible exchanges.

I should point out that in all of my interviews and discussions, none of my interlocutors referred to himself or herself as being *zalamat al-amn*. However, it was common that this label or category of identification was ascribed to someone else they knew at work, in university or in their neighbourhood. During a conversation on the question of artistic freedom and censorship, a playwright with whom I was speaking invoked the subjectivity of *zalamat al-amn* to explain the constraints on independent artistic production that she and others faced. My interlocutor identified a known figure in the Ministry of Culture as being *zalamat al-amn* and then asserted that no appointment or promotion to a senior position in the Ministry can be made without this person's input. A former government minister, removed after a brief term in office, reflecting on the reasons for the removal, stated: 'I just could not be a *zalamat al-amn*. It is not something I would do or accept to do.' This reasoning and assessment could not be taken at face value, as all high-level positions are vetted by the security services and many are thought of as nominations by the heads of security forces. In fact, removal may signal the services' dissatisfaction with the subject's performance or the presence of some other security and political considerations of the moment.

The anticipation of *zalamat al-amn* – their being conjured up in the course of interaction or communication – informs such civilities as the use of rumours to circulate information. During my periods of fieldwork, rumours, as a mode of communication, appeared to perform well in Damascus, connecting the city through criss-crossing social networks springing from a multitude of localities and connective nodes. I became conscious of dense connections for the circulation of rumours among individuals and institutions as I moved from one circle of interviewees to another in the intellectual and artistic fields. As a mode of communication, rumours require secretiveness in the telling and sharing of news. A counter-public that passes on the latest analyses and stories operates with a code of secrecy that relies as much on distrust as on trust, for there exist doubts as to the purpose of the telling: for example, does the speaker want to ensnare the listener? At any moment, an ordinary exchange can turn into a dangerous incrimination of oneself. If a speaker is designated as *mahsub 'ala* (literally 'counted on someone' and denoting a client of a security officer or a powerful figure) her or his speech could be interpreted as an attempt at entrapment. Vigilance against such a possibility is honed in order to qualify or locate an interlocution. One can imagine that distrust-guided communication creates a fertile ground for Kafkaesque exchanges where doubts and different planes of enunciation and reception structure exchanges and could culminate in mutual indictments that need not be stated, but, nonetheless, take the form of strongly held personal convictions about one's interlocutors. Such modes of communication, while seen as necessary to protect oneself against being drawn into making self-incriminating statements, destabilise personal relations and cause rancour among the subjects. For example, Ruba, an interviewee, spoke about feeling pain at being identified with the regime because she grew up in an Alawi family and was associated with the Alawi community.

In my observations of the public intellectual scene and in my conversations with civil-society activists in Syria prior to the Uprising, I noted the entrenchment of this mode of communication. It was still common for opposition figures and civil-society activists to invoke an intellectual opponent's alleged security links or to point to a colleague as being *zalamat al-amn*. This tendency to connect public speakers, journalists and artists to the security apparatus emerges out of governmental practices in which security clearances are required for a wide range of both professional and mundane activities. The security services operate by recruiting agents inside all government departments and institutions. Agents in positions higher up the ladder cultivate direct relations with the heads of the security services and provide them with the necessary information to approve a nominated appointee to a given position. As such, in acceding to a position of authority in any government department or in holding state office, an individual is suspected of having compromised her independence and as having received the approval of the security services.

The discursive civilities highlighted here undoubtedly belong to mundane interaction, but they acquire their full effect when they orient political engagements and relations. For instance, civil-society activists pointed out and acknowledged to me, during interviews, the limitations they faced on open communication among themselves.

Zalamat al-amn, as a subjectivity conjured up in conversations and in interaction among fellow citizens, performs alongside a host of supporting subjects such as *mahsub 'ala*, *mad'um*, and *min jama'at fulan*. These subjectivities embody relations of clientelisation and incorporation. They circulate in the mental maps that the subjects draw of their political fields of action to identify intermediaries who can intercede on their behalf or to develop a protective shield from a potentially predatory relation. As noted by Khalaf (1981), it is common for middle- and low-level state functionaries to view themselves as supporters and protégés of higher-up officials and to see their job security and promotion as being tied to the fortunes of their patron.

In her novel entitled *Kursi (Chair)*, Dima Wannous portrays a *zalamat al-amn* subjectivity in great detail. Wannous' writing possesses an ethnographic quality and documentary features, allowing for insights from the immediate setting and offering reflections on social and political relations. It is worth noting that she grew up in Syria in the 1990s and was a young writer when she wrote *Kursi*. It was published in 2009, just prior to the Uprising, and was greeted with much acclaim in literary circles in Syria. To get a sense of the inscription of *zalamat al-amn* in the socio-political landscape, I draw on Wannous' protagonist, Dorgham, a migrant to Damascus who practically severed his relations to his natal village in Tartous and who works in state media propagating the regime's political discourse. Dorgham's rise in his profession is facilitated and advanced by the services he renders, namely report writing and surveillance – activities in which he engaged starting from his time in university when he informed on his friend and roommate, a political dissident, leading to the latter's arrest. This betrayal is cast in Dorgham's recollections/flashbacks as saving his friend from a worse fate. He asserts to himself his love for his friend, though he also broods over his betrayal in a manner that intimates that he may be troubled by his act. As for others on whom he informed, he has no remorse, but, rather, feels vindication by his sense of self-importance.

How should we read Dorgham's self-authoring and political subjectivity? Wannous locates Dorgham in the macro social and political changes of the period. Yet the account of Dorgham's conduct can, nonetheless, be viewed as pertaining to a mere idiosyncratic character and individual psychology. There is more, here, however. Dorgham's professional ambition is shaped within a system of rewards and sanctions based on assessments of loyalty to the regime and subscription to its claims. Within this system, flexibility is a prized quality. For example, Dorgham is at ease altering his political positions and views to accommodate the unaccounted for shifts in regime alliances and proclamations. He follows the official line without being troubled by apparent inconsistencies and contradictions.

The account of Dorgham's background reveals the antagonisms of the social field: poverty and dispossession as the backdrop for the appeal of the party's and the state's ideological pronouncements on progress; political opportunism encouraged by regime officials. In Dorgham, Wannous draws a portrait of the kind of subjectivity fashioned when one is enlisted as an informant by the Ba'th Party or the security services. A number of other recent literary works delve into the fashioning of the Ba'thist subject from the early stages of a person's entry into the Vanguard Organisation (al-Tala'i'), to their co-optation in the National Union of Students and, eventually, to the assumption of a position within the apparatuses of rule.

Zalamat al-amn is the subject in relation to whom other subjects modulate their speech and adjust their performance. Similarly, subjects fashion themselves in interaction with the security services and with other institutions of government as 'wanted citizens' (*muwatin taht al-talab*) – a subject who has committed an infraction against some rules or regulations – perhaps encouraged and ensnared by the state into illegality and now is a compromised and silenced subject. My interviewees spoke of the sense of compulsion felt by citizens to commit infractions. They saw themselves and others as being drawn into illegal practices through regulations and practices designed precisely to compromise them. This ensnarement was perceived to be at work in all spheres of social life. Iyad, a journalist working at one of the state-owned newspapers when I interviewed him in 2005, illustrated this compulsion to transgress by giving the example of his university professor who sold class notes and marks. He explained that the professor's salary was 15,000 Syrian pounds, a sum insufficient to feed his family. Nora, a lawyer, admitted to bribing court officials to process the release of political prisoners who completed their sentences, but who would languish in prison if the bribe was not paid. The infractions are not unique to the Syrian case and, indeed, occur in other settings. However, what emerges in the Syrian case is that the infringement of rules becomes an enactment of a particular citizen subjectivity – a criminalised subject wanted by the same authorities that compelled him/her to commit the infraction. In assuming this subjectivity, the citizen forsakes the right to political engagement, to demand accountability or to press for rights.

The production of 'wanted citizen' may be a *homo sacer* in waiting: the transgressing citizen who is being pursued and who must keep a low profile and not open his eyes. In this, the subject is bound by similar rules to those operative in Tadmur Prison where prisoners were expected to lower their gaze and not look the guards and security officers in the eye.

A Shadow State: The Political Economy of Subjectivation

Zalamat al-amn and clientelisation associate with a hierarchy of relations of domination in which those in the lower strata are followers of a patron or a boss. The *zalamat* follows and answers to a *m'allim* (a boss) ('Udwan 2003). The same applies to the *shabiha* groups. In this hierarchy, a *zalamat al-amn* can also be a patron or a boss of someone to whom he provides security clearances and contacts. 'Bossism', as discussed by John Sidel (1999), has an equivalent in the Syrian context in a patronage network centred on the *m'allim* and operating within the apparatus of coercion and the networks of smuggling and trafficking. Often bosses have been tribal leaders and heads of clans who, through relations of patronage and business partnership, became part of the shadow state and formed their own economic fiefdoms, smuggling goods from Lebanon, Turkey and Jordan. Many of the bosses are known by name and their activities and areas of control are defined and delimited. For example, control of the ports of Latakiyya and Tartous in the 1980s and 1990s was maintained by members of the al-Asad family. Members of the regime clan, high-ranking army officers and high-level state personnel made substantial profits from access and control over state resources and, in the process, they built extensive clientelist networks, which furnished them with power bases among segments of the population. Sidel (1999), in reference to the Philippines, notes that the strength of local bosses is derived from the subordination of the state apparatus to elected state officials. In Syria, however, the bosses rely on either direct control over powerful state offices, in particular in the military and security services, or on having close ties with the holders of these offices.

The regime's practices of government encouraged local bosses to emerge and entrench themselves throughout the Syrian territory. Often, bosses accumulated wealth and power through smuggling and trafficking activities. According to Deeb (2011, 436), smuggling became an important economic activity in Syria with the formation of the United

Arab Republic in 1958 (the short-lived unification of Syria and Egypt) and the introduction of restrictive measures on imports and domestic trade. However, smuggling became institutionalised after the entry of the Syrian army into Lebanon, in 1976, and its deployment along main regional roads and in the Lebanese port city of Tripoli. According to some estimates, 70 per cent of annual imports into Syria in the 1980s were smuggled goods (Sadowski 1985, 6). Goods were also trafficked out of Syria. For instance, goods sold at subsidised prices inside Syria, such as cement, sugar and petrol, were redirected for sale in Lebanon and Jordan (Sadowski 1985, 6). Sadowski also notes that directors of state firms worked with private agents to procure foreign currency and to process foreign contracts. In turn, private-sector actors paid bribes to obtain permits and licensing requirements and to secure public-sector contracts, thus bypassing tendering regulations. This mode of operation was routine and encompassed a wide range of exchanges within networks of patronage (Sadowski 1985, 6). The brokering of influence permeated the apparatuses of government and reached its apex with influential ministers and Ba'th Party command members mediating access to resources and assets.

With the entry and stationing of Syrian troops in Lebanon, high-ranking officers supervised smuggling networks which comprised large numbers of conscripts and non-commissioned officers (see Deeb 2011, 406; Hinnebusch 1990, 165). Deeb (2011, 437) estimates the number of smugglers to have been in the tens of thousands and to have included security officers, customs officials, militiamen, merchants, gang members, petrol-station proprietors and many others. Smuggling and trafficking networks constitute parallel authority structures anchoring social and political relations (see Barout 2012; Dalila 2002; Deeb 2011; Sadiq 1992).[12] The widespread scale of smuggling is attested to by the fact that commercial streets in many informal neighbourhoods and towns in Syria are named *shari' al-tahrib*, meaning 'street of smuggled goods'. With the Syrian intervention in Lebanon, the intricate links between the shadow networks and state institutions were formalised in the inauguration of a military route to facilitate the movement of military leaders between the two countries.[13] This military route was part of the infrastructure of smuggling, blurring the lines between the formal state and the shadow state. In recollections of everyday life during the period of

---

[12] The entanglement of ordinary citizens in these networks is captured in the film *Shay' ma yahtariq* by Ghassan Shmayt (1993).
[13] Additionally, thousands of permits were distributed to Syrian elite families for shopping in Shtura, Lebanon, the main depot of mostly illegally imported goods.

shortages in the 1980s, some of my interviewees from small towns in rural Damascus recalled that wives of low-rank military officers were part of the networks of distribution of trafficked goods (interviews, Beirut, 2015). A wide range of goods unavailable on the local market, such as washing soap, blankets, apples and paper tissues, was procured from the military spouses. Local products destined for public cooperatives also circulated in this underground economy. Smuggled luxury items, including western-made clothes, geared to the better-off and those who had access to foreign currency, could be found in the exclusive boutiques of Damascus, some of whose proprietors were identified as the wives of officers in the highest military echelons (interviews, Damascus, 2005).

Smuggling and trafficking were normalised in everyday life for many ordinary Syrians by virtue of being the only means through which they could acquire basic goods in the 1980s and early 1990s. Certain items such as household appliances and electrical goods could be procured on the black market more readily and cheaply than in state cooperatives. While clandestine importation of many of these goods declined as a result of the economic opening, smuggling expanded in the 1990s and 2000s. Smuggling continued as an avenue of employment in many border towns that suffered economic hardship. For example, in Qusayr, in the Homs Governorate, youth ferried subsidised heating oil (*mazot*) across the border to Lebanon (Hassoun 2004). In border towns in the north-east, cheap goods procured from China and elsewhere were smuggled into Iraq for sale on the local market (Asfour 2006). Further, smugglers' markets could still be found in major urban centres such as Aleppo where pro-regime clans and clients in the Chamber of Commerce ran underground import networks.[14] Ordinary citizens became entangled in this parallel economy. In the process, they were drawn into conflicts along lines of societal division that structured the networks of smuggling and trafficking through the regime's practices of co-optation and exclusion. Tensions and, at times, outright conflicts developed between smugglers protected by military officers and others without such connections.[15]

---

[14] Prominent among these pro-regime clans in Aleppo reputed to be part of the smuggling network is the Berri clan, one of whose members served as a Member of Parliament and was thought to be one of the most powerful figures in the Aleppo Governorate. By some accounts, the Berri clan paid thousands of fighters (referred to as shabiha) to confront protesters during the 2011 Uprising (interview, Montreal, 31 August 2015; Abi Samra 2012b). Tobacco from Lebanon and Cyprus was smuggled into Syria in cooperation with the trafficking networks based in the coastal region.

[15] In a testimonial, a former resident of Homs, drawing on his own father's smuggling activities, traces the complex webs of trafficking involving customs officers, security men and transport workers and drivers who ferried passengers and goods between Homs and Beirut from the 1970s to the 2000s (Abi Samra 2012a, 155, 204). This narrator's

Included in the smuggling and trafficking networks is a thriving drug trade, involving bosses originating from within the shadow state. An impetus to drug trafficking came with the formalised presence of Syrian forces in Lebanon under the auspices of the Arab Peacekeeping Forces. From then on, according to observers from the period, Syrian military figures oversaw the increase in hashish and heroin production and trade, with half of the value of the trade going into Syrian hands (Herbert 2014). Alongside the drug trade, illegal tobacco smuggling flourished throughout the 1980s and 1990s. In the early 2000s, Syrian economist and dissident 'Aref Dalila (2002) estimated the loss to the Syrian treasury resulting from tobacco smuggling to be in the millions of dollars. The continued trade in smuggled tobacco, with the liberalisation of the economy, is noteworthy given that the traffickers competed with a regime-backed rival who controls the newly established duty-free shops located at Syrian borders with Jordan and Lebanon. The operation of these parallel markets and their political economy had implications beyond the privatisation of public assets, engagement in criminal and illegal commerce, and the loss of public financial resources. Of relevance here is how this political economy of the shadow state rested on and consolidated the patronage networks and relations of power which structured the subjectivities of the boss (*m'allim* or *Khal*) and *zalama* or *tabi'* (hireling) and that, at a later stage, metamorphosed into the *shabih* in the shadow state, taking the form of what Yassin al-Haj Saleh (2012b) called the 'State of *Shabiha*' (*dawlat al-shabiha*).

The term 'State of *shabiha*' is used as a descriptor of a particular permutation of the shadow state during the Uprising, when *shabiha* gangs were recruited to crush the demonstrations. However, the terms *shabiha* and *tashbih* (an act that is transgressive against others' rights and properties) have been in circulation from much earlier. The origin of the term *shabiha* is uncertain, and its meaning is multivocal. It is thought to have been coined to refer to the gangs of thugs surrounding the influential bosses of an earlier period. The term, in some definitions, is understood to be derived from *shabah*, meaning ghost, an allusion to a particular model of Mercedes automobile driven by gangsters. However, as explained by Mamdouh 'Udwan (2003), it is likely to denote the act of enlarging and extending an object, including stretching one's arm.

father was a driver who, enjoying familial links to a security officer, smuggled weapons to Lebanon in the 1970s, then food items, including bananas and nuts, in the 1980s. Trafficking in autoparts and antiquities, according to this narrator, was the preserve of tribes that settled on the peripheries of Old Homs, working in conjunction with security agents and high-ranking officers (Abi Samra 2012a, 217).

In this sense, *shabah* refers to accumulation that involves stretching and pushing the extremities (the act of extending an object is denoted in the term '*shabha al-shay*", see 'Udwan 2003; see also Sliman 2011). As observed by al-Haj Saleh (2012b), the boundaries between *shabiha* gangs and state institutions were hazy and fluid. At origin, as he points out, were the kin ties binding membership in the Asad family and clan. The model *shabiha* network was established around various members of the immediate and extended family of Hafez al-Asad, with figures such as Fawaz al-Asad and Mohammed al-Asad (known as Shaykh al-Jabal) being prominent players. Although other members of the extended Asad family, such as the Shalishes (paternal cousins of Bashar al-Asad) and the Makhloufs (maternal cousins), obtained privileged access to public contracts without proper tendering, they do not fit into the original *shabiha* activities that involved outright criminality in the form of extortion, armed burglary and theft. In time, the *shabiha* label and mode of operation extended to include outsiders from various religious and social backgrounds. Thus, several clans in Aleppo wielded similar power to that of the inner-circle *shabiha*. The *shabiha* are enlisted for similar services to those performed by the *baltagiyya* (thugs) in Egypt. That is, they serve as a reserve pool of muscle-for-hire – sometimes with criminal records – called upon to serve the interests of the bosses of the shadow state or of their protectors in public institutions and to safeguard the regime, the ultimate patron of these networks.

The Political Economy and Identitarian Dimensions of Clientelised Subjects

In the state of permanent war – resting on an 'us' and 'them' caesura drawn in the ideo-theology of the Eternal Leader – social lines of identification and sources of selfhood, namely family, tribe, sect and region, are called upon in the making of political subjectivities. These lines of division are deployed in a recomposition and realignment of social and political forces. It should be noted that state practices of co-optation, incorporation and exclusion are operative in the processes of reproduction of social forces and in the constitution of any political agency they might have.

It is relevant to sketch briefly here the socio-economic transformations in which state social engineering played a vital part. Studies of Ba'thist politics in Syria tend to highlight its populism, in particular during its early phase (Hinnebusch 1989; Perthes 1997; Van Dam 1996). Indeed, this populism was instrumental to the formulae of rule. It worked both as a mode of incorporation and as a frame for the organisation and management of the state of war – the maintenance and the upkeep of the caesura and the deployment of violence, as will be illustrated below. First, however, we will look at the terms of recomposition and realignment of social forces instituted by Ba'th populism as it evolved under Hafez al-Asad.

To trace the contours of this recomposition and realignment, it is important to note the interplay between the statist and developmentalist policies – which enabled large segments of the rural lower classes to abandon their villages in pursuit of education and employment in cities and towns – and regime-sponsored practices of enframing and clientelisation aimed at enlisting these classes as its social base. Despite the land redistribution policies intended to break down large estates and help small- and middle-sized farmlands to consolidate, rural areas in many regions were left underdeveloped in crucial respects. The coastal villages of the regions of Latakiyya and Tartous are a good case in point. For many young, rural families in these regions, volunteering in the army and moving to the cities of Tartous, Latakiyya and Damascus presented a way out of the limited opportunities of life in the countryside. From the 1970s onward, the army and security services drew most of their rank-and-file from this segment of the population – the lower-middle class with a noted sectarian and regional inflection, as with the recruitment of individuals of Alawi background from the Sahel (coast) and from rural Hama, and of lower rank non-commissioned officers drawn from the rural poor in the north-eastern peninsula. The enlistment of the poor and disadvantaged in the apparatuses of coercion provided a nodal connection with these sectors of the population while inscribing lines of division between the agents of violence and control and other societal forces. The loyalty to the president that would later make the army and the security services guardians and protectors of his regime can be traced back to these early patterns of populist co-optation.

Patterns of rural migration and urban settlement further reinforced societal divisions as they were tied to the regime's mode of governance with its entrenchment of lines of social differentiation. If we consider how the rural migrants – the regime's social base and key nodal connectors in its clientelist network – were integrated into a city like Damascus, we get a clear sense of the reproduction of traditional societal divisions in identitarian terms. This manner of integration preserves social rupture, thus perpetuating fears about the possible outbreak of violence. I draw on my fieldwork in Damascus to illustrate the reconfiguration and realignment of social forces that capture dynamics of conflict and division – dynamics which shape the formation of subjectivities and the positioning of subjects vis-à-vis the state and fellow citizens.

How have the statist, developmentalist and populist politics given rise to new social formations and a reconfiguration of forces? One point of entry to an answer is to examine the changes of the urban setting of Damascus as the centre of government.[16] In the early phases of these changes, the military and security forces expanded significantly and, in the process, absorbed a large proportion of the migrants into their ranks. The regime pursued spatial control by erecting military and security facilities in strategic urban areas and by managing housing settlements connected to the apparatuses of violence. Associated with this development was the emergence of urban quarters to house the low-level military volunteer recruits and conscripts. These quarters were differentiated along various lines such as position and rank in the military, regional origin and religious affiliation. For example, the quarter of Mezzeh 86 emerged to house the non-commissioned officers in one of Rif'at al-Asad's military divisions. Located in the Mezzeh Mountain, the quarter grew on a rocky terrain, lying north of the Damascene quarter of Sheikh Saad. Originally unplanned and lacking basic infrastructural services, the quarter was, in time, extended the services on order of the president (interview with residents, Damascus, March and April 2005). In terms of confessional affiliation, 85 per cent of the residents of Mezzeh 86 are Alawi. Their establishment in the city follows a pattern of incorporation into the state through its organs of coercion. Yet their form and degree of integration into the urban sector also captures societal divisions manipulated by the regime. Based on my interviews with residents, it is evident that Mezzeh 86 remains on the margin of the city, un-integrated economically and socially. While the first-generation migrants found employment in the army, their children occupy the lower rungs of the service sector, remaining on the margins of the commercial and productive activities of traditional Damascus. What is important about the terms of integration is what they reveal about the entrenchment of divisions along lines of class, sect, regional origin and place of residence and how these overlap and intersect (a point I will return to below).

The Qaboun quarter serves as a point of comparison with Mezzeh 86. Built on agricultural land, Qaboun houses rural migrants mostly from Idlib and rural Damascus. A portion of the quarter residents from Idlib came to voluntarily join the military and work in the army, but most came as conscripts who remained in the city after completing their military service. The economic activities of the residents point to other elements of

---

[16] The following discussion, over the next few pages, of informal neighbourhoods in Damascus draws substantially on Ismail (2013) and is based on fieldwork that I conducted in 2005 in the neighbourhoods of Mezzeh 86, Qaboun and Barzeh.

the political economy of Ba'thist rule. Notably, many are involved in the trafficking of smuggled goods. Trafficking was, at one time, a source of income made possible by the fact that the conscripts served in Lebanon and entered into the smuggling networks bringing in clothes, electrical goods and spare automobile parts. Other residents entered the service industries, running and operating minibuses (primarily migrants from the village of Hafir in rural Damascus) and working in informal outdoor markets. Some set up small textile workshops. Like Mezzeh 86, the Qaboun residents are not integrated into the part of the Damascene economy that is based in the city's traditional markets, but, unlike the Mezzeh residents, they are not dependent on the state for employment. This distinction in patterns of employment between these two informal quarters, both with largely rural-origin migrant populations, embodies differing patterns of co-optation and exclusion by the regime.

The dynamics of incorporation and exclusion could help explain the sense of precariousness that Mezzeh 86 residents felt after the death of Hafez al-Asad in 2000 when, it is said, some prepared to leave the city and return to their villages of origin, sensing uncertainty and fearing retribution that would be aimed at regime supporters. In their narrative of the history of the quarter's establishment – from the allocation of space or permission to squat, to the provision and regularisation of infrastructural services – the existence of the place is projected as an appendage of the rulers, first Rif'at al-Asad as benefactor, and then Hafez al-Asad and Bashar al-Asad as protectors. One of the residents I interviewed ended his reflections of his personal journey by stating: 'life is good, we thank the president'. In this utterance, and others like it, there is more at work than being versed in the language of the cult of the president. Indeed, there is an acknowledgement of the clientelist relations that take the form, euphemistically, of gratitude but are, in fact, expressions of the symbolic violence that is an inbuilt element of the 'gift'.

Mezzeh 86 may represent the extreme case of clientelisation through employment in the army and bureaucracy and through residential arrangements, but it exemplifies spatial and demographic patterns of change associated with the militarisation of rule and of society: the emergence of residential quarters on the peripheries of the city to house army personnel and their families. A number of peripheral quarters have entire sections identified with the military: for example, the housing adjacent to the military barracks in Qaboun; the settlement of 'Ish al-Warwar established on the communal lands of Barzeh community in North Damascus; and the settlement of Summariyya constructed on the land of Mu'adamiyya. These urban spatial arrangements, along with the demographic characteristics, are a dimension of the social differentiation expressed in identitarian terms. With Mezzeh 86 and 'Ish al-Warwar, as with tribal co-optation, we discern the dynamics of incorporation of segments of the population into the web of authority and power through employment as retainers, informants and regime guards.

What are the identitarian dimensions of these different political positionings, albeit expressed at different socio-historical junctures? Qaboun and Mezzeh 86 embody the 'us' and 'them' division patterned along socio-economic lines, with overlapping affiliation to or member- ship in a sect, and also along rural–urban distinctions. Both quarters are on the margins of the city's economic and cultural life. The fact that Qaboun's population is predominately Sunni has not translated into closer ties with the city's social elites, namely the Sunni Damascene merchants and entrepreneurs who are the regime's historical allies. The distinction between Sunni and Alawi in reference to the migrant populations of Qaboun and Mezzeh 86, respectively, has to do with the functionalisation of sect as an element in the institutions of coercion and with the articulation of this distinction with the social, spatial and eco- nomic realignments of the populist conjuncture.

The socio-spatial divisions, in which relations with the regime were a determining factor, overlapped with sectarian distinctions. However, the divisions are primarily, and more appropriately, political, being drawn around distinctions that set those who are co-opted by the regime against others who are marginalised or denied access to the apparatuses of power (in particular the army and the security forces). Added to this is the enmity or antagonism that arose in processes of land expropriation that appeared to benefit one group at the expense of another. The cases of Barzeh and 'Ish al-Warwar can serve as a model for understanding developments in other strategic territories throughout greater Damascus and across Syria.

Barzeh, an informal quarter built on agricultural land on the nor- thern gate of Damascus, maintains a nucleus of its original inhabitants in a section known as Barzeh al-Balad. These long-time inhabitants are referred to as Barzawis to denote their territorialised identity. Barzeh's expansion and urban build-up began in the 1970s with the state expro- priation of land for the middle-class residential project of Masakin Barzeh (Barzeh Housing). Further land expropriation took place for the purpose of erecting military facilities, including a military hospital. The break-up of Barzeh land and the inscription of antagonisms towards the regime deepened when the families of a military unit of Rif'at al-Asad's brigades were settled on land in a rocky area adjacent to Barzeh al-Balad. The area, known as 'Ish al-Warwar, was considered as part of the communal terri- tory of the original Barzeh inhabitants. The settlement of 'Ish al-Warwar (also know as 'al-'Ish') was associated with tensions from the start. The antagonism was marked in an early incident of violence, which is now referred to as *ahdath Barzeh* (the Barzeh events). According to my informants' accounts, in 1975 the new neighbours from 'Ish al-Warwar attacked a coffee shop where community elders had gathered to decide a question of access to water wells for the irrigation of fields. A fight broke out and some of the elders of Barzeh al-Balad were killed. As the 'Ish was considered to be under Rif'at al-Asad's protection, the Barzeh residents believed that there was little they could do to get redress and, in fact, some, fearing retribution for their role in the fight, fled from the area. These historical antagonisms resurfaced at the time of the Uprising in 2011 and afterwards, and were expressed in the positioning that both quarters took vis-à-vis the regime: Barzeh al-Balad was at the forefront of anti-regime demonstrations, while 'Ish al-Warwar sided with the regime and mobilised against the protesters.

As with Barzeh, the district of Mu'adamiyya, in al-Ghuta al-Gharbiyya (to the south of Damascus), had much of its land expropriated to build military installations including the Mezzeh Military Airport, and to create a housing area, known as the Sumarayya neighbourhood, for officers in the Fourth Division. Mu'adamiyya's original inhabitants came to harbour grievances towards the regime and their neighbours in Sumarayya who were Alawi and were the beneficiaries of land appropriation. Antagonism towards these beneficiaries, the regime and the military would also come to be expressed during the Uprising. In interviews, young men and women from the area who participated in the demonstrations noted the seizure of agricultural lots by the regime, and the loss of cultivation rights and of real estate as driving their grievances (*mazlumiyya*) against the regime. One activist from Darayya, who was incarcerated for a time at the Mezzeh Military Airport, recounted a telling anecdote in which a fellow detainee, who came from Mu'adamiyya, is said to have proclaimed to a cell guard that the entire facility and his division were sitting on *her* land (interview with activist in Beirut, 2015).

Land conflicts overlaid with sectarian particularism, articulated with forms of differentiation relating to employment, access to education and so on. The patterns of migration and settlement reinforced socio-spatial differentiation, with new quarters established to house military personnel of rural origin juxtaposed to neighbourhoods where private and informal employment was dominant. An often-repeated assertion by interviewees residing in places like Qatana, Mu'adamiyya and Barzeh, is that the family members of army officers had privileged access to government employment (interviews, in 2015, with former Qatana and Mu'adamiyya residents, displaced in Lebanon; interviews with Barzeh residents in 2011). This view is given credence if we review the profile of economic activities in Barzeh al-Balad when compared with 'Ish al-Warwar. As in Qaboun, Barzeh's original inhabitants work in construction, private transport and manufacturing. The predominance of employment in private and informal sectors of the economy is viewed by youths from these areas as evidence of their exclusion from public employment and the preferential status that neighbouring migrants (of Alawi origin) enjoy (interviews with youth activists from Barzeh, Qaboun and Mu'adamiyya, Damascus, April 2011, and subsequent correspondence, October and November 2011). It should be noted, however, that opportunities for employment in the public sector underwent a significant decline during the 1990s. The public sector could not absorb most of the new entrants into the labour market.[17]

Patterns of migration and urban settlement in other cities such as Homs also reinforced differentiation along sectarian lines as well as grouping according to regional origin and kinship ties. Of Syria's major cities, Homs received among the largest number of rural migrants over the last thirty to forty years (Barout 2012, 301). New urban quarters emerged with communally differentiated populations. For example, Akrama, Nuzha and al-Zahira had predominately Alawi populations working, in large part, in public-sector employment or in the army and security services (see Balanche 2000; interviews Beirut, October 2015, with youth from Homs). Sunnis from rural areas and of Bedouin origin, on the other hand, settled in the existing old-city quarters and in the peripheral quarters that had previously been rural fringe areas and were incorporated into the city (for example, Baba Amro). Residents of these latter areas, especially, relied on trade, transport and smuggling activities to earn their livings. Accounts of the relationships between inhabitants of quarters differentiated along communal lines indicate that conflict was infrequent and that harmonious relations were maintained (Bishara 2013, 121). However, as with the Barzeh events referred to above, at the time of the Uprising incidents of conflict were recalled and antagonisms arising from the differing positioning in relation to the regime came to the surface (Nakkash 2013; on Barzeh-'Ish al-Warwar antagonisms, see discussion above). Friction lines, as found between Barzeh and 'Ish al-Warwar, could

---

[17] Data from governorate labour offices for levels of unemployment confirm the vast chasm between opportunities for state employment and the labour needs of the yearly numbers of market entrants. For example, in 2012 the Labour Office in Hama had 190,000 registered job seekers, of which only 7.6 per cent were able to find work (*Tishrin*, 5 November 2012; see also Habib, 2004). In the meantime, figures on workers in the informal economy confirm a marked increase from the 1990s onwards throughout the country (Hayan 2007).

be discerned in the relations between Sunni-majority neighbourhoods such as Khaldiyya and Bab Al-Siba', on one hand, and Alawi-majority neighbourhoods such as 'Akrama and al-Zahira, on the other. Residents of these neighbourhoods clashed during the Uprising (Barout 2012, 287; see also Balanche 2011).

Equally contentious to the matters of land conflict noted above was the issue of the disproportionate employment, in the municipality, of migrants linked to the officers' networks. Employment in the state bureaucracy is construed as an example of differentiation in identitarian terms. In testimonies and interviews with Syrians, a recurrent theme is that a number of state offices and institutions draw their personnel primarily from among Alawi migrants (interviews with activists from Homs, Beirut, 2015). In cities like Hama and Homs, it is asserted that the newcomers took most of the jobs in the civil registry office.[18] In Banyas, figures are used to demonstrate that posts in certain establishments, such as the city's port, are occupied, in absolute majority, by Alawis (Abi Samra 2012a, 293). The same perceptions hold for the military firms (ma'amil al-difa'). Employment in these firms necessitates contacts within the security forces and the military, hence reproducing a mode of functioning that ultimately amounts to politicising and instrumentalising sectarian affiliation and thus reinforcing identitarian divisions.

Without the benefit of full or reliable statistical data on the demographic and social composition of public-service personnel, it is difficult to establish the extent of possible preferential access to public-sector jobs for Alawi migrants by virtue of their network links.[19] Yet the appearance of favouritism has created a sense of discrimination, which could be construed along sectarian lines, even though the clientelist networks entrenching differentiation are neither religious nor necessarily communitarian. Rather, what is widely known to be the case is that military officers promote the interests of their families and friends. An activist from Baba Amro noted that many Alawi families had 'one of their own' serving in the military in some capacity and on whom they could rely for help with such things as processing paperwork in the public administration, getting public services or obtaining a job (interview in Beirut, October 2015).

---

[18] Similar assertions regarding the Alawis' privileged access to public employment are made with reference to registry offices in Deir al-Zour. This favouritism is attributed to the influence of the head of military security for the Eastern Department (Kuluna Shurka' fi al-Watan 2012b).

[19] For data on Alawi employment, see Balanche (2000).

Favouritism and clientelism facilitated the development of communally-based recruitment into different sectors of the economy. It should be noted that an implicit understanding of spheres of influence emerged in places like Damascus and Aleppo, whereby traditional markets and manufacturing continued to be the preserve of these cities' traditional families who were mostly Sunni and Christian. In accounts of settlement in Damascus, 'outsiders' contend that Damascenes were closed to newcomers (interviews in Beirut, October 2015, and Damascus, 2005). For example, a Syrian journalist from a town in Idlib stated that after two decades of living in Damascus, he was still an outsider to Damascene networks of sociability. In his words, '*al-shawam ananiyyin fi shamiyyithum*' ('Damascenes selfishly guard their Damasceneness') (interview, Damascus, 16 March 2005). A multitude of factors contributed to the persistence of these patterns, notably the merchant class's association with conservative religious preachers and exclusionary market practices (see Ismail 2009; Pierret 2013). Regional origin, urban–rural and sect divides were indexed in relation to cultural practices in complex and intersecting terms. The divide along the lines of sect invoked distinctions between conservative values associated with Sunnis and liberal attitudes attributed to Alawis. However, differentiation in terms of lifestyle lumped together all rural migrants of diverse religious backgrounds in terms of lacking the urbane manners of Damascenes, both Sunni and Christian.[20] Societal prejudices articulated with the divisions that arose from citizens' differentiated relations to the regime.

Parallel dynamics of subjectivation are at work in the communal corporatist policies adopted by the regime during 'the state of war' that came to the surface in the late 1970s and early 1980s. In addition to co-optation on the basis of sect, the regime incorporated segments of the population along clan and tribal lines. Heads of clans and tribes served as relay points with the security services and the Ba'th to reproduce their authority and to deliver their constituencies to government. It is these frames of association and social ties and relations with the regime that were mobilised in the battle with the Islamists and the broader opposition at that time. Similarly, since the 2011 Uprising clans active in the trafficking and smuggling networks have been deployed against the population, as transpired with the *shabiha* and the Aleppo smuggling clans in 2011 and afterwards.[21]

---

[20] On Damascenes' attitudes towards rural migrants in Damascus, see Salamandra (2004).
[21] In the shadow of the shadow state, such groups and formations proliferate and grow. One may wonder if these are the formations that Bashar al-Asad spoke of when, in his

Clientelisation served to reinforce the lines of division bringing popular forces into the orbit of rule, thus creating the veneer of a populist state. However, it would not be correct to see the regime/state as populist in a manner that promotes social inclusion. Rather, this populism develops in an exclusionary fashion, sustained by and sustaining the ideo-theology of the sacredness of the ruler (see 'Udwan's (2003) discussion along the same lines in *Haywanat al-Insan*). It is this populist face of rule that appears clearly at times of open conflict with the regime, as seen in the events of the 2011 Uprising. As the challenge to the regime grew and spread, the diehard supporters, fans and cult followers who came to be referred to as the *minhibakji* ('the we love you camp') intensified their practices of adulation and their expressions of devotion, as shouted in such slogans as *Allah, Bashar, Suriyya wi bas* (God, Syria, Bashar and that is all), *Bashar ila al abad* (Bashar until eternity), *Bashar aw la ahad* (Bashar or no one). It is also from the same popular forces or lower social strata that the shadow state retained the networks of *shabiha* who are deployed against the demonstrators. These various social forces constituted important actors in the management of the state of war in its civil war form.

Clientelisation and *istizlam* are mechanisms of subjectivation produ-cing subject dispositions and informing norms of action and interaction. In this way, these mechanisms define fields of action operative in various spheres such as schools, workplaces, public spaces and infiltrating into the private sphere as well through organs of enframing like the Ba'th Vanguards (Tala'i') and the Revolutionary Youth Federation (*Shabibat al-Thawra*).

From Homogenised Subjects to Exposed Subjects

Ba'thist enframing of citizens through its various popular organisations intersects with a particular experience of discipline of the subject that is grounded in material conditions of 'the state of war'. As will be discussed when we turn to an examination of Syrians' memories of both violence and life under Hafez al-Asad's dictatorship, the militarisation of different spheres of social life is a structuring theme of narratives of that period. It was common for my interviewees to recall that their school days were experienced as a form of mobilisation for war. They often made reference to school uniforms as resembling military uniforms – khaki in colour and styled in a military cut. Further, the classes in national education and the *futuwwa* (physical training) classes figured prominently in these

---

June 2011 speech, he affirmed that there were 64,000 armed criminals on the loose in Syria and that they represented the equivalent of a number of military divisions (see al-Asad 2011).

recollections. The shared experience of a particular type of discipline points to a homogenisation experiment and homogenisation practices. However, this should not be understood to mean that subjectivation is necessarily productive of uniform outcomes.

Self-proclaimed as 'socialist', the state controlled consumption by the citizen through bans on certain imports, guided consumption of national products and so on. In my interviews with Syrians in their late twenties and older, and from a diversity of backgrounds, the experience of deprivation and exhaustion had a great bearing on their sense of self as political subjects. This invocation of deprivation as defining of life before the Uprising was part of an explanatory narrative as to why they believed that sensations of fatigue and exhaustion kept them from political engagement and undermined their strength to organise and act for change. One businessman in Damascus, commenting on regime mobilisation for support against international pressures on Syria during the investigation into the Rafiq al-Hariri assassination, stated: 'I am tired of being told you cannot convert local currency into foreign funds because the national economy needs foreign reserves. I am tired of the injunctions to do one thing or another to maintain the national front. I am tired of being told not to eat bananas' (interview, Damascus, 17 April 2005). In this commentary, the various bans in effect during different periods were merged together: the ban on bananas and on currency conversion, dating back to the 1980s, with restrictions on currency exchange during the mid 2000s. The recollections come with a certain felt irony at the injunctions to sacrifice for the national good and with a sense that citizens were pawns used by government rather than being actual contributors or participants. These same experiences are being recollected today. So are the performances the subjects were compelled to enact in the Ba'th organisations, such as the marches in support of the leaders and the 'spontaneous' processions.

A key theme in the recollections and in the self-presentation of 'the subject of lack' is the struggle for survival and self-preservation and being reduced to conditions of bare life. A related theme is that of being the subject of neglect, being left to one's devices and, worse, being exposed to abusive treatment. The self-understandings that arise within these regimes of subjectivities align with the divisions drawn in relation to the ruler and between the ruler and the ruled. Access to goods and services, protection from the heavy hand of security, from exposure to false accusation and from the criminality of state agents or criminal networks growing in the shadow of the illegal state, can be achieved by assuming the subjectivities cultivated through clientalisation and *istizlam*.

Narratives of exposure to theft, false accusations, becoming victims of *salbata* (that is, predatory practices) became more common in the period preceding the Uprising. By the time of the Uprising, criminality was given the shorthand of *shabiha* and *tashbih*. The narrative of exposure to criminality extends an existing repertoire of accounts of abuse by agents and officers of the state. During the Uprising, and with an unleashed stream of recollections, many narratives surfaced illuminating the sliding of ordinary citizens from the homogenised subjects of authoritarian government to the precarious and exposed subjects of the shadow state.

Conclusion

In this chapter, I examined regime practices of government and control, which shaped the formation of Syrian political subjectivities. Within the apparatuses of rule, the enframing of citizens and the practices and programmes of securitisation combined to delimit fields of action and modes of interaction between citizens and the regime, and between and among citizens themselves. The Ba'th Party and its auxiliary organisations worked to form, co-opt and enframe citizens. Through indoctrination activities, clientalisation and its penetration into various aspects of everyday life, the party has been instrumental in the propagation of regime rhetoric and the cultivation of core regime supporters. The party's activities of enframing citizens combined with the securitisation of mundane activities and aspects of everyday life. Regime practices of securitisation, in turn, informed discursive civilities and communicative competencies among citizens. These civilities and competencies enter into the making of political subjectivities. In quotidian conversations and exchanges between citizen-subjects the *zalamat al-amn* arises as an 'anticipated subject' orienting communication.

The chapter brings to light the material anchoring of political subjectivities in the informal networks of the shadow state. It shows how these latter are enmeshed in practices of government, as is the case when the networks are mobilised in political contests to suppress dissidence and opposition. In this respect, we find that clientelist networks structure citizens' interaction and political positionality. Illegal economic activities, such as smuggling and trafficking, furnished the resources of bosses/patrons and followers who emerged from among the ranks of the security apparatuses, clans and the regime's inner circle. Relatedly, regime practices of co-optation and exclusion reinforce and politicise differentiation along regional and sectarian lines. Through these practices, the polarisation and fragmentation of society are articulated in identitarian terms. This is particularly evident in the manner of integration of rural migrants into the urban space, the labour market and the apparatuses of coercion.

3   Memories of Life under Dictatorship: The Everyday of Ba'thist Syria

Regime violence, as a mechanism of government, has been formative of Syrian political subjectivities under al-Asad rule. While apprehending the role of state violence as a dimension of subject formation in Syria is crucial for the examination of state–citizen relations, it is necessary to bring to this enquiry an understanding of other interlinked formative state/regime practices, in particular practices that are devised in relation to the postcolonial national projects of development and liberation. In pursuit of these projects and with the declared goal of bringing about a radical societal transformation, successive Ba'thist regimes, beginning with the first Ba'thist coup in 1963, embarked on a programme of political, social and cultural remake. Integral to the developmentalist project – resting on industrialisation through large projects such as land reclamation and the building of the Euphrates Dam – was the remaking of the Syrian subject. Even though the Ba'thist radical vision of social change was attenuated, if not completely abandoned, under the rule of Hafez al-Asad and his associates following the 1970 military coup, the rhetoric of crafting 'a new man' persisted and, alongside it, grew the drive to enlist popular forces in the projects of transformation – a task that was entrusted to the Ba'th Party. As observers and analysts have noted, the idea of class as the basis of party membership was forsaken in favour of mass recruitment. Still, the party aspired to train cadres, and to create a core of committed adherents who would be the pioneers and guardians of the project of Arab revival. Enlistment in this cause was to begin at the early stages of subject formation through the work of 'popular organisations' led and controlled by the Ba'th Party. Key among these organisations was the Revolutionary Youth Federation established in 1968 and the Pioneers Organisation created in 1974.

This chapter examines memories of everyday life under the dictatorship that the regime of Hafez al-Asad erected and put into effect during the postcolonial period. In particular, it focuses on the structuring themes and narratives in the memories of individual and collective life under this system of rule. In Syrians' recollections of the past, as the chapter will show, we see how governmental techniques of rule and national projects of transformation shape understandings of self and orient self-positioning. In a manner similar to the Chilean experience under Pinochet (Stern 2006, 1), Syrians' everyday experience of the national life under Hafez al-Asad indelibly marked their sense of self and personhood. Individual memories, as discussed by Steve Stern in reference to Chile, arise in dialogue with 'emblematic frameworks', understood as frames of recollection that enable individuals to make sense of their personal experiences and to locate these experiences within remembrances of a collective or shared national life (Stern 2006, 1). As elaborated by Stern (2006, 105), 'Emblematic memory refers not to a single remembrance of a specific content, not to a concrete or substantive "thing," but to a framework that organizes meaning, selectivity, and countermemory'. Following Stern, one of the concerns of this chapter is to draw the contours of the frames of meaning, which organise Syrians' memories of life under dictatorship. A related concern is to identify those remembrances, which are narrated as emblems of shared societal experiences. Through these narratives, it is possible to discern the terms in which individual memories of everyday life aggregate to form a composite of the national experience, and to create emblematic frames of that experience. Memories of everyday life events and daily happenings furnish the raw material out of which emblems of the national life are made. This is illustrated by the intersection in Syrians' social memories of recollections of school and family life with narratives of political events and encounters with government, and by the emergence, through and in narratives, of repertoires of ostensibly commonly shared national experiences, social codes and meanings.

Relatedly, narratives of the national life – referenced by official interpellation and ideological affiliation – provide frames for reflecting on personal experiences and making sense of the processes and factors that shape individual and collective dispositions and action. In other words, authoring the self is undertaken within national frames of memory and history which, themselves, are the product of the interplay between official rhetoric and counter narratives and interpretative frames that emerge in everyday life experience. To trace this process of moving from the national frames to the individual self, in a second part the chapter draws on interviews with Syrians and on artistic works that narrate the national experience through the life stories of Syrians, both activists and ordinary people. These narratives bring to light the interconnections of the mundane events of life and those taking place on the national stage. They offer insights into how the national experience is woven into narratives of the self or self-authoring in a manner of giving account of the self and of the factors that shape self-positioning.[1]

The following discussion of memories of everyday life under the Hafez al-Asad dictatorship is divided into two parts. The first part looks at memories of growing up and coming of age that specifically narrate everyday life as an experience of the national life and as an orienting frame of recollection. The themes and motifs sketched out in personal and intimate remembrances unfold within emblematic frames that are appropriated and created through recollection. Two emblematic frameworks organise remembrances of everyday life and shared experiences, namely 'abjection and precarity' and 'national salvation'. The second part of the chapter examines how narratives of the self by publicly engaged actors – primarily intellectuals, writers, artists and activists – chart personal trajectories that interweave the lived experience and the national experience. These self-narratives articulate concerns with questions of compromise and complicity with the regime and are oriented towards accounting for the subject's political positioning and, ultimately, for her/his political responsibility.

Everyday Life under Dictatorship

This section examines the memories of growing up as sources for discerning the societal frames within which Syrians' understandings of their selfhood were shaped. As will be shown, the school, youth organisations and the family crystallise as sites of recollections that shed light on practices of subjectivation. The analysis draws on interviews with Syrians who belong to the generations that grew up and went to school in the 1980s and 1990s, coming of age under the rule of Hafez al-Asad. These generations are referred to in Syrian public discourse as 'the Ba'th generation' (*Jil al-Ba'th*), an appellation that is also used in self-identification by the subjects themselves. This appellation emphasises the role that Ba'th institutions played in shaping the generation's self-understandings and positionality. I began, in 2005, to gather Syrians' recollections of everyday life and continued to do so until the Uprising in 2011 and then in its aftermath. In this part of the discussion, I identify common formative experiences as well as social processes and junctures

---

[1] The documentaries of Omar Amiralay (1997) and Ossama Mohammed (1979) and the novels of Khaled Khalifa (2008), Mundhir Badr Hallum (2009a, 2009b), Nabil Sliman (2005), Rosa Yassin Hassan (2011a, 2011b), Samar Yazbek (2010) and the films of Mohammad Malas, Ossama Mohammed and Abd al-Latif Abd al-Hamid lay out the threads that weave together the individual experience with the collective.

that contributed to a general transformation that altered Syrians' positioning vis-à-vis the regime and government. The examination of memories of growing up in Syria aims to elucidate experiences formative of Syrian political subjectivities under the Ba'thist formula of rule which, as discussed in the previous chapters, rested on the cult of the leader, on the security apparatus and on the enframing of citizens through the Ba'th Party and its auxiliaries. This understanding of the terms of rule in Syria could be read as approximating a totalitarian form of government. However, I refrain from using the term 'totalitarian' even though it would be appropriate to consider the degree to which, at certain junctures, the regime had totalitarian aspirations. A more immediate question is, in light of the pervasive role of the security services and of the politics of enframing citizens, can we speak of a Syrian Ba'thist subject in the same terms that studies of totalitarian government in the Soviet Union speak of the Soviet subject or the Stalinist subject? This question helps to identify core dimensions of the problematic in this chapter, namely how Syrians experienced the workings of an authoritarian/dictatorial system of rule in the everyday; how Syrians' social memories narrate experiences that are formative of their political subjectivities; how Syrians deploy narratives of the national in their self-authoring and their account of their political positionality as subject-citizens.

Growing up in Ba'thist Syria

The Ba'th Generation: The School and the Youth of the Revolution
In her analysis of the politics of public rhetoric in Syria, Lisa Wedeen (1999) argues that the Asad regime did not demand or expect its subjects to believe its rhetoric. Rather, Wedeen contends, the regime aimed at generating compliance expressed performatively wherein the subjects publicly act as if they believed its outlandish and hyperbolic claims and representations. Although this analytical lens explains aspects of the subjects' interaction with the regime, there is a need to widen the problematic of citizen–state interaction to enquire into practices of government and rule that were deployed in the everyday, beyond the parades and public spectacles of the leader's grandeur. As such, in this investigation, consideration will be given to how the regime insinuated itself into the everyday beyond the rhetoric of the cult of the president. The guiding question here is how have Syrians and, in particular, the Ba'th generation, interpreted and related to life conditions, structures of authority and government in the everyday? Answering this question by drawing the contours of the typical subject or subjectivity would be

neither possible nor informative analytically. However, recollections and self-authoring narratives can give us a sense of the selves formed and performed. Notably, these come to light in interviews and in published memoirs of the period as the subjects' affective dispositions and practices are recalled in the act of recollection: for example, disaffection, dread and disgust emerge as affects associated with the formative years of many Syrians of the Ba'th generation. This affective register contrasts with another where feelings of gratitude and loyalty structure the memories of supporters and adherents of the regime and the party.

I begin with Ba'thist education and the processes of subjectivation that were part of the educational experience. These are summoned up in critical self-distancing enacted by subjects who, through their remembering, articulate an oppositional positioning vis-à-vis the regime. For the generations that grew up under the rule of Hafez al-Asad, memories of school life structure the narratives of their lived experience and at the same time are understood and interpreted as emblematic of the national and also as formative of both the self and the collectivity. These memories are recalled in interpreting and making sense of the self within the national experience. There are common themes and motifs that are sketched out in recollections of school days. At the same time, social memories are inflected with regional, socio-economic and religious associations.

A recurrent motif in the recollections of school life is that of the militarisation of everyday life. In her recollections of school, Ruba, who was twenty-seven years of age in 2011 when I interviewed her, depicts vividly how, as a young girl, she came to recognise the military dominance of her personal space and surroundings. Ruba grew up in Rukn al-Din neighbourhood, a Kurdish quarter of Damascus. Her family was originally from a village in the Sahel and is of Alawi descent. Ruba does not self-identify as Alawi, but that identity is ascribed to her by virtue of the terms in which her family's religious affiliation and place of origin are worked into identitarian discourses and practices operating in the social body. In meta-narratives of sectarian rule, Ruba's family trajectory typifies the experience of rural Alawi families from the Sahel that migrated to the capital in search of work opportunities and a better life for their children. Her father found work as a non-commissioned officer and the family settled in Rukn al-Din. This family trajectory places her, by default, as a regime beneficiary and supporter, a projection that is not borne out by her own terms of self-identification and by her self-positioning as a dissident. Ruba began to articulate a critical perspective on the regime during her university years in the 2000s. When I met Ruba in Damascus in early 2011, she was engaged in media work supporting the Uprising and she was also providing logistical aid to other activists. Reflecting on her school days, she said:

[T]he call of the assembly line has rung in my head since primary school. We used to shout 'al-Ba'th, al-Ba'th, al-Ba'th.' For many years, I shouted this word, but I did not know what it meant. I still see the colour of the uniform which is colourless … saluting the flag on Mondays and Thursdays. Khaki surrounds me from the age of thirteen to eighteen. This ugly colour still besieges me. I used to hate it and I continue to hate it. I recall crawling on the stomach as discipline for any transgression.

Ruba's visceral sentiments in recalling these early experiences were expressed in emotive terms. She began her recollections by expressing her sense of surprise at the rancour and unhappiness that her remembrances brought forth. In reflecting on how she feels when remembering these early days of schooling, she stated: 'I did not know that my memories would come out in this festered condition.'

The khaki colour of the uniform triggers unpleasant associations and elicits unhappy affects as illustrated in the sentiments expressed by Tha'ir, a man who was in his thirties when I interviewed him in 2005, at a time when the regime appeared to be faltering. Tha'ir shared Ruba's repulsion towards khaki. He stated that it had affected him in an intimate way, rendering him unable to have a sense of colour and to have a personal aesthetic sensibility. In 1995, Tha'ir moved to Damascus from a town in the Sahel. By the early 2000s, he had established a small business in electronic goods and was relatively well off. Like Ruba, he is of rural background and, therefore, belongs to the strata whose interests the Ba'thists claimed to champion. In assessing his training and education, Tha'ir found them wanting, citing, by way of example, his lack of skill in speaking a foreign language. This he attributed to the deficiencies of Ba'thist education, which devoted time to military training and doctrinal teaching, but left him with no practical skills. He drew connections between this pedagogy and what he called the 'ruination' (al-kharab) that pervaded his surroundings: ruination was everywhere, as evidenced in the loss of agricultural land in the Ghuta.

For Ruba and Tha'ir, the ugliness of Khaki invaded their person and left its sediments.[2] Khaki, in these recollections, is a metonym for the Ba'thist system. This metonymy is deployed in Mundhir Badr Hallum's novel *Children of Sakiba* (2009a). Set in a coastal village, the children of a local school give the school guide (al-muwajih), who is in charge of student discipline and national civics training, the nickname 'Khaki-suit' (badla al-khaki). Many of my interviewees recalled attendance at the

---

[2] The affective relation to khaki finds parallels with grey as a colour used to describe a sense of oppressive atmosphere in Eastern Europe before the 1980s (Fehérváry 2009).

civics training classes and the role played by its *muwajih* (guide). In the words of one, 'the guide' was the most important teacher in administrative terms. Each year, at the beginning of the first year of high school, the guide distributed application forms for membership in the Ba'th Party. All accounts of the guide's role and authority invoke the ties and connections that he or she has with the security services. These connections translated into the *muwajih* having greater authority than the school principal and intervening in many aspects of school life, from disputes among pupils or between them and teachers, to the organisation of parades, to the running of elections for school units of the Ba'th Party's Revolutionary Youth Federation (Shabiba).

Military training, as recalled by Ruba, draws out the intimate experience that the subject had of regime/state power as embodied in the person of the military trainer: 'We used to have a military trainer in preparatory school. She was severe like lightning, and we feared her very much. She walked like a cat and was alert to any move. She looked for the slightest transgression of the rules to punish the girls. She became known as "slow-walking Nahla" (*Nahla bitmshi 'ala mahla*).' Figures like the military trainer and the guide signalled the everyday presence of the state/regime and populated the lifeworld of ordinary subjects. Walking in the school halls and the schoolyard, the guide elicited feelings of fear.[3]

Reflecting on his school days in the 1990s, Mustafa, a thirty-one-year-old playwright at the time I interviewed him in Beirut in May 2012, stated:

[T]aming and moulding begin at an early stage. The self-evident premise that is engraved in all Syrians' memory is the military uniform. At the time when I was a teenager, the uniform meant maturity and early adulthood. Through habit, things become acceptable. The rule was that we shout slogans every morning: 'Our Goals are One: Socialism, Freedom … ' A slogan from childhood. I remember in seventh grade the complicated slogan 'We swear to crush Imperialism, Zionism and their destructive tools, the treacherous gang of the Muslim Brothers'. I recall that it was difficult to pronounce it correctly.

Memorising slogans and repeating them daily and memorising the words of 'the Eternal Leader' may, as Wedeen (1999) argues, have had as their aim the production of compliant performances and not necessarily indoctrination and firm convictions. Yet the performance unsettles, and in their recollections many of my interviewees expressed their dismay at the compulsion they felt to participate in these performances. In reflecting on the slogans they shouted during the school assembly lines, many Syrians like Ruba and Mustafa recalled the sense of unease in the

---

[3] The figure of the *muwajih* is vividly drawn in the works of Hallum (2009a) and Khaled Khalifa (2008).

compulsion to proclaim statements that they did not understand or with which they could not identify. To some extent, they are refuting the idea that the regime's ideological proclamations had ever appealed to them.

Both Ruba and Mustafa were students in the 1990s. Their recollections resonate in many respects with those made by Fadwa who belongs to the 1980s generation. Both generations, as noted above, have been labelled the Ba'th generation (*Jil al-Ba'th*). The regime conferred the label on the youth in a move aimed at appropriating them. However, in many of the recollections, the term is used to signify practices of subjugation at school: 'When we were students [in the 1980s] in school we used to be very alert to the *futuwwa* teacher because punishment was being forced to crawl on the stomach and elbows. Punishment for mistakes included additional military training. We were required to spy on schoolmates and report them and, if we refused, we became targets of discipline.' Ruba's and Fadwa's recollections underscore certain commonalities of experience among different generations schooled during the period of Hafez al-Asad's rule. However, there are also contextual differences. Although the motifs of military-style discipline and Ba'thist indoctrination were present in the recollections of Mustafa, who was born in 1980, he pointed to a predicament particular to the post-1980 generation, describing himself as 'belonging to the generation that came of age when Hafez al-Asad was omnipotent (*kuli al-qudra*)'. This sense of al-Asad's omnipotence was shared by Ruba when she reflected on her sentiments upon learning of Hafez al-Asad's death. Although she was critical of Ba'thist indoctrination at school and of regime propaganda, she recalls her disbelief that 'the Eternal Leader' had died. Ruba explained that her shock and disbelief arose because she had, at some level, accepted that the leader *was* eternal.

Narratives of school life expose other dimensions of practices of taming and moulding of which Mustafa spoke. Of these, spying, monitoring and reporting on schoolmates were encouraged by the *muwajih*. Ba'thist socialisation in the school was reinforced by the work of Tala'i' and the Shabiba organisations. Both organisations enframed student life, organising training and competition in such extra-curricular activities as horticulture, drawing, poetry and sports. Watchers and informers were recruited among the *futuwwa* teachers and students active in the Tala'i' and Shabiba. Mustafa remembers being called in by the *futuwwa* teacher for failing to show up for a rally organised to meet the then French president (Jacques Chirac) upon his visit to Damascus. He remembers his feeling of dread as he was summoned to explain his absence. Some accounts highlight that the performative aspect of showing loyalty and adherence during rallies and commemorative events was subject to monitoring. A bad performance put the subject at risk. In his memoir, Maher Sharaf al-Din (2007) describes his fear of being denounced by a schoolmate or a teacher for laughing during an event that required public displays of loyalty. The fear persisted as he anticipated the denunciation. When he is eventually denounced to the security services by one of his classmates and by his teachers, it is because of a love poem that he wrote for a girl in his class. A visit by a security officer and a warning from him served to communicate the immediate presence of surveillance agents.

School experience, in my interviewees' recollections, is punctuated by national political happenings such as party congresses, referenda and the death of prominent regime figures. Not only were the personal memories marked in reference to these events, but also the school experiences were entangled in the national happenings as the events intruded into the teaching and other conventional school activities. Muhammad al-Abdallah, a thirty-year-old dissident, recounts in poignant terms how as a young schoolboy, following the death of Basil al-Asad (President Hafez al-Asad's eldest son) in a car accident in 1994, he was made to pin the latter's photo on his school uniform as he was herded, along with other pupils, in a march of condolence to Hafez al-Asad.[4] Muhammad's father was a political prisoner at the time and, in the circumstance, Muhammad's forced participation was especially troubling to him. In time, he saw that it also evidences the coercive and surreal dimensions of the staging of loyalty and dedication to the ruler.

Present in all recollections are the Ba'thist structures of enframing citizens such as the Tala'i' al-Thawra (Vanguard of the Revolution) and Shabiba-t al-Thawra (Revolutionary Youth). These organisations, proclaimed as 'popular organisations' (*munazamat sha'biyya*), enframed the lives of citizens. Not only were the security and military apparatuses strongly present in the body politic, but also, in various respects, civil or popular organisations were extensions of these apparatuses, serving as their appendages.[5] Dissidents and critics of the regime among the youth tend to distance themselves from the party and its auxiliary youth organisations. However, it should be noted that indoctrination activities

---

[4] This recollection was made by al-'Abdallah during a televised interview in 2011.
[5] The Ba'thist institutional set-up and practices of government, modelled after both Soviet and North Korean examples, acquired specificity following the regime's confrontation with the armed Islamic militants in the late 1970s (al-Attasi 2003, 325) and its onslaught on independent civil groupings such as the professional syndicates. The regime pursued a policy of absorption (*isti'ab*) of the entire generation of youth (al-Attasi 2003, 326) through enlistment of all pupils in these organisations operating throughout the different stages of school life, and then later at university level through the organ of the National Federation of University Students.

and rituals of the type studied by Raymond Hinnebusch (1980 and 1990) in the 1970s continued at a highly intense level into the 1990s and 2000s. Party recruitment and ideological education and training (*tarbiyya 'aqa'idiyya*) were carried out on a large scale during that time.

The widespread engagement of high school and university youth in political parties pre-dates the Ba'thist rise to power. Indeed, revolutionary ideologies had attracted segments of the youth population from the 1940s onward. For example, the Arab Socialist Party and the Communist Party, which drew youth adherence, advanced programmes of social and political transformation that went beyond the nationalist goals of the 1920s. Thus, the youth generations of the 1950s and 1960s subscribed to revolutionary ideals and aspirations. Not only were disadvantaged rural youth who joined the military recruited into militant and left-leaning organisations, but so were urban and educated youths from the middle classes who were attracted to radical organisations, which mobilised among the peasants (al-Faysal 2007). The question that arises here is how the 1970s to 2000s youth generations related to the Ba'thist project and to the enforcement of the cult of the leader.

What emerges from my interviews is that dynamics of engagement and distancing characterise how *Jil al-Ba'th* (the Ba'th generation) relates to the regime and the leader. In considering the scope of Tala'i' and Shabiba activities – their regularity and intensity – the self-distancing that many Syrians aver does not fully exhaust the terms of the relationship that Syrian youth have with these mobilisational organisations. The scope, range and reach of the Shabiba's activities indicate a not-so-negligible degree of youth engagement. A wide range of activities organised by the Shabiba drew in participation throughout the 1980s, 1990s and 2000s. In that period, among the different generations there were youths who adhered formally to the organisation and those who simply found in its activities a space for self-expression and realisation. In the 1980s, subscription to the nationalist and patriotic claims, and not only opportunism, motivated the drive to take part in such military training as the parachutist and the paratrooper courses. In addition to the rewards given in the form of extra marks on the high school diploma, the youth in these camps attained an elite status in symbolic terms. As exemplars of the ideal 'Shabiba personality', they were addressed directly by the president in the speeches he gave on the occasions of their organisation's national congresses. In an echo of Mussolini's fascist pronouncements, al-Asad repeatedly proclaimed: '[W]hoever controls the youth, controls the future.'

The regime sought to invest the elite Shabiba groups with a heroic, if not a mythological, quality. Significantly, this dimension is obscured in contemporary references to the parachutists that associate them exclusively with material privileges and with the documented incidents of aggression against veiled women in public in 1981. During that same period, figures from among the Shabiba were represented as the ultimate model of self-sacrifice for the nation and commitment to the leader. Of particular note is the example the regime set using the martyrdom of a number of youths who undertook, in the mid 1980s, suicide missions against the Israeli military presence in Lebanon. Of these martyred youths, Hamida al-Taher, a seventeen-year-old member of the Shabiba from Raqqa, acquired an iconic status. Al-Taher, following a period of training at al-Qaboun military camp in Damascus, went to South Lebanon where she drove a car full of explosives to a checkpoint jointly run by the Israeli military and the South Lebanon Army and detonated it. Al-Taher's spectacular act was deployed and understood within the dominant interpretative frames. In fact, as part of the framing of her particular act, she penned a letter, written in blood, to the leader/president confirming her loyalty and dedication to the cause he leads. Details of her life, her training and her commitment, were supplied by the army officers who trained her and accompanied her on her mission. Newspapers and TV covered the story extensively, including publication of her letter and photos of her penning it. The life and sacrificial act of Hamida al-Taher served as evidence of uncontested belief in the leader, the nationalist mission and the dominant narratives.

According to the official, public account of her suicide mission, al-Taher was a member of the Shabiba who, after completing a military training course, took the decision to actively fight for the nationalist cause. This account does not provide the reasons why she was selected and then trained to undertake this particular mission in Lebanon. The emphasis was consistently put on al-Taher as a subject who acted in an exemplary and heroic fashion and thereby validated the leader's proclamations of resistance and steadfastness. Both in its tutoring and mythologising dimensions, the story/staging of Hamida al-Taher's sacrifice is multifaceted: it belongs to the order of nation-making spectacles/narratives as an element of repertoires called upon to renew national identification, pride and obligation to the nation; it demands faith in the national project even when the sacrifice provokes cynicism relating to the corruption and greed that plagued the party and its upper ranks (see Sadowski 1985).

The staging of Hamida al-Taher's suicide mission and sacrifice fit into the regime's nationalist narrative and discourse on martyrdom, and was part of a strategy to enlist the youth in both internal and external battles in defence of the regime.[6] Indeed, in the party's ideological proclamations it was asserted that the imperative was for the youth to become 'the tool of the Party in all of its battles: in construction, confrontation … to be the equivalent of the armed forces' (*al-Munadil*, May 1983, 160). Notwithstanding the regime's claims about the youth's loyal adherence to Ba'thist organisations, the Syrian opposition and many analysts have tended to view these proclamations with scepticism on account of the Ba'th Party's ideological impoverishment. Thus, the value of youth engagement in these organisations tends to be solely linked to careerist and opportunistic motivations on the part of the youth and to coercive and similarly opportunistic rationales at work in the activities of the party and its auxiliary organisations.

However, even into the 2000s, the narratives of some Shabiba enthusiasts continued to exhibit a degree of commitment and aspiration to improve their surroundings and contribute to progress and development, however vaguely defined. A review of Syrian newspapers in the 2000s reveals the scope of Tala'i' and Shabiba activities. Party cadres visited schools and organised elections to the Youth Federation (Shabiba).[7] Both the Tala'i' and the Shabiba organised summer camps which, by all accounts, were well attended. In Tarin, a village in Idlib, the summer camp in 2003 drew 495 male and female Shabiba adherents from nearby villages. These youths were given lessons in nationalism and love of country and leader, and they were instructed on political developments and reminded of the achievements of the Corrective Revolution. The crafting of the Shabiba personality included military and national defence training and training in the arts of intimate combat (*al-qital al-qarib*). In 2008, the executive of the Homs branch of the Shabiba set up the Al-Basil Training Programme and attracted 850 youths from Shabiba branches across the governorate. These activities are presided over by the Ba'th leadership at branch level and attended by high-ranking military officers. The Shabiba and the National Union of Students would come to supply the core of regime supporters during the Uprising. Key in all of these activities

[6] The valorisation of martyrdom is referenced to Hafez al-Asad's statement that 'martyrs are the virtuous ones, the saints' ('*al-shuhada' hum al-shurafa' … al-qidisun*') (cited in *al-Munadil*, May 1985). Propagation of martyrdom could be found in articles penned by prominent figures of the party such as Abdallah al-Ahmar, president of the Party National Executive, and by Bouthaina Sha'ban, President Hafez al-Asad's Chief English-language Interpreter (*Al-Munadil*, May 1985).
[7] Data on Shabiba activities is drawn from reports in the Syrian newspapers of *al-Ba'th* and *Tishrin* for the years cited in this paragraph, namely 2003 and 2008.

is the work of ideological guidance and partisan training, along with the formation of the Shabiba personality. Such were the declared objectives of these popular youth organisations. Undoubtedly, they also aimed at creating a space outside the family that would ground allegiance to the leader and the ruling party.

Despite the far-reaching scale of absorption of youth into the Shabiba and the National Union of Students, oppositional activism continued with different levels of intensity from the 1970s until the Uprising. In the 1970s, oppositional action was channelled either through the Muslim Brothers and smaller militant Islamist factions, until their crushing in the early 1980s, or through communist groups, which were also subject to sweeping arrest campaigns. With the crushing of the Muslim Brothers and the armed group known as the Combatant Vanguard, and with the banning of all independent political groupings, some youth found that Sufi orders were suitable alternative sites for distancing themselves from the regime.[8] Yet this option was not entirely satisfactory in light of the fact that the Sufi orders were tolerated by the regime and, in some sense, worked within the lines drawn by it.[9] The co-optation of religious figures and organisations at times involved the use of such organisations in surveillance and reporting activities.[10]

During the 2011 Uprising, oppositional youth activists distanced themselves from the Shabiba and the National Union of Students. However, it should be noted that the organisations provided a base of support to the regime during times of crises. They did so in 2005, when the regime faced pressures from regional and international players for its role in Lebanon and for the assassination of Rafiq al-Hariri for which some of its army generals were reputed to be responsible. At that time the Shabiba and Ba'thist university students took a leading part in silencing internal opposition and in mobilising public support for the regime (Saleh 2005a, 2005b). Later, during the Uprising, the two organisations helped regroup loyalist constituencies and were instrumental in organising parades and demonstrations in support of the regime. Further, armed

---

[8] On the appeal of Sufism, see Pinto (2006). On the re-emergence of men's religious study circles, see Pierret and Selvik (2009).

[9] According to some accounts, in the 1990s, youth in Banyas and Aleppo opted to join Sufi groups, but many were disenchanted by the perceived connections between these groups and the security services (Abi Samra 2012a; Tayyara 2011).

[10] One of my interviewees from Old Damascus related that during the security sweeps and arrests of the early 1980s, the priest in her local church reported to the security services on a group of Christian youth whom she claimed had links with underground communist organisations. Among the group was her older sister who was called in by the security services and detained for interrogation for a period of time (interview with a playwright in her early forties in Damascus, February 2005).

militias such as *al-lijan al-sha'biyya* (the popular committees) and *kata'ib al-Ba'th* (the Ba'th militia) recruited their membership from the loyalist youth in these organisations (Mustafa 2014). Indeed, in the aftermath of the Uprising, the party embarked on a revival of its auxiliaries and pressed forward with enlistment of youth in areas of the country still under regime control.

Familial Life   Remembrances of family life underscore the links between the processes of enframing at school and in popular organisations, on one hand, and in conventional family settings, on the other. The latter functioned especially to discourage children from involvement in politics and public affairs. Indeed, in stories of childhood and growing up, Syrians I interviewed recall their parents advising and warning them against any political talk. Family relations were entangled in regime politics. Reflecting on parents' injunctions to 'walk by the wall' (*imshi janb al-hit*), a number of young men, who were later active in the civil-society forums of the early 2000s and then in the 2011 Uprising, viewed the protective shield of the family as inhibiting political activism and thereby contributing to the authoritarianism of everyday life (interviews, Damascus, March and April 2011). The family's vigilance against political engagement included discouraging speech about politics even at home, where it was often said all talk could be overheard because 'the walls have ears' (*al-hitan laha adhan*). In Ruba's words: '[T]he phrase "walls have ears" is one of the remnants of the Ba'thist period that we, as Syrians, have not yet transcended. This phrase means that each one of us had two informers watching over each shoulder, registering every word and every breath … saving us from making a mistake that would lead to self-ruin and the destruction of one's family.' The injunctions communicated the warning that great perils attended the family if the children engaged in political talk – a specific and common warning that many recalled was that of being told by a family member that the security men will come and get their father if they were to utter any critical statements about the party or the leader. Thus, within family circles, certain practices of self-censorship were cultivated as, for example, learning to excise from public mention the names of family members who were dissidents and lived in exile. The banned close relatives joined the lists of other forbidden names (*al-asma' al-mamnu'a*) to whom no reference should be made.[11] Within

---

[11] The notion of a list of banned names is derived from the public practice, on the part of the official media and regime institutions, to forbid the mention of the names of regime critics and dissidents. This mostly applied to external critics, given that internal dissension was extremely circumscribed.

the same circles, children learnt about possible informants and the need to exercise vigilance in their presence.

The involvement of the family in constraining political activism was cultivated through regime practices of surveillance and control. Governing through the family in authoritarian regimes can be pursued in a direct manner, as in the case of the North Korean 'five-unit household' that positioned family members as informers on one another (Kang 2011). While no such system was set up in Syria, the family was nonetheless rendered a site of control through a host of security techniques. For instance, questioning and interrogation by security personnel targeted family members of a dissident or a suspect, sometimes before speaking to the subject in question. In this way, familial ties brought political responsibilities. Relatives of dissidents risked losing employment, or not getting a place in university, and they could potentially be arrested and imprisoned in lieu of the dissenting subject. Mundane inequities, as much as severe punishment, raised the cost of opposition and generalised it within families and social circles. Additionally, with many families broken up by incarceration and forced disappearance, parents assumed a protective role by steering their children away from any form of political engagement. Whereas in the North Korean or Chinese surveillance systems family members were made to report on one another, the Syrian system worked by cultivating the family as a constraining force. Several imprisoned communist dissidents recount in their memoirs that family members, under the influence of the security services, exerted pressure on the dissidents to renounce their political views and declare their loyalty to Hafez al-Asad in exchange for being released from prison (Hebo 2001).

In commentaries and reflections on their oppositional activities in the early days of the Uprising, activist youth expressed the view that the Uprising was a 'revolution against the generation of fathers' (*thawra 'ala jil al'aba'*) (interviews with a number of activists, Damascus, March and April 2011). The statement carries the implication that the generation of fathers had contributed to normalising a culture of obedience to those in positions of power within the state. As children, many were witnesses to rituals of disavowal of any political engagement. Youth recalled the burning of books by parents who feared inspection and raids on their homes by the state security (*mukhabarat*). Nadir Karim, a civil society activist in his late thirties, recounted how his father set his own brother's books on fire.

Mustafa, the playwright whom I interviewed in Beirut in 2012 (mentioned above), described the family as 'a miniature/microcosm repressive regime'. Drawing on his personal experience and his observations of his friends' family relations, he put forward the view that '[F]or the father, as a defeated citizen, the family was the only site for the exercise of power' (interview with Mustafa, Beirut, 2012). In his recollections of the early days of his youth in the 1990s, Mustafa spoke of the continuity between the family and the school as apparatuses of coercion. In his words: '[I]f the teacher beat me, I knew that I could not go home and complain to my father as it was certain that he would think that the teacher had a good reason to do so. And I could not turn to my teacher if my father hit me.' For Mustafa, this continuity in authoritarian governance between home and school went deeper, as he starkly states: 'I was seeing that there was Hafez al-Asad, and there was my father and there was a direct relationship.' Mustafa's father was a Ba'thist, though not particularly active in the party and not overtly expressive of support for the regime. For Mustafa, the relationship between the regime and the family had to do with the father's exercise of patriarchal authority in a compensatory manner for his defeat as a citizen. What was the father's defeat? In Mustafa's narrative, it emerges as the tale of frustrated middle-class aspirations linked with failed national projects. As a college teacher and a Ba'thist, Mustafa's father was an 'ideal citizen' enlisted in the regime's developmentalist and nationalist projects. He was also 'an idealist', in Mustafa's description, 'he was not a bribe-taker'. In the 1970s and 1980s, he was a beneficiary of the regime's policies, securing a respectable position in a state institution. He also procured an apartment in Damascus' Dummar housing project for professionals. With the economic opening and liberalisation in the 1990s, the symbolic and material success gave way to middle-class disadvantage in both normative and material senses (education lost its value, and public employment salaries could no longer support middle-class status).[12] In Mustafa's view, the loss of this status represented personal defeat for someone like his father, who was against *wasta*, *da'm* and *mahsubiyya* (terms denoting connections and patronage) and who strove to preserve his integrity.

In his memoir entitled *My Father, the Ba'thist*, Maher Sharaf al-Din also draws a connection between the family and the system of rule and, in particular, between his oppressive and physically abusive father and Ba'thist rule. In Sharaf al-Din's narrative, the beatings meted out to political dissidents and minor offenders paralleled the beatings that he and his siblings received at the hands of their father. Indeed, Sharaf al-Din hones in on how his father's hand becomes a metonym for absolute power.

---

[12] On the economic conditions of the wage-earning middle classes in Syria in the 1980s and 1990s, see Perthes (1997, 106–9).

The hand is not only the instrument of physical punishment. Rather, in Sharaf al-Din's memoir, the hand stands for an absolutist sovereign power that, in its crushing effects, acquires a metaphysical dimension. This is captured in Sharaf al-Din's account of how he and his younger brother marvelled at their father's hand – at its seeming physiognomic uniqueness. They fantasised about acquiring the hand to the point that they asked him if they could borrow it. Eventually, Sharaf al-Din begins to fantasise about the hand being cut off. At one point, he finds solace in the idea that a relief from this heavy hand could be achieved through the application of an Islamic ordinance decreeing the cutting off of the hands of thieves.

In the literature on how authoritarian and totalitarian regimes draw the family into the web of rule and control, it is noted that allegiance to the party supersedes family ties in some cases, as evidenced by instances in which children reported on their parents (Fitzpatrick 1999). At the same time, it is noted that the family offers a sense of cohesion in individual life (Fitzpatrick 1999). In the Syrian narratives and recollections, we get an equally complex depiction of the family as both constraining and protecting – a site of domineering patriarchy, as reinforced by the state, but also a shield against that very state. This duality is mirrored in the regime's practices. The Ba'thist regime appears to have been driven by contradictory impulses: to saturate all spaces and incorporate them, on the one hand, and to subcontract governmental functions to societal structures such as the family, the clan and religion, on the other. Not necessarily co-opted, the family perpetuated practices of silencing and hierarchical control.

The constraining role of the family was weakened with the Uprising and, in effect, parents were not able to prevent the involvement of their children in oppositional activities. However, family cohesion was strained as a result. This was due not only to political differences within the family, but by virtue of different positionalities in relation to the regime. As noted above, in recollections of family life under Hafez al-Asad and then under Bashar al-Asad, the family discouraged activism but also provided a protective shield. This was not possible to maintain in a state of widespread and deep upheaval. Divisions within families arose between those who continued to cooperate with the regime and those who joined the ranks of the opposition and participated in demonstrations. Some regime opponents talked of betrayal by family members – immediate and extended – who reported to the security services on dissidence and participation in demonstrations. In the early days of the Uprising, I gained an appreciation of the divisions that pitted family members against one another. In one conversation about the evolution of the Ba'th Party and the challenges of the Uprising, my interlocutor, a long-time Ba'thist cadre from Raqqa, opined about the arrest of his twenty-two-year-old activist nephew (who had been engaged in social media work for the opposition). The arrest and imprisonment, he said, was a necessary 'ear pinch' (*qarsit udhun*) to straighten out his nephew and to keep him from being lured into the foreign conspiracies against the country (interview, Damascus, April 2011).

Emblematic Frames of Everyday Life

Individual memories of Ba'thist schooling and of family upbringing, as shown above, bring to light particular institutional practices and social experiences formative of Syrian subjectivities. In this section, I turn to a discussion of emblematic frames through which Syrians interpreted their everyday life experience of government. I draw the contours of two frames of meaning which emerge in the recollections and memoirs of the period. The first frame, namely 'abjection and precarity', captures the terms in which conditions of living and senses of self are most often described in the remembrances. The second frame of 'national salvation' has as a reference point the events of Hama but, in effect, also furnishes a horizon of meaning for negotiating everyday life under dictatorship.

Abjection and Precarity   Recollections of life under Hafez al-Asad's dictatorship depict conditions and states of being for ordinary citizens that characterise a lived experience of 'abjection' and that detail processes of fashioning and constituting 'abject subjects'. The concept of abjection, as used here, describes lived social processes that debase subjects and that cast them as unworthy and degraded. As such, it refers to both the acts of debasement and humiliation that make or render the abject subject and the state of being that is brought forth through these acts. Abjection also entails attributes and ascriptions of debasement, degradation and defilement to both objects and subjects in the life world. In Julia Kristeva's foundational theorisation, abjection is conceived of in terms of qualities and conditions of being that are considered repulsive and that unsettle the natural order of things. Within Kristeva's psychoanalytic approach, these qualities are associated with a universal (western) psychic evolution resting on the child's expulsion from the maternal. Some critics (Tyler 2009) have argued, however, that this 'maternal abject' is not prehistoric or universal, but socially constructed. Yet Kristeva's account offers an exploration of abjection as a state of being and a process centred on the body wherein the body is a site and vehicle through which borders or boundaries of self-integrity and self-hood are drawn, preserved, unsettled and violated. Abjection describes embodied affect through which the self negotiates, through expulsion and drawing boundaries, that which threatens its integrity (see Kristeva 1982; see also Tyler 2013, 27).

Conditions of imprisonment and practices of control and power in prisons (discussed in Chapter 1) rendered subjects abject through bodily debasement and defilement. The prisoners, as figures of 'the national outcast', embody the horrors and threats from which other subjects should instinctively recoil. At the same time, everyday life experiences of ordinary citizens were marked by humiliation, threat and exposure to danger, also rendering them abject. Themes of abject conditions and experiences intersperse remembrances of the hardships of daily life in the 1980s and 1990s, a time of political crises and economic shortages. Indeed, abjection is spoken about by some of my interviewees as a shared condition of life, conveyed in an often-repeated phrase: '*ihna 'ishna al-dhul*' ('we lived abjection').

In reflecting on the possibility of political action and resistance, many interviewees narrated experiences of abjection to signal the sense of powerlessness that they felt. They presented testimonials of degradation, which were also intended as an alibi for enforced silence and inaction. Economic conditions, from the early 1980s until the mid 1990s – marked, as they were, by serious and prolonged periods of shortages in fuel, basic foodstuffs and everyday necessities – figure prominently in recollections of the period and in the sense of self that has been formed under such conditions. Shortages and material deprivation were themes in many of the narratives and are associated with experiences of debasement and humiliation that are formative of the self in the present. The travails of obtaining rations and of procuring foodstuffs such as oil and rice or items of simple comfort such as paper tissues, were now constitutive experiences entering into self-definition and self-understanding.

Before the Uprising, these recollections framed articulations of disengagement from politics. Narratives of lack and constraint underscored a sense of diminishment and were presented as an argument or reason for withdrawal from civic and public life. The orientation of such accounts is that it was not possible to assume individual responsibility in collective political life. In 2005, in response to my questions as to what avenues of change existed or what role civic action could play, one interviewee, Mazen, a playwright in his mid fifties, responded:

What could I do under the conditions of life then? We had to queue for hours for everything from toilet paper (which was mostly unavailable) to rice? Do you know that I had to buy rice on the black market to feed my children? Do you know that it was illegal and that I got the rice as a favour? I did this and I risked being charged with a contravention of the rules on "guided consumption". And then, when the rice came, it had mice excrement in it.

For Mazen, the memory of procuring soiled food captured the experience of abjection that made or formed him as a disengaged subject, despairing of the benefits of action, engagement and resistance. The experience of lack and want recalled and conjured up tired bodies – weakened and humiliated. Shortages, and the struggle to gain access to basic necessities, were experiences of embodied humiliation. The long queues to obtain rations on food staples such as sugar, rice, oil and ghee and on household items like toilet paper, as well as the hours-long, if not days-long, line-ups in front of state cooperatives, are recounted as instances of having lived *dhul*, a mixture of humiliation and abjection (*'ihna 'ishna al-dhul*).[13]

The interdiction on the importation and sale of bananas and the prolonged scarcity of facial tissues and toilet paper became ciphers of lived subjugation and debasement. Scarcity and shortages, referred to in Arabic as *azamat* or crises, are understood by many of my Syrian interlocutors as a mode of government. The idea that the regime governed Syria through crises (*al-nizam hakam Suriyya bil azamat*) appears to have taken hold among regime critics and ordinary citizens alike. Crises (*al-azamat*) ranged from food shortages to actual tensions and confrontations with other states regionally and internationally. Rather than scarcity being seen as resulting from economic conditions, and more specifically limited foreign currency induced by boycott, it was viewed as an instrument of rule that rendered citizens abject.

During the early weeks of the Uprising, a former Syrian TV presenter-turned-dissident drew a self-portrait in a few suggestive words: 'I grew up in the 1980s. I am the daughter of lack, of long queues for bread, for ghee, and for a box of tissues. I am the daughter of poor school buildings, of hysterical *futuwwa* teachers.' The statement reflects on life and experience in abject conditions and, given its timing, is an expression of the view that there was no longer much to lose from explicit public dissent. The statement is also indicative of how abjection, as a condition and an affective practice, lingered on and became defining and constitutive of the subject. In these narratives, elements of the material world and the exhaustion suffered in the pursuit of everyday needs symbolise abjection (*dhul*). Invested with a particular logic in these recollections, exhaustion

---

[13] The experience of lack was differentiated along class lines. Upper-middle-class families were able to shop in Shtura in Lebanon. Indeed, thousands of permits for passing through 'the military route' to Shtura were distributed to networked families, political figures and upper-echelon army personnel (Deeb 2011, 437). Some of my interviewees recalled trips to buy basic foods, paper tissues and bananas. Such privileges were paid for in bribes and generated a sense of complicity as subjects engaged in condoned transgressions of import bans.

explains withdrawal into oneself, retreating from public engagement. We can see parallels here with certain accounts from Eastern Europe in the 1950s and 1960s (Fehérváry 2009, 427). Yet a different logic unfolds during the Uprising. The abject subject, previously forced to hide, has reasoned – on the basis of that very experience of want and fatigue – that she has nothing to lose.

Shortages and scarcity, as defining elements of the material world of subjectivity, are not experienced in the same manner by all Syrians and are not exhaustive of that materiality. For better-off Syrians and those with connections to high-ranking regime figures, allowances were made for such things as purchasing products in Lebanon and, depending on one's means, accessing goods on the thriving black market (interview with Haytham, a Damascene in his mid thirties, Damascus, 2005). Among the less well-off, those who were Ba'thists or state employees working in showcase industries or involved in large-scale national projects (e.g. the management of the Euphrates Dam) enjoyed better access to subsidised goods and were beneficiaries in other respects; for example, having free access to public services such as water and electricity. Thus, for some, the state delivered on its promise of plenitude. In an illustration of the benefits conferred in conditions of abjection, Sharaf al-Din (2007) recounts how his mother consumed excessive amounts of freely supplied electricity by leaving the houselights switched on at all times: '[S]he said it was "*bibalash*" (for free).' According to Sharaf al-Din (2007), '*bibalash*' was a reason for the gratitude felt towards the regime by his mother and neighbouring families in his small town in the north-eastern governorate of Hasaka. In this respect, the free electricity service validated aspects of the developmentalist claims of the regime, and thereby secured it the gratitude of this group of beneficiaries. Yet at the same time, in Sharaf al-Din's description, the town's streets, schools, children and workers bear the marks of abjection. Sharaf al-Din portrays abject existence in his depiction of poor hygiene conditions of the pupils, a broken sewage system and general filth in the surroundings.

In memories of growing up and coming of age, the experiences of humiliation are narrated as formative of the self (Abi Samra 2012a; Sharaf al-Din 2007). Humiliation in interaction with the state is a structuring theme of recollection. For the post-Hama generations, recollections of daily life in Syria include narratives of scenes of everyday violence that were witnessed. In interviews carried out after the start of the Uprising, some of these recollections were responding to videos, viewed during the first few months of the Uprising – of beatings at the hands of military personnel or regime loyalist militias. They were recounted, in part, to validate the recorded images and also to insert oneself into the unfolding events as a narrator and witness of the brutality of the regime. Thus on Facebook pages many young Syrians who grew up in the 1990s, and who supported the Uprising, recounted stories about having witnessed during their youth incidents of security men beating up ordinary citizens who were going about their daily business. Typical episodes are those of security men, either in uniform or undercover, stopping taxi drivers and other car drivers and hitting them as punishment for what they judged to be offences against traffic regulations or simply against their positions of power and authority. Popular narratives of such encounters with security and police agents emphasise the practices of humiliation of ordinary citizens, instanced in disrespectful forms of address such as '*ta'a lahun wela*' ('come here boy'), and in physical assaults both on the street and at checkpoints (Abi Samra 2012a, 159). The recollection of witnessing security men abuse a fellow citizen – sometimes a family member, a neighbour or a friend – emerges as emblematic of everyday experience and as formative of particular affective states (in some instances, there are traces of trauma in the narrative, for having been a witness and for feeling powerless to stop the abuse).

In some of the narratives, the episodes of routine violence witnessed in the everyday acquire a surreal character and convey a lived quotidian horror that articulates with the horror of spectacular violence. For instance, Fadia Ladhiqani (2013), a journalist and former political prisoner, recounts in an essay the type of memory-marking incidents that many ordinary Syrians experienced and remember. The incident unfolded during a brief bus ride on a hot day in Damascus in August 1980. Ladhiqani describes the prevalence of a surreal and menacing atmosphere and how ordinary citizens devised tactics and practices that allowed them to manage the threats that it represented to them. In this episode, riding through the city at a heavy traffic junction in the summer heat, one passenger turned to the person sitting next to him and slapped him. There was no apparent reason for the slap. Shortly after his unaccountable act, the passenger who inflicted the slap got up and got off the bus. Ladhiqani's comments on the incident are instructive. She notes that no one intervened and that other passengers knew intuitively that the aggressive passenger was a security agent. To confirm their suspicion, they discreetly attempted to get a view of his waist belt to see if he had a pistol hanging there. To avoid being implicated, various distancing postures were adopted (Ladhiqani 2013).

In their vivid manner of recounting such incidents, Syrians underline the extent to which memories are present for them, noting the impact of these past experiences. A number of Syrians who reside outside Syria asserted that it was witnessing such daily humiliation and abuse of ordinary citizens that led them to leave the country. Hussam, an engineer from Damascus who moved to Lebanon in the early 1990s, asserted that his decision to leave Syria was motivated by his sense of insecurity and his feelings of personal affront at seeing armed military and security men occupying the sidewalks (interview, Beirut, 2012). He referred to them as the *sarsariyya* (loafers). He described feeling estranged and disconnected from the place, reasoning that he would not be able to protect himself if the security men were to obstruct his way for any reason. In his words, 'It was a terrible feeling'. More than a mundane feeling, Hussam is referring here to the sentiment of dread that inhabited him as he went about his everyday chores and work. The presence of security men on the sidewalks and the demarcation of the street through the installation of security kiosks (*mafrazat al-amn*) engender a range of affective practices centred on the sense of precariousness. Hussam's feeling of precarity is qualified in terms of his class standing. As a descendant of an aristocratic Damascene family whose land and properties were nationalised, he belonged to a stratum that was constructed in Ba'thist discourse as the exploiters of the people. Yet by the 1970s, the regime had made overtures towards the traditional Damascene families. For Hussam's family, this translated into having connections with individuals in high-ranking positions who could provide some protection. In his terms, his family benefited from 'the presence of those who can cover [read: protect] us' (*fi min yighatina*). Yet this form of patronage or network relationship was not entirely sufficient for him to feel secure. In this respect, he stated that 'at any time, they can falsely charge you with a crime … and there comes a point where no one can shield you'.

The sense of precarity of one's life and of being exposed to danger emerged in relation to the regime's modes of operation, including its shadow networks that comprised the gangs known as the *shabiha*. Rosa Yassin Hassan's (2011b) account of the presence of these gangs brings to light how fear was cultivated in everyday life. She recounts how *shabiha* figures contributed to the sense of insecurity in the coastal areas. They adopted an aggressive posture and trespassed on the rights of fellow citizens. Hassan recalls an instance in which a neighbour, identified with the *shabiha* gangs in Latakiyya, encroached on neighbourhood collective spaces, and on others' private property. Another example of the transgressive conduct of the *shabiha*, especially those from powerful *shabiha* families, is their threatening pursuit of young women. It is important to note that practices of extortion and intimidation of ordinary citizens were not carried out only by the *shabiha*. Members of the security forces, as well as individuals with connections to them, also imposed levies on citizens in extortionate ways. In his *Haywanat al-Insan* (*The Bestialisation of the Human*) Mamdouh 'Udwan (2003) identifies these practices as *salbata* (predation).

In ordinary Syrians' accounts of their lived experience, abjection and precarity appear not only as affects emergent in encounters with security agents or the infrastructures of violence. Rather, these affects form as structures of feeling shaping subjects' dispositional relations to one another and to their environment. Abjection and precarity infuse tactics and manoeuvres of everyday living such as, for example, plotting one's route so as to avoid passing by a security kiosk, or locating one's interlocutor in the web of power and control so as not to get entrapped. Abjection set the terms of making intelligible the sense of self and self-responsibility as can be discerned in Mazen's account: procuring soiled food was emblematic of a condition that exceeds him, pervading the environment and setting the limits on his experience and his capacities to act. Abjection resonated with precarity. That is, it co-existed with the sense that one is exposed and had no cover: 'any time they can get you'; 'any time they can falsely charge you'. Referencing common encounters and modes of interaction with government, abjection and precarity form as affective relations and dispositions. In this case, the individual and collective resonate with and mediate each other. Imbued in the soiled food, dwelling in the long queues for basic food items, and circulating between military-training teachers and students, abjection came to pervade the environment.

National Salvation   Subjects sympathetic to the regime's ideological proclamations and narratives framed their recollections, during interviews, within what could be termed the theme of 'national salvation'. This is particularly the case in the accounts and memories of the period narrated by individuals in high office and members of the social elite. That is, they corroborated the regime's account. In these narratives, Hafez al-Asad was cast as a figure of national salvation in the face of threats of sectarian division and splintering. Within this account of salvation, the assault on Hama in 1982 is said to have been directed against the Muslim Brothers who had taken up arms and who were threatening the national fabric. To maintain consistency, this frame homogenises the entire population of Hama as Muslim Brothers, disregards that a significant number of unarmed civilians were killed and that the killing and destruction went on for an extended period of time. This fits within the regime's interpretation of social reality as a life-and-death struggle in which the regime is the community's protector and its life guarantor.

The narrative of salvation is premised on a view of Syrian society as fragile and in danger of break-up on sectarian lines. As articulated by a one-time member of the regime whom I interviewed (Damascus, 2005), the narrative includes an analysis of Syrian society to the effect that it is composed of dozens of sects and communities that could potentially be warring with each other if not for the regime's firm hand keeping a grip on divisions. The fear of breakdown and chaos was manipulated by the regime. Authoritarian regimes' manipulation of fear is a common tactic, as noted by South America scholars (see Coronil and Skurski 1991; Suarez-Orozco 1990). The justifications given by regime supporters cannot simply be explained by their being its economic beneficiaries. The fear of societal breakdown and of an evil that is greater than the regime helps the regime garner and preserve support. Further, as discussed by Suarez-Orozco (1990), denial and internalisation of the dominant narrative are mechanisms of the self to cope with the violence. Thus, regime violence is constructed as an appropriate response to the threat and danger posed to society by the insurgents, using particular episodes of violence as rationalisations. In a brief memoir of everyday life in Syria in the 1980s, one woman, who was a teenager during the period of the conflict, described the time as:

terrifying, particularly after the explosion in Azbakiyya … Homes were destroyed, and many citizens were blown up on the street. People then forgot [the shortage of] paper tissues, lemon … and the long queues waiting for bread. We closed ranks for the safety and security of the country. Syrian TV showed images from the Azbakiyya explosion … images of men and women with blown limbs. These are images that could not be forgotten … Sometimes we recall these events, their terror and the fear we used to feel … When we consider the events of Hama caused by the Muslim Brothers, we agree that they were dealt with appropriately. In any other way, the country would have fallen into civil war. This was a time that civil war in Lebanon was a source of dread for Syrians. (Bassam 2005)

Interpreted within the nationalist frame, the regime's violence in Hama is viewed as having been necessary to respond to foreign plots and threats. The public and media discourse of the time is woven into individual remembrances in such a manner as to rationalise and justify the course of action and to make the discourse one's own. As such, personal recollections would weave in content from the official account, as in: '[A]t the time, Saddam Hussein sponsored militants and supplied them with weapons and so on.' The reiteration, in this manner, of rationalisations and justifications projected by the media and the elites, indicates that, for some Syrians, the official narrative was adopted and became part of personalised memory.

Retrieving the Self in Narratives of the National

Personal and intimate everyday life experiences – from the daily wearing of khaki-coloured school uniforms, to the witnessing of the random humiliation of citizens by state security personnel in everyday situations – aggregate in the life of an individual to form a composite of the national experience of living under dictatorship. Meanwhile, the life of the nation, construed in terms of collective goals and projects, orients narratives of individual life and the terms of self-authoring. In some respects it is in relation to the aspirations for national liberation and independence that subjects situate themselves and develop understandings of their life trajectories and political positionality. Inserting the self into the national, the subject embarks on journeys of self-retrieval. The narration and authoring of the self in the works of remembering also entail assessment, judgement and reckoning. Similarly, outspoken dissidence confronts silent disengagement and self-distancing. Hence, critical revisiting of the past in recollections are also revisions of earlier convictions and positions. Exercises of self-retrieval and critical self-authoring orient much of independent artistic and intellectual works in the 1990s and 2000s. In what follows, I present vignettes of these exercises of self-criticism and of accounting for oneself as found in cultural works, conversations among intellectuals and journeys into the past by politically engaged actors both in the ranks of the opposition and on the side of the regime. My exposé of these vignettes, drawn on the basis of interviews and extended conversations I had with activists, dissidents and writers, is intended to bring to light the aspects of the memory struggles running through these actors' accounts of their personal trajectories. The concerns articulated in the interplay between personal trajectories and national-oriented frames of meaning focus on one's political responsibility, complicity and compromises. These concerns transcend the individual stories to reflect the social and political struggles framed by national politics and projects while, at the same time, revealing the terms in which the memories of the national unfold in specific life histories.

Needless to say, the meanings and symbolism of both official and oppositional articulations of the national are not fixed. For the 1960s and 1970s generations, we see the construction of identity in the terms defined by national narratives and aspirations in which the liberation of Palestine and of occupied Arab land was a constitutive element of the political. The liberation objectives and the project of modernisation – envisioned in terms of building an independent national economy and an egalitarian and materially prosperous society – combined to define the horizons of the subject as a member of a national community.[14] The Ba'thist state propagated itself as leading a project of remaking the people, individuals and the nation. Beyond its constitutionally enshrined role of 'leader of state and society', the Ba'th proclaimed its leadership of the mission of Arab unity (best captured in its slogan '*umma Arabiya wahida*'), and the party took charge of the creation of 'a new man' and the remaking of the people through its various organs.

In the context of struggles for nationhood and peoplehood, the aspirations of the nationalist and developmentalist projects for Syria had wide resonance among intellectuals and broader social forces. Looking at the cultural scene as it unfolded from the 1990s onward, we find that a growing number among the Syrian intelligentsia embarked on projects of rereading the self in the national narrative. A number of documentaries made by Omar Amiralay during this period seek to revisit the past and, in the process, give account of individual positionality and responsibility.[15] Illustrative of this type of exercise is Amiralay's *And There Are Many Other Things One Could Have Talked About* (1997), a documentary film about prominent playwright Saad-Allah Wannous. In this documentary, Wannous, who was at a terminal stage of cancer at the time of filming, journeys into the past to scrutinise his trajectory as a public intellectual and to open a window onto the self as it is formed in national struggles of liberation. Wannous critically reflects on his engagement in

---

[14] The formation of Syrians as national subjects is a historical process that can be traced to the struggle for independence from French mandatory rule. People's engagement in this struggle was not uniform but rather involved diverse imaginaries and forms of action (see Gelvin 1998; Thompson 2000 for discussions of the formation of political subjectivities, in particular popular and subaltern subjectivities in contrast to elite subjectivities). Various political groups and parties connected with these struggles and sought to take on the mantle of leadership and representation. Nationalist imaginaries and modernist aspirations were structuring frames of subjectivities (see memoirs by Akram al-Hourani (2000) among others). Emblematic signs of the developmentalist state were such grand projects as the Euphrates Dam. The Euphrates project, perhaps more than any other, came to embody the drive for transformation and making the 'new citizen'. For an account of the great aspirations invested in the Dam project and the subsequent disappointments, see Rabo (1985).

[15] Omar Amiralay's 2003 documentary *Flood in the Country of the Ba'th*, a study of Ba'thist socialisation in school and of the intermeshing of patriarchal power and dictatorial power, is offered as a text to be read in conjunction with his 1970 documentary *An Essay on the Euphrates Dam*. In this juxtaposition, *Flood* confronts the earlier representations made at the time of great hopes and aspirations. The enthusiasm for the project of remaking is faced starkly with the desolation and destruction that was brought about and that was not, for Amiralay, just an outcome of mistaken implementation but a result of a faulty design to begin with. This assessment is more than a self-rebuke for the enthusiasm afforded the great projects.

the struggle against Israel and how this struggle came to inhabit him and, in the process, overshadowed other battles, including the battle against the conditions of subordination created by the Syrian regime. Wannous' intellectual and personal trajectory is enmeshed in the nationalist project of a united Arab nation and in the drive to liberate Palestine. In the film, Wannous reviews various historical stages of his public engagement, from the shattering impact of the 1967 defeat and Nasser's announcement of his resignation, to Sadat's trip to Israel in 1977 (which occasioned Wannous' attempted suicide and a long period of abstention from writing), to a later stage of self-criticism and re-evaluation of his ideological givens. At one point he states, 'Israel stole my life'.

Wannous' statement speaks of the dilemma that his generation, as well as later generations, faced. As nationalist and progressive subjects, the liberation of occupied land represented their primary cause and put a check on their opposition to regimes that claimed steadfastness against Israel, as was the case with the Ba'thist regime in Syria. Yet the subject is also cognisant of the fact that the regime is using its claimed nationalist role to suppress the citizen. When I brought Wannous' statement up in discussions with activists of different generations, they tended to concur with his assessment and share his sentiment, but sought to nuance the meanings that can be drawn from it. During a discussion following a showing of Amiralay's film at the Institut Français du Proche Orient (IFPO) in Damascus, in 2005, one of the participants, a sociologist and leftist academic, conceding the regime's instrumentalisation of the national liberation objective, reminded the audience that Syria was *still* an occupied country. This, the participant continued, meant that Syria's fight with the external enemy necessitated a united domestic front which, by implication, put constraints on political activism against the regime.

Through an introspective mode of recollection, Wannous scrutinises his political positioning and responsibility as necessarily framed by nationalist projects and aspirations and by anti-imperialist politics. The nationalist imperative of a united front will come back to haunt Syrians over and again. During the Uprising, Mustafa, a playwright and a member of the Ba'th generation, shared Wannous' view that Israel stole his life while, at the same time, believing that the Syrian regime, using the claims that it was leading the fight to liberate Palestine, also stole his life. Acknowledging that the regime's claims to be a force of liberation were mere rhetoric, Mustafa noted a dilemma that he and other dissident Syrians faced, namely that his opposition could play into the hands of imperial powers with their own regional agenda. Mustafa drew parallels with a similar dilemma he faced when supporting Iraq's liberation from Saddam Hussein's dictatorship, while opposing US intervention. He averred that grappling with this dilemma was not only a matter of rhetoric but also a question of ethical and political responsibility. The implication of nationalist rhetoric in the consolidation of dictatorship and patriarchal authority is nonetheless interrogated by Mustafa and many of his generation through their questioning of the official discourse on liberation and through recognition of how it is functionalised to maintain the regime's hold on power. Thus a critique develops around the idea of a disjuncture between the official rhetoric of nationhood and regime practices.[16] All the same, writers and artists brought 'the national burden' to bear on their understanding of their personal trajectories and public engagement.

While different generations of Syrians anchored their stories of self in the national, their accounts were informed by changing socio-political contexts and by differing personal aspirations. For example, 'the national burden' was given a less grand articulation in Ayman's self-authoring which emerged in the course of interviews and informal conversations I had with him in Damascus in late 2004 and early 2005. Born in 1959, Ayman, a writer and cultural commentator, moved to Damascus from the Syrian Peninsula in the early 1980s. Although he self-identified as an intellectual (*muthaqaf*), his preoccupations spoke to the personal and the everyday, reframing the national in terms of regime practices and their impact on his generation. Ayman labelled himself as one of those who suffered 'small defeats' (*haza'im saghira*), distinguishing his generation from the previous generation, which suffered 'big defeats', namely that of 1967. In his account, his generation suffered 'the terrorising power of the police state in the details of everyday life'. Recalling his experience of life in Damascus in the 1980s, he retraced the practices and events that formed the generation of small defeats: 'I could not walk in the street late at night without being stopped and questioned and having to produce my identity card. I feared reports by others, by neighbours and acquaintances' (interview, Damascus, 26 December 2004). Ayman includes in his autobiographical narration an incident of arrest at a private social gathering of young artists. An evening of singing and 'pseudo-intellectual conversations' was interrupted when the security men arrived and hauled him and everyone else at the gathering to a police interrogation post. After being duly humiliated by the interrogators, they were let go.

---

[16] The sense of betrayal of the national aspirations and the awareness of complicity with the declared enemies destabilise the subject and, at the same time, give rise to dilemmas. In the face of constraints on oppositional politics, the subject's unhinged docility came to be expressed in irony, cynicism and ambiguity.

Ayman weaves this episode of arrest – one incident in a catalogue of 'small defeats' – into a narrative of a clandestine life and the pseudo-intellectualism of artists who led a bohemian life, inhabiting basement rooms and holding small social gatherings, rebelling in matters of social and sexual mores. He recalled this rebellion in mocking and somewhat bitter terms: '[A]t the time, the leftists' struggle turned to raising money to help their girlfriends obtain abortions.' In his satirical and somewhat cynical self-authoring, Ayman retraces the making of a diminished national subject preoccupied with the exigencies of daily living and constrained from engaging politically on the loftier plane of the 'national burden' to which the previous generation dedicated itself. In Ayman's narrative, the account of self, and its reckoning, develops in relation to regime practices and is dialogic. The unsaid in this narrative is that the regime, not Israel per se, stole Ayman's life because, through repression, he was denied true agency. Instead, he became content to live a pseudo-intellectual, clandestine life. He sought to belittle this life by placing the effort to pay for an abortion as a top priority on the leftists' agenda. Ayman's critique of the leftist circles to which he belonged in the 1980s could be read as an anchoring frame for addressing, in an indirect manner, questions about the compromises he as a writer, by necessity, made by taking up employment in a state-owned newspaper in the 1990s.

Different sensibilities with respect to political engagement about one's past actions, decisions and choices relative to life under dictatorship are expressed in the acts of self-retrieval and in conversations among activists who came of age in the 1980s and 1990s. The narratives and dialogues point to polarisation and division around trajectories of activism and around positions taken vis-à-vis the regime. Ultimately, these latter express contests about agency and political responsibility. The dilemmas and paradoxes with respect to action are revealed through self-criticism as much as through confrontational stances and disagreement with others from rival camps. My conversation with Nadim, an activist from Salamiyya (a town in the governorate of Hama) who was imprisoned between 1991 and 2000 on the charge of being a member of the Communist Action Party, illuminates further the complexities of activist engagement during the period. In an approach similar to Ayman's parody of the left (though not a self-distancing narrative), Nadim spoke of the intellectual labour of his party at the time and how removed it was from reality. He critically referred to how party members, who had never travelled outside Syria, discussed social and political conditions in Eritrea and theorised about syndicalism in that country. He then mused that 'perhaps today they would be theorising about civil society in Togo' (interview, Damascus, 7 February 2005). In pointing out his party's limitations, Nadim noted that he was not rejecting his political involvement and that when comparing it to that of others who 'sold out to the regime or who remained on the margin', he deemed that his experience was still a positive one.

Nadim's trajectory of activism is one that is shared by opposition activists who joined communist parties that remained outside the National Front formed under the tutelage of the Ba'th Party. The Communist Party Political Bureau and the Communist Action Front (later renamed the Communist Action Party) adopted independent political lines and agitated against the regime during its most repressive period in the 1980s and 1990s. The Front organised Marxist discussion circles in areas such as Salamiyya and Misyaf in Hama. Members wrote pamphlets for discussion and published a magazine that was distributed by hand. These activities drew the attention of the security services and through successive and relentless security services campaigns almost all members of the Front were arrested and imprisoned (Abbas 2006; Abu Nijm 2017). The activists spent long periods in prison and many refused to retreat and declare allegiance to the regime in exchange for their freedom (Hebo 2002). Nadim's self-critique addresses intellectual and organisational deficiencies, but upholds the rightfulness of oppositional politics even at the high price he and his companions paid. The normative valuation of the independent left's trajectory is an important undertaking in remembrances by different groupings. At stake are questions having to do with complicity and compromise and, ultimately, political responsibility.

The question of complicity and compromise with the regime and being co-opted into its institution of rule arises as a pressing issue in introspective accounts of selfhood. The recollections are elements of the interpretative frames making sense of the political set-up and of social relations and of one's location. Narratives of the self are drawn in relational terms, that is, in terms of where one stood in relation to the organs of the Ba'th and the security services. In authoring the self or narrating one's personal story and pulling through the threads of the past, Syrians endeavour to locate the self and others vis-à-vis the institutions of rule. Thus the question of membership in the Ba'th, and other organs of popular mobilisation, comes up as an element of the recollections. Many of my interviewees and interlocutors reflected on how they dealt with the injunction to join the Shabiba and the National Union of Students. Their narratives emphasised the pressure exerted on them to join and the feeling of being compelled to do so. At the same time, many stressed that they made efforts to dissociate themselves. Ruba recalled that it was her school friend who paid her membership fees to protect her from possible punishment for not being a member. She stated that she did not take part in any activities. Nominal membership was possible in the late 1990s and in the 2000s, but active membership was required or viewed as a necessary condition for academic, social or professional advancement. In this context, narratives of dissociation are important to the construction of the self. Indeed, as will be discussed below, they belong to the discursive civilities deployed to locate complicit subjects – those who compromised.

Subjects who acknowledge compromise offer explanations as to the reasons that compelled them to maintain active membership. Malik, a newspaper editor who wrote critically about economic corruption and who was a respected investigative reporter, strove during different periods of his Ba'thist career to reconcile his nationalist identity and his sense of personal integrity with his party membership. Concerns about making compromises with the regime are not necessarily present throughout one's time in the party. In Malik's case, he framed his period of active membership and political affiliation in nationalist terms and in terms of the exigencies of different junctures and events. Thus in 2005 his active membership and his candidacy in elections for a party branch executive position are explained as part of a desire to contribute to the promised reform to rejuvenate the party and to make it truly representative. When he failed to win the branch nomination, he attributed his electoral loss to the persistence of the influence of clan and family relations in party politics. In 2011 he agonised about whom he should hold responsible for the violence of the security forces in suppressing the demonstrations. He continued to uphold an estimation of the president as a good leader who was surrounded and hampered by disloyal advisers and untrustworthy local leaders. Yet this account was troubling and, ultimately, he acknowledged that the president must assume responsibility for events occurring on his watch. It would take until eighteen months after the start of the Uprising before Malik declared his break with the regime and left Syria with his family.

For Malik, the events of the early days of the Uprising, and particularly the regime's response to the demonstrations, necessitated that he revisit his own political affiliations – an exercise which entailed self-authoring of sorts. In considering the implication of the regime in violence, Malik reflected on his own commitment and implication in the events, going back to the time he joined the Ba'th Party. In a stream of consciousness mode during a conversation that I had with him in Damascus in April 2011, he rhetorically asked me: '[D]o you think that had Salam [a mutual friend] and I not been members of the Ba'th, we would have been admitted to the Media Faculty in Damascus University?' He then recalled coming to Damascus with Salam from his village in Northern Syria to be interviewed by a Ba'thist faculty committee at the University. He asserted that both adherence to the party and loyalty to the regime were required for entry into the Media Studies programme. Malik's recollections articulate a desire to come to terms with earlier choices and positions. In his account, the notion of compulsion, of having had little choice but to join, is an orienting term of memory and of self-construction. The account is dialogic: it speaks to a critical self – within and without – that demands explanation. A counter-narrative is implicit and must be engaged at some point. Malik's account seeks to address questions that arise in conversation between dissidents – those who paid for their opposition and others who kept silent or, when they spoke out, were careful not to go beyond the red lines.

In the 2000s it became common in intellectual and activist circles, and beyond, to revisit in conversation personal political trajectories and positionality vis-à-vis the Hafez al-Asad regime during the preceding two decades. These conversations often returned to the period of the insurgency in the early 1980s and its aftermath. In such a review of trajectories of activism, a line of division was drawn between those who spent time in prison and those who bent with the tide of repression. The divisions were expressed in accusations and indictments. For example, the 'pacifists' blame communist activists for committing a fatal strategic mistake by spurring on a bloody confrontation with the regime in the early 1980s. In response some public dissidents, who spent years in prison, indict the quietists for being beneficiaries of regime largess. These lines of division and polarisation form as a backdrop to emergent trajectories of activism that began with the civil-society movement in the early 2000s and that culminated in the 2011 Uprising.

Conclusion

In this chapter, I have attempted to show that memories of everyday life aggregate to form a composite of the national experience of how life under dictatorship was lived. The school and the family are salient sites in recollections that often developed around the themes and motifs of Ba'thist practices of enframing citizens through party auxiliary organisations and through monitoring. For many, the accounts of the personal experiences of these practices articulate a self-distancing from the Ba'th and the regime. This dissociation, it should be noted, is retrospective and informed as much by the concerns of the present as by the events of the past that is being recounted. The emblematic frames through which the past is narrated illuminate the subject's self-understandings and political positionality. In this respect, abjection and precarity, as emblematic of conditions of everyday living, serve as ciphers of tired and disengaged subjects under repressive rule and of contesting subjects in the context of the Uprising.

In self-authoring narratives by publicly engaged actors – in particular intellectuals, artists, writers and political activists – individual life trajectories are interpreted through the lens of the national, and as such are anchored in aspirations and projects of the nation, or in the political formula of rule. In some respects, self-authoring unfolds as a revisiting of the past aimed at accounting for the self's political responsibility. These exercises of self-authoring are dialogic and expressive of the social polarisation and the political contests that have marked the social and the body politic under the rule of the Asad regime.

4 Memories of Violence: Hama 1982

As discussed in Chapter 1, violence was an ever present mechanism of government under the rule of Hafez al-Asad. The centrality of violence to the terms of rule continued under his successor and became especially manifest during the 2011 Uprising. The regime's propensity to use violence on a wide scale if challenged or opposed has long been a consideration of Syrian dissidents, activists and ordinary citizens in their thinking about oppositional strategies and politics. Indeed, under the Asads' rule, Syrians lived in a state of anticipation of regime violence. The anticipation of violent acts, and the projection of regime terror as the inevitable response to any questioning of its power practices, arise in Syrians' interpretative horizons in relation to memories of violent events and experiences involving the state. Such memories hearken back, most notably, to the period 1976 to 1982, referred to, variously, as 'the time of the events' (*fatrat al-ahdath*) or 'the events of Hama' (*ahdath hama*). These characterisations euphemistically designate a violent period in Syrian history – a glossing over of massacres and the toll of civilian deaths that resulted (estimated to be at least 10,000).

Just prior to the 2011 Uprising, and during its early days, in conversations with Syrian youth activists, seasoned observers and political dissidents, it was often pressed to me that the regime was ready, willing and capable of killing a large number of people to maintain its rule. For instance, a prominent political dissident, reporting 'insider information', stated, in the course of a meeting I had with him, that a high-ranking figure in the Syrian military had expressed readiness to sacrifice 100,000 people (meeting in Damascus, April 2011). Further, in explaining why Damascene merchants seemed reluctant or cautious to express support for the Uprising, a Damascene merchant in his mid forties asserted to me, with conviction, that he believed that, on his deathbed, Hafez al-Asad convened his sons, Bashar and Maher, and told them that if their rule was ever threatened, they should 'do Hama again' (Damascus, May 2011). 'Doing Hama again' is what many Syrians suspected to be in store for them should they ever stray from the public script of loyalty to the regime. Hama inaugurated a model of violence and a frame of power relations. Regime brutality in Hama was constructed as a template for the regime's anticipated use of violence to suppress opposition. It was understood as a lesson (*al-dars al-hamawi*).

In light of this, there is a need to consider the impact of the Hama violence on Syrian politics and society and, more specifically, on how Syrians came to understand themselves as subjects of the regime. I want to approach this question by looking at the social memories of violence and of events during the period, culminating in the Hama massacres in 1982. The apprehensions and anxieties about regime violence and about an impending civil war and sectarian strife, expressed through the invocation of past events of violence, raise the question of the kind of shared understandings that Syrians have had about the past. This is especially so since this period of Syrian history was not only marginalised in public discourse but was a taboo subject. At the time of their occurrence, the events were subject to regime rhetoric which set the terms for referring to and interpreting them: broadly, the Islamist insurrection was the work of the Muslim Brothers – agents of enemy foreign powers – and the regime, the leader and the people rose against this criminal plot until its defeat. Within this narrative frame, official media and regime figures provided corroborating evidence to flesh out the details of the official story.

Following the Hama massacres and the destruction of some of the city's old quarters, the public account receded into the background, attaining narrative closure, in the sense of not being open to revisiting or discussion in the public sphere. For example, 'the events' (*al-ahdath*) were not the subject of any kind of official memorialisation (in the terms sanctioned by the regime). Nor were they integrated into the official history of the country taught in school history books.[1] School and university curricula on modern Syrian political history make no reference to the violent Hama events. Thus, the generation schooled in the aftermath of Hama received virtually no information about it. Yet in school assembly

---

[1] Syrian history textbooks at the ninth-grade Baccalaureate levels cover Arab World history from the time of Ottoman rule to the post-independence period. The textbooks adopt a chronological approach with key events named and explained. The historical chronology is geared to providing *points de repère* that would symbolise or stand for the story of colonialism and nationalism ultimately crowned by the rise of the national hero and saviour, Hafez al-Asad. In this story, national historical events that do not fit within the narrative are omitted, including the episode of confrontation with the Islamist opposition and 'the Hama events'.

lines, pupils were made to declare oaths to fight against the criminal gang of the Muslim Brothers. Further, in published works of fiction and in commentary by critical and dissident writers, the Hama massacres remained an unspoken subject (see Kahf 2001).[2]

Despite the enforced public silence, social memories of the Hama events (and of the experience of imprisonment and torture) became constitutive of understandings of the regime and its modes of operation. My enquiry into memories of the Hama violence interrogates the place of past violence in understandings of the present, in interpretations of political norms of interaction and in the formation of political subjectivities. This question requires that we examine Syrians' constructions of the past to discern the terms in which it is negotiated, claimed, managed and mobilised in contests in the present. An extension of this examination is to look at how the past is lived in the present. Writing about the Latin American experience of violent military rule, Elizabeth Jelin (2003) notes that the passage of time, when it comes to political contexts of violence, does not lead to closure or forgetting. Rather, settling accounts with the past and making sense of the individual and societal experiences is a continuous endeavour. Memory, in this sense, is not a stored or fixed narrative but a processual undertaking, whereby memories are material for negotiation and understanding, as well as for conflict and resolution (Argenti and Schramm 2010, 7; Trouillot 1995).

With the aim of probing the politically formative role of the Hama violence, the chapter enquires into the ways in which memory practices have managed relations with the past, and have fashioned individual and collective modes of understanding atrocity and living with it. It begins with a tracing of fragments of narratives and accounts, as told by protagonists in the conflict. It then moves into an examination of different practices of remembering that can be discerned in recollections of the events in the narratives of witnesses and survivors and in works of fiction set in the period or hearkening back to it. My investigation of social memories is focused on the forms that recollections of Hama take and on the workings of technologies of remembering understood as embodied practices of memory. The final section widens the optic of the investigation to include the remembrances that take shape and find expression in dialogue with the Hama violence.

---

[2] A semi-fictional account by Abdallah al-Dahamsha (2009), first published in 1982 outside Syria, titled *Adhra' Hama* (*Hama Virgin*), and films such as Mohammad Malas' *al-Layl* (1994), make reference to the city, with allusions to its experience of destruction.

The Hama Events in Fragments

Dear Brothers and Sons: What these criminals [reference to the Muslim Brotherhood] did in Hama, what these criminals committed in the city of Hama, these paid agents, cannot be rationally believed. They left no act forbidden by God without committing it, they made licit all that is illicit, they enter a home, kill all its inhabitants including its women, children and men to turn this home into a hideout, placing themselves by its windows and doors to fire in all directions. They distribute death on all passers-by, forbidding groups of women and children from leaving the neighbourhood to avoid the danger of bullets and forcing them to enter into their hideout, and if a woman who works as a nurse in Hama objects, this woman is sprayed with bullets. (From a speech by Hafez al-Asad, 7 March 1982)

According to news reports and information received by Amnesty International, shortly after dark on 2 February, regular Syrian soldiers tried to raid a house in the ancient, western part of the city of Hama. Ninety soldiers led by a lieutenant surrounded a house believed to contain a large cache of arms belonging to the outlawed Muslim Brotherhood. As they started their raid, the troops were ambushed by armed Mujahideen. They were captured and killed and their uniforms removed. The insurgents then posted themselves on the rooves and turrets of the city.

The next morning, the citizens of Hama were apparently informed from the minarets of several mosques that the city had been 'liberated' and that the 'liberation' of the rest of the country will follow. The insurgents occupied government and security forces buildings, ransacked the local armoury and began executing government officials and 'collaborators'. At least 50 people are reported to have been killed by the anti-government demonstrators on this first day of protests.

According to some observers, old parts of the city were bombarded from the air and shelled in order to facilitate the entry of troops and tanks along the narrow streets. The ancient quarter of Hadra [sic] was apparently bombarded and raised [sic] to the ground by tanks during the first four days of fighting. On 15 February, after several days of heavy bombardments, Major General Mustafa Tlas, the Syrian defence minister, stated that the Uprising in Hama had been suppressed. However, the city remained surrounded and cut off. Two weeks of house-to-house searches and mass arrests followed, with conflicting reports of atrocities and collective killings of unarmed, innocent inhabitants by the security forces. It is difficult to establish for certain what happened, but Amnesty International has heard that there was, among other things, a collective execution of 70 people outside the municipal hospital on 19 February, the Hadra [sic] quarter residents were executed by Saraya al-difaʿ troops the same day; that cyanide gas containers were alleged to have been brought into the city, connected to rubber pipes to the entrance of buildings believed to house insurgents and turned on, killing the building's occupants, that people were assembled at the military airfield, at the sports stadium and at the military barracks and left out in the open for days without food or shelter.

On 22 February, the Syrian authorities broadcast a telegram of support addressed to President Assad from the Hama branch of the Ba'th Party. The message referred to the Muslim Brotherhood fighters killing party activists and their families and leaving their mutilated bodies in the streets. It said the security forces had taken fierce reprisals against the Brotherhood and their sympathisers 'which stopped them breathing forever'.

When order was restored, estimates of the number of dead on all sides ranged from 10,000 to 25,000. (Amnesty International 1983, 36–7)

These extracts, from longer accounts, relate the events of Hama from the perspectives of one of the protagonists and of an outside observer. There are general contours of the events on which these and other accounts agree: the existence of an Islamist insurgency and its crushing by the security and armed forces. Beyond these broad lines, there are contesting claims about the actual events – for example, the number of insurgents, the number of civilian victims who were killed during the military operations, the specific terms of the orders that guided the security operations and the actual conduct of the security forces. Further, accounts of the Muslim Brothers' role in the insurgency remain confined to regime rhetoric and to the defensive narratives given in memoirs of the organisation's leaders. On the whole, the Muslim Brotherhood dissociates itself from the violence of the Combatant Vanguard group (al-Tali'a al-Muqatila) and only acknowledges taking up arms as a tool of resistance after the regime declared war on the organisation. For example, in his published memoirs of the period, Adnan Sa'd al-Din, leader and general guide of one of the Muslim Brother factions at the time, states that followers of Marwan Hadid – a radical Islamist activist spurred on by what he believed to be discriminatory state policies against Sunnis – were pushed to take a confrontational route. He then asserts that the Muslim Brotherhood only later became aware of the militant activities of that period (Sa'd al-Din 2010, 27). In an interview in 2012, Yassin al-Ghadban, a prominent member of the Muslim Brotherhood, asserted that the Brotherhood had no connection with the violence of the Tali'a, though he acknowledged that 'Adnan Sa'd al-Din, who operated from Iraq, maintained links with them (interview in Amman, May 2012). The Muslim Brotherhood's official line is that the group was compromised by the Tali'a activities and was dragged into armed resistance in self-defence once the regime started attacking Muslim Brotherhood activists and their families. Memoirs by Tali'a militants, on the other hand, assert that the leadership of the Brotherhood encouraged the armed struggle, but that they reneged on their promises of help (Abd al-Hakim 1991).[3]

---

[3] In the account of a Tali'a activist, coordination with certain leaders within the Syrian Muslim Brotherhood organisation – specifically with the Aleppo-Hama axis that enjoyed the International Muslim Brotherhood organisation's backing – was initiated by Abd

The Muslim Brotherhood's continued refusal to open its own records of that period for investigation and scrutiny has been pointed to by some civil-society activists as a reason why they should not be part of a national coalition working for transition from the Asad regime (interviews in Damascus, March 2011). For some Hamawis, the demand for Muslim Brotherhood accountability is more focused on the issue of ethical responsibility, in particular, their role in encouraging the turn to violence (interviews in Damascus, March 2011). In the appraisal of some of my Hamawi interviewees, the Muslim Brotherhood betrayed an attitude of ease in sacrificing human life in the name of religiously sanctified goals.

The regime-managed official history of the events and the wide-reaching repression contributed to practices of self-censoring and public silencing that muted alternative accounts. This is especially the case for those who lived the events. Independent media coverage at the time was limited and, hence, what happened in Hama has preserved a murky and uncertain character. Further, without the benefit of archival records or access to oral history sources, critical and sustained historical scholarship has been constrained.[4] An added consideration for current research into this period is whether the events of the 2011 Uprising have altered the optical field from which the past could be viewed. This is particularly relevant as different parties to the conflict reconstruct the past with a view to validating their accounts and interpretations of the present.

For the most part, the events of Hama are recounted in fragments: human rights reports and journalistic reportages and sketches. However, an effort at documenting and recording the circumstances of Hama was undertaken by the Syrian Human Rights Committee (SHRC). In a series of reports, killing, detention and abduction are detailed in a catalogue of destruction and ruination. One of the SHRC reports names localities where violence occurred and records the acts of destruction that occurred there. It also documents the names of individuals and families that perished and the manner in which they were killed. All is

al-Satar al-Za'im, who took up the Tali'a group's leadership upon the death in 1976 of Marwan Hadid in prison (Abd al-Hakim 1991, 93). Letters attributed to 'Adnan 'Uqla, responsible for the group's military training and operations in Aleppo, charge the Brotherhood leadership, which was based outside Syria, with having reneged on promises of financial and military support to the group (Abd al-Hakim 1991, 110–28). For an account of the Brotherhood's role in the armed confrontation with the regime, see Abd-Allah (1983) and Lefèvre (2013).

[4] Seale (1988) discusses the insurgency and the armed confrontation but does not delve into the impact the violence had on the people of Hama and on Syrians in general. Batatu (1982), Lawson (1982) and Michaud (1982) have addressed social, political economy, and systemic dimensions of the conflict. Lefèvre (2013) examines the politics of the Muslim Brotherhood during the insurgency and the period leading up to it.

organised and set out both chronologically – laying out an account of daily massacres – and thematically according to categories of the population that were victims of massacre – women and children, young men, religious figures – or according to the sites of massacres, for example the Porcelain factory.

These SHRC reports are similar in content to the account presented by a group close to the Muslim Brothers in the book titled *Hama: The Tragedy of the Age* (Majmu'a min al-Bahithin 2003). Indeed, there appears to be much overlap between the two accounts. The SHRC account also draws on reports by international human rights organisations such as Amnesty International. This work of *documenting* the Hama events is concerned with facticity and truth, both of which can be and would be contested through other sources of documentary evidence or evidentiary pieces. Despite the possible challenges to which these documents are subject, they do allow for threading together an account of the events. Even if verified and authenticated as 'the record' of events, they do not tell the full story. There are other fragments and other stories that can be told in an open narrative. Importantly, the accounts pursue the 'factual' as can be documented by reference to evidentiary information such as the number killed, the site of killing and the instruments used. The affective and cognitive 'evidence' of the aftermath, the lived experience and the formative and transformative work of violence are not the object of these documentary works.

There are different and multiple stakes in the work of recollection. My purpose, here, is not to examine contested claims, let alone to adjudicate between them, but to elucidate various relations to the past in the present. Ultimately, I am interested in the afterlife of violence and in the question of how violence folds into everyday life (in the sense articulated by Veena Das (2009)), and into the struggles to create a past that can be inhabited and a memory that can be meaningfully lived (McDougall 2010, 47). Inhabiting the past, as James McDougall (2010, 47) notes, is a distinct endeavour, different from the 'idealised historiographic, or juridical, procedures of establishing the facts'.

However, in certain accounts, inhabiting the past is presented as a historiographical procedure. This, for instance, is evident in a number of interviews that I conducted in the spring of 2005, with individuals who were once part of the regime, either serving in ministerial positions under Hafez al-Asad or having risen up in the ranks of the Ba'th Party. My interviewees reiterated the official account of Hama, complemented with personal views and opinions that justified the regime's assault on the city. One former government minister recalled the explosion of bombs in al-Azbakiyya in central Damascus, not very far from his office, sometime prior to the assault on Hama. He stated that people were being blown to pieces and asserted that the anti-regime violence was orchestrated from Iraq and that the Iraqi Ba'th had supplied weapons to the perpetrators. The lines of this narrative were reiterated by another interviewee who was a member of the Damascene political elite. My interlocutors in the higher political echelons also expounded on the particularities and characteristics of Syrian society, asserting that it is composed of a fragile mosaic of ethnicities and religions, which, in turn, necessitates a firm grip and a strong leader like Hafez al-Asad. Such observations displace the details of the violence and forego a closer examination of the human cost of 'political imperatives'.

My interviews with Damascene merchants yielded what can best be termed a historiographical rehearsal aimed at accounting for their position and role during the Hama events. Such narratives identify the protagonists as the regime and the Islamists, with the rest of society being caught in the crossfire. The contours of this historiographical rehearsal in the recollection of one merchant – a member of the Board of Directors of the Damascus Chamber of Commerce – were drawn around a meeting with Hafez al-Asad in 1980 in which the latter made clear his intention to contain the challenge of the Muslim Brothers in Aleppo (interview in Damascus, 20 March 2005). My narrator recalled his attempt to plead on behalf of Aleppo and its people and to sway the president to adopt a softer approach. In his recollections, it appears that he is responding to the charge of betrayal for not joining the general national strike called in 1980 by Aleppo merchants. The Damascene merchants' decision to decline or to withdraw support for the strike is accounted for in the assertion that Damascus was besieged by the troops of Rif'at al-Asad who threatened violence.

In contrast to the self-exonerating recollections of merchants close to the regime, other Damascene merchants charge collusion and manipulation by the Damascus Chamber of Commerce. A number of my interviewees recalled being contacted by Badr al-Din al-Shallah (the then president of the chamber) or by other chamber board members and being warned not to participate in the planned strike. Some stated that they were advised that their shops would be forced open by the security forces and that they may be looted. One merchant recalled having heard that some merchants who supported the call to strike had been murdered.

These recollections are offered not only as supposedly factual or objective accounts of what happened, but they also aim at attributing responsibility, at self-exoneration from charges of complicity and at justifying a particular position and action. For example, in a programme called *al-Sanduq al-Aswad* (The Black Box) aired by Al Jazeera Satellite

TV (2015), As'ad Mustafa, a former governor of Hama and a high-echelon Ba'th member who defected, reiterated that Rif'at al-Asad was in command of the violence and that two local officers, namely Ayman al-As'ad and Yahya Zidan, were key figures on the ground. As'ad Mustafa, who rose in the ranks and assumed the governorship of Hama in 1985, placed himself outside the circle of actors. However, other testimonials would point to Mr Mustafa's implication in the events, if not necessarily his complicity. In an undated memoir, a high school teacher in Hama in the 1970s, who was an acquaintance of Mr Mustafa, casts a different light on the latter's role, portraying him as being loyal to Hafez al-Asad and having collaborated closely with the party to secure his rise in the ranks (Shantut ND). Memory and narrative are offered as historiography, with an attendant claim to be representing objective history. The competing claims made in these recollections are intended for the historical record. Narratives of what happened, as a mode of remembering, attempt to fill in some of the gaps in the historical record and in available information.

The documentary objective is also pursued in numerous first-hand accounts offered with a view to bearing witness and providing testimonies on the part of the survivors. A number of these testimonials appeared during the 2011 Uprising and aimed primarily to disclose the details of the violence of Hama, to expose the brutality of the culprits and to bear witness to the harms to which the victims were subjected. These accounts are also intended to invalidate denials and misrepresentations in the public record maintained by the regime and to speak with the objective of 'truth-telling'. In the context of the Uprising, the intention was also to establish Hama as a precedent, which would furnish further evidence for the regime's willingness to use violence in suppressing the protests and opposition in 2011 and afterwards.

Remembering Hama: Managing and Inhabiting the Past

As discussed in the Introduction, social memories of political violence develop intersubjectively in relation to events and experiences in the past. If experiences of regime violence are formative of political subjects, so too are social memories of violence. In this regard, the terms in which violent events are remembered, recalled or silenced inform and shape the subject's positioning vis-à-vis political government, the regime and fellow citizens. In this sense, social memories of violence are components of the subject's interpretative horizons: contending with a violent past and finding individual and collective terms of negotiating one's relations to it has been formative of Syrians as subject-citizens under the Asad regime. In the following discussion, I draw on literary writings and on Syrians' personal recollections about the Hama events to sketch out the practices of memory through which the violence was lived and negotiated. Relatedly, I probe the politically constitutive role of social memories of violence.

The most extensive recollections of the Hama events and their aftermath are offered in the narrative work of Manhal al-Sarraj, a writer from Hama. Al-Sarraj's work stands as a repository of social memory, of how the events folded into the everyday. The imperative of telling arises in al-Sarraj's work as an ethical practice in the sense in which remembering is undertaken with a view to giving account.[5] The ethical imperative of remembering entails a struggle against a forgetting that denies the truth of the subject's experience of violence and her quest for a reckoning and not forcibly for retribution (see Lambek 1996; Ricoeur 2004). Drawing on al-Sarraj's narratives and on recollections and remembrances that I gathered in interviews with Hamawis and other Syrians who lived the events, I highlight different practices of memory at work: analytic retrospections that reconstruct a social history of Hama and deploy social categories for understanding and explanation; spatialised remembering and memorialisation; and embodied practices of memory revealing how the past is lived and inhabited.

Remembering as a Reconstructed Social History: Religion, Class and Piety

The official version of the events of Hama not only set the terms of framing them but also brought about a forced closure by banishing any reference to them from the public sphere. In this spirit, the regime did not seek to commemorate even its own version of the events. It would appear that, from the perspective of the rulers, the historical record was settled in the form of Hafez al-Asad's speeches during the period and in Syrian media accounts. In this sense, the life experiences of Hama

---

[5] In al-Sarraj's work, acknowledging the events of violence and understanding the suffering that they caused guide the documentary-like narratives and the memory work of the characters in her novels. In conversation with Manhal al-Sarraj (over the telephone on 22 November 2011), she stressed the importance of recognising the pain and acknowledging it, and of communicating and understanding it (*tafahum al-alam*). She also spoke of many places in Syria that became *hamida* (lifeless or still) after being subjected to disciplining violence.

residents were not allowed voice and remained suppressed. With the 2011 Uprising, there was a rush to produce testimonials and recollections. One notable testimony is that of Khaled al-Khani (2013). Al-Khani's father was a prominent eye doctor who, during the siege of the city, had one eye gouged out before being killed by regime forces. Al-Khani titled his recollections 'I lived to recount to you: the story of my childhood, my father's eye and the Hama Massacre'. The testimony tells of security forces' assaults on homes, summary executions and assaults on young women. Al-Khani's testimony shows a preoccupation with evidentiary and documentary requirements. To some extent, the context of the 2011 Uprising highlights the privileging of the evidentiary and documentary dimensions of testimonials about Hama.

The imposed silencing also drove the impulse to offer factual accounts of events that were either personally witnessed or were socially verified in earlier telling and corroboration by multiple witnesses. In my interviews with Hamawis before and after the 2011 Uprising, the recollections of the events tended to be told in the style of formalised testimonies. Many of the interviewees wove similar tales of what they experienced. This formalised testimonial style is initially puzzling as it appears to correspond to the documentary work done by the Syrian Human Rights Organisation. The stories are reiterative of the same occurrences such as the witnessing of neighbours and family members being lined up against a wall and shot. Another recurrent theme in the recollections is that of soldiers coming into homes, destroying furniture and possessions, looting and threatening to rape the women. In some sense, the personal narratives, disallowed from public discourse and, at best, confined to the most intimate spaces, assimilated the generalised narratives of the human rights organisations. Although personal, the remembrances are permeated by the collective. An important element in understanding the forms of telling and the stakes of memory is the long period of enforced silence and the contests surrounding what actually happened. The similarity in survivors' testimonials of the massacres, as noted by Liisa Malkki (1995), entails a degree of for-malisation, a quality that should not diminish the importance of the accounts. Concurring with Malkki, Laleh Khalili (2008) asserts that formalisation conveys the systematisation of the mechanics of violence and, as such, it is a means of attaining coherence within the survivors' sense of the overall order.

Moving beyond stylised or formalised testimonies concerned with facts and validation, an analytic mode of retrospection could be discerned in the work of memory that offers a fleshed-out social history of the city and its people. In this analytic mode of recollection, Hama is read through the categories of class, social status, piety and the rural–urban divide. Also, in some of the narratives, a historical reading of the nationalist and Ba'thist eras is developed. The recollections are made through the prism of the polarisation of society and the political lines of division. Modes of retrospection of the events reveal a concern with the dynamics of the struggle and of where one was positioned in relation to it. The personal memories mobilise knowledge and particular understandings of the political context at the time. In vivid recollections, my Hamawi interviewees endeavoured to bring forth their perceptions of the unfolding events as they were lived and experienced. For example, some recalled, in evocative terms, the widely held view that the regime was weakened and that its demise was near. Integrated into the frames of narrating the events, and situating the self and the collective in relation to them, are social and political categories such as sect, party alignment and class. For some, there is an urge to locate where one stood in relation to the conflict and to societal divisions.

An analytic mode of retrospection also runs through the narratives in Manhal al-Sarraj's works. By virtue of her extensive writing as a narrator, a chronicler and a witness, she has come to occupy an important place with reference to the work of remembering. In her first novel, *Kama Yanbaghi li-Nahr*, al-Sarraj narrates the story of Hama as it sinks into a duel between the regime, in the person of strong man, Abi Shama, and his men, and the Islamists, in the person of Uncle Nazir and his followers. Fatima, the narrator, recounts the events through introspective recollections as well as in exchanges with others around her. She keeps the memories present in her thoughts and her surroundings. Fatima's account is a kind of bearing witness. In her narratives, the two sides are pitted against each other, though they are unequal: soldiers in uniform against youths in delicate pyjamas. However, the unequal physical power does not occlude the extremism that drives each side – extremism in thought on one side, and absolutism of power, on the other – making the confrontation unavoidable.

Al-Sarraj's narrative is instructive for what it tells us about where to stand vis-à-vis past violence: To remember or not to remember? To assign responsibility? To hold to account? How? In simple terms, there are victors and losers, but where should one stand? In the work of recollection, the subject is challenged to take sides, to allocate responsibility and identify the guilty party.[6] In a number of interviews with Syrians from

---

[6] Fatima, as the agent of remembering in the novel, transcends the challenge. Although she explores the reasons behind Abi Shama's attack on the alleys, and delves into the manipulations of Uncle Nazir, she does not take sides as such. All the same, the extent of violence shocks and angers. It is not the rectitude of one of the opposing parties (i.e. the

Hama, the question of how the entire city was drawn into a deadly duel between the regime and the insurgents figures prominently in attempts to come to terms with the past. For some, the question is about assuming responsibility and, for others, it is about providing explanation, though these are interlinked issues. Interrogation about responsibility is often directed at the Muslim Brothers. There remain unanswered questions about their role in the violence. The official position of the Brotherhood is that the insurgents were members of al-Tali'a al-Muqatila who acted to avenge the death of Marwan Hadid in prison. In this account, the Tali'a members acted on their own and they were misguided about the legitimacy and merits of the use of violence. It is only after the regime's declaration of war on the Brotherhood, that its leadership endorsed the use of violence to defend its members.

The credibility of this account is questioned on various grounds expressing differing political and ethical positions. For example, Tareq, who grew up in Hama in the 1970s, expressed his deep dissatisfaction with the Brotherhood's account. In his thinking, the Brotherhood contributed, through their *da'wa* work (religious teaching akin to proselytisation), to fostering the objective of removing the regime by force. His recollections leave him with the sense that the youths were misled to believe that the MB would provide aid and succour in their confrontation with the regime. Instead, they were abandoned. In addition to demanding both a truthful accounting of events and the Brotherhood's assumption of responsibility, Tareq's questions, derived from his recollections, offer a kind of witnessing. In his questions, it is implicit that he was sympathetic to the insurgency, but now he has feelings of anger and rancour that the young militants were misled and manipulated.

Remembrances of a number of my interviewees bring to light the influence exerted by the Muslim Brothers through religious-teaching circles and other *da'wa* activities. Although religious piety and conservatism characterised the lifestyle of large segments of the population in Hama in the modern period, adherence to the Brotherhood was not wide in its reach until the early 1970s. In the 1950s and 1960s, secular political movements such as the Arab Socialists and the Ba'th had a significant following. These Parties garnered followings among the burgeoning segment of educated youths, many of whom were from

---

Islamist youths) that motivates the condemnation of Abi Shama and his men, rather it is the brutality of the acts in themselves. The youths in pyjamas are victims of Abi Shama and dupes of Uncle Nazir (the Islamist agitator).

rural areas or from the urban middle classes. Incidents of confrontation occurred between Ba'thists and religiously oriented groups, notably in 1964 (see al-Hourani's (2000) memoirs). Then, the 1970s saw a
widening of support for the Brotherhood. According to some Hamawis,
this development is attributable to the need of Hamawis to lean on some
force in the face of a Ba'thist takeover of all institutions of government
and their exclusion from these institutions, whether as a result of deliberate or systemic barriers to entry or access or because many had voluntarily opted out of joining the Ba'th Party (interview with self-exiled
Hamawis in Beirut, May 2012, and London, December 2011).[7]

Social memories of the period that followed the ascendancy of Hafez
al-Asad to state power crystallise around recollections of increased
religiosity and growing sympathies with the Muslim Brotherhood.
A number of my interviewees recalled that an atmosphere of religiosity
began to set in: religious books were more frequently found in homes,
older male siblings joined the Muslim Brothers and female religious
preachers became popular. One interviewee observed the shifts in her
own surroundings. For example, her mother began wearing a *monteau*
(long coat) and attending religious lessons. Further, young girls from
her neighbourhood gathered in homes for Quranic and exegesis lessons.
Young men went to mosques in various districts of the city to attend
lessons by renowned preachers. Tareq, who was one of these young
men attending such sermons, recalls the period preceding the assault
on Hama:

I used to attend the lessons of Sheikh Adib al-Kilani in zawiyyat al-Kilaniyya.
I was still in preparatory school and was attending Quranic memorisation
lessons. I was also attending the Friday sermon of Sheikh Ahmad al-Murad in
al-Jadid mosque.

In Manhal al-Sarraj's analytic narrative, piety took an ideological form
and became an affirmation of a distinct identity.[8] Further, opposition to
the regime was articulated in a nominal identification with the Muslim
Brotherhood. In the words of a Hamawi exile: 'we were all Ikhwan without
the Organisation' (*kuna kuliyatna Ikhwan bidun tanzim*) (interview,
December 2011). This statement underscores the prevailing sentiment
of opposition to the regime, which was put to me by another interviewee,
Tareq, in terms of Hama, the city, being 'instinctively oppositional'

---

[7] The use of 'Hamawi' refers to city residents, predominately Sunni, but inclusive of long-
time Christian residents.
[8] I conducted three extensive interviews with Manhal al-Sarraj, one over the telephone and
two in person during meetings in Stockholm where she resides.

(*Hama mu 'arida bil-fitra*) (interview, November 2011). According to Tareq, 'integral to Hama's set up (*manzumat Hama*) was hatred for the Ba'th'. At the same time, many of my interviewees dissociated themselves from the Ikhwan:

> those who were killed were Hamawi, they had no relation with the Ikhwan. The armed men were killed in the first couple of days. In al-Mal'ab al-Janubi [a district of Hama City], many people were killed … ordinary people. The killing was systematic. They [the security men] entered the alleyways. They searched, they stole, they gathered people, stood them against a wall and killed them … They entered homes like beasts. The girl they like, they take her. (Interview with Manar, Hama survivor, London, December 2011)

At the time, the Muslim Brothers were distributing leaflets about Alawi rule, which resonated with the more generalised anti-regime feelings and with widespread resentment. This resentment of regime and party practices is conveyed in these observations of one of my Hamawi interviewees:

> [T]he poor strata had now come to govern us. They took everything from the people of the city. They took the government jobs, and they withdrew all support from the city people. They came from the surrounding villages and took over the high positions in institutions such as the Organisation for Grains. In Hama, the people who assumed positions of responsibility were from poor families. They benefited from the Ba'th. There was the idea that the poor of the city (Sunnis) were not respectable people, they were *mukhabarat*. Everyone knew who the informants in their midst were and avoided them. The powerful (*al-mutanafidhin*) were from the surrounding villages. (Interview with a Hamawi exile, December 2011)

Similarly, Tareq recalls his grandmother saying that 'the outsiders' had invaded the city and would be taking retribution on its people. In these recollections, both class and the rural–urban divisions serve as categories mediating and framing social memories.

Through an analytic mode of retrospection, Hamawis who lived through the events reconstruct the social and political context of the bloody confrontation. They recall how the Muslim Brotherhood came to be perceived as a serious contender to the regime. There was a strong conviction that the MB would win. In her recollections, Manhal al-Sarraj recounts that one of the common rumours during the period leading up to the events was of Hafez al-Asad dead and of his body being placed in the morgue (assertions were being made that he was in the refrigerator '*Hafez bil barad*'). Recalling the certainty of an Islamist victory invites a call for an accounting, not for failure to deliver, but for the role of leaders in misleading the followers and sympathisers about the likely outcome of the confrontation with the regime.

Practices of Forgetting and Practices of Remembering:
Ruins and Spatialised Remembrance

Questions of accountability and responsibility for the 1982 violence have been raised publicly in the period following the 2011 Uprising. Previously, under conditions of enforced silence, recollections were muted. This is captured in al-Sarraj's *Kama Yanbaghi li-Nahr* (discussed above), where Fatima's remembering unsettles society and its practices of forgetting. In the market, the vegetable vendor and the milkman fear her speaking of Abi Shama and Black Friday, though they themselves have marked the day in stories of escape: 'in the memory of the kind of sprint each ran' on that fateful day. Even Fatima's brother, who spent many years in prison, resents her for raking up the past and urges her to stop talking about the events.

The moral dilemma facing the survivors of the violence is that the demands of mundane living require a degree of forgetting and perhaps complicity. Fatima records complicity in the aftermath. As Abi Shama passes in parades, she remarks: 'they cheer him for killing their children, destroying their homes, stealing their trades. They cheer with unparalleled enthusiasm.' The exigencies of life implicate the survivors in the death of their kin.[9] Thus, the practice, of mainly wives and mothers, of registering their missing relatives – usually husbands and sons – as dead, is described by Fatima as 'women who kill their husbands, women who kill their sons to collect compensation'. This complicity becomes formalised in the setting up, in Fatima's neighbourhood, of a syndicate called 'Yes, a Donkey and Without Shame' (*na'am himar wa la 'ar*). Residents of the alleys join the new syndicate to communicate their compliance. Such practices are also practices of forgetting in al-Sarraj's account: 'people forgetting the alleys that were uprooted, the children and the youths who were tortured, and they become preoccupied with crumbs' (al-Sarraj 2007a, 156). Daily living, in itself, becomes an act of forgetting and, in the process, violence is routinised: 'brother eats brother and mothers deform their children to protect them from being taken by the men of Abi Shama' (al-Sarraj 2007a, 157). Thus, the spectre of violence remains in the aftermath of spectacular violence.

Kama Yanbaghi li-Nahr underscores the practices of forgetting and the tacit understandings that develop to stifle remembering. Yet other

---

[9] This depiction of the subjects' implication in their own subjugation carries resonance with Mbembe's (2001) account in his work on the postcolony of ordinary citizens' applause at the public hanging of fellow citizens.

narratives reveal the impossibility of forgetting because the violence has memorialised itself in the wreckage, destruction and ruination that the city suffered. Remembrance of the city before and after the destruction is a structuring theme in narratives of Hama. The stories of places have shaped individual and community histories and served as commemorative practices under conditions of forced silence and in the absence of public memorialisation. Remembrances of the events of Hama conjure old quarters and scenes of their destruction. Narratives of place turn sites of memory into memorials of the events. In some instances, they excavate the heritage and life that lay below the rubble or that was bulldozed and evened out. In others, they transform the sites of erasure that came with the construction of new quarters into monuments of the death and desecration that the city and its people underwent.

Memories of the destruction of the city, as lived by Hamawis, are the subtext of 'Ala Sadri (2007b), another of al-Sarraj's novels. The memory of the city that seeped into the ruins is the burden carried by the main protagonist, Najla, in her continuous journeys through the city of Hama and in her efforts to document its history. Najla works in the Heritage and Preservation Department of the city's municipal office. She is earnestly, and against all odds and doubts, moved by a desire to restore the old places to their glory, to repair and to preserve. In her relations and interactions with others around her, Najla wants to recreate the moments of the past – going up to the citadel, walking slowly and casting a long look over the al-Asi river waterbed. Like Kama Yanbaghi li-Nahr's Fatima, she wants to remember, but not the events in particular. Rather, she wants to recall a life before the events, to revive the legends and myths and to summon up the nooks and crannies of the alleyways (110).

Reconnecting with the past and returning Hama to its splendour is the future for which Najla yearns. Indeed, she has restoration plans for all the quarters. She adopts these plans as factual and outlines them to the tourists that she guides through the city. She projects life into the abandoned dwellings. As she glances into the deserted dwellings, she conjures up inhabitants and their lives – imagining a woman listening to a radio, taking a nap, and preparing lunch for her children. She goes on in her city tours to achieve what the director of the Heritage and Preservation Department (the state authority) could not accomplish. She populates homes and alleyways, opens the doors and windows of abandoned homes, fills rooms with inhabitants, fills squares and courtyards with children, rebuilds half-destroyed homes, restores latticed windows and renews entire quarters (186). Najla, the daughter of Hama, weaves the story of the city. She lays out city plans before revival and after revival. Najla's enterprise of restoration is a work of tahqiq (186). In a manner analogous to the Arab-Islamic tradition of *tahqiq* – the authentication, verification and restoration of an old manuscript to its original form – Najla is proceeding with her work, and with her life in Hama (lifework), exerting a great labour to be true to the author's original text (the author, here, being the city and its people).

In some respects, the work of restoration lies in spatialised practices of memory and remembering, in walkabouts and tours wherein the subject names what was there, describes spaces once lived and once invested emotionally. Memories lodge in the walls, in the stones and pavements that once were, and in the gap between what was, then, and what is, now. The ruins and trail of destruction become summonses to the past and testaments to a monumental injustice committed against the city and its people. The city's physical destruction and ruination are structuring themes of recollections of Hamawis who witnessed the assault and who lost relatives, friends and neighbours. In her recollections of the events, Manar, who was eighteen years old at the time, spoke to me, in interview, of the demolition of al-Suq al-Tawil (a market area). She reflected:

why did they destroy it? Because it leads to all of Hama. It is full of alleyways. It branches into Hadir, Suq and Baraziyyah [all old quarters of the city]. They also destroyed Suq al-Shajarah because in its homes you can jump from one roof to the next. They destroyed the features of Hama, like the baths in the suq (*hamammat al-Suq*). Tourists used to come to them. They built a park and a swimming pool over a cemetery. They do not respect the dead. Tanks rolled over the dead. (Interview with Manar, London, December 2011)

Bara' al-Sarraj, who grew up in Hama and who was studying in Damascus at the time of the military and security forces' assault on the city, recalls returning to it with his twin brother in early March immediately after the siege was lifted. In his recollections, he sketches out the streets, the homes and the familiar sites that were destroyed:

We got off at al-Alamayn Street and al-Asi Square. The homes were destroyed, the shops looted. There were unexploded shells everywhere. We walked to al-Suq where our old house was. Its columns were damaged, but the building did not fall. We walked to the mosque at the last incline of al-Dabaggha on Ibn Rushd Street – the mosque was destroyed. We went to a friend's home and it was burned and swollen. I went inside and found the skull of my friend. I touched it and it dissolved in my hands. We walked to al-Hadir. We were thinking of the historical importance of the city. We wanted to make sure the historical part was still standing. Al-Hadir was the most affected area. Al-Kilaniyya at the beginning of al-Hadir was all destroyed, there were no people. In al-Hadir, we went to check my grandmother's house, it was shelled and there was blood on the roof. We walked in Kilaniyya, but we could not recognise the streets. The streets were raised by a meter and a half. The bulldozers had flattened the rubble from the demolished homes. We walked over corpses. There was the smell of fire, a distinct smell mixed with the corpses and the humidity. It was raining. It smelt like charcoaled flesh. The scene of Kilaniyya rendered us speechless. We said nothing. We could not talk. In the evening, we went back. (Interview with Bara' al-Sarraj, 20 November 2011)

The memory of place – the traces of the past in the old homes, in the alleyways, the cobbled stones – is where the past spills into the present and is lived. In a similar vein to Najla's relations with the city, Hamawi practices of memory present an aesthetic of place formed in recollections of living it, and in the meanings invested in it. In this work of remembering, memory is inscribed in the lived space and the damage it underwent which cuts deep into the lives of the living – the survivors who cannot speak about it, as articulated by Manhal al-Sarraj, Bara' al-Sarraj, Manar, Tareq, Rula and others. My Hamawi interviewees undertook journeys into the past that unfolded as spatialised practices of remembering. In these spatialised recollections, as when recalling walkabouts in the city, the subject's relationship with space develops as a counter-memory practice. In their narratives, they transmit their memory of space – space which has been radically altered or erased. Bara' al-Sarraj, for example, recalled his grandmother's description of al-Kilaniyya and its aristocratic homes that, when she was growing up, were not to be approached by the less well-off. In such stories, Hamawis remind themselves and others of the history of the obliterated spaces. As borne out by witness accounts and documentary reports, al-Kilaniyya was subjected to heavy shelling and many of its homes and streets were bulldozed. Recollections of al-Kilaniyya and of other quarters summon up the city before the events.[10]

Many of my interviewees spoke of the erasure of al-Kilaniyya and the construction of the hotel Afamia and other modern buildings in its place, and they poignantly noted the symbolism of erecting leisure places over a site in which victims of massacres were buried. The old sites and destruction are recalled to conjure up the ruins that are now covered by new buildings. Under Afamia, there lies the rubble of al-Kilaniyya and the bodies of the dead. In a commentary on the relationship that developed between the people of Hama and the spaces of destruction

---

[10] The 'holding onto' in remembering is a practice against loss. Hama, as place, its history, beauty, legends, sociability and ways of life, is disappearing. Nostalgia emerges as a mode of remembering. Against death and destruction, Hama lives in memory. In 'Ala Sadri, Hama lives in the ghost of Najla's grandmother Hayat (the noun hayat means life and Hayat's apparition also stands for the ghost of life), who appears to Najla in dream-like visions and whom she summons in her imagination. Najla interrogates the temporal relation between past and present: 'How can the past be present if all the events are past once they happen, the past is past, the present is past, and the future is past. Why do the happenings of the story not pass and not end' (101).

and massacres, Manhal al-Sarraj emphasises how practices of recol-lection superimpose layers of meanings and connections on the space ensuring that the events are not buried in some recesses of memory but are brought to the fore. The coffee shops and restaurants built on the grounds of the destroyed quarter double as memorial sites and spaces of betrayal and abandonment of one's commitment for redress (interview with Manhal al-Sarraj, Stockholm, 3 and 4 December 2011; interviews with Hamawis in Damascus, April 2008; and in London, December 2011). The spaces of the present do not accomplish the regime's intended erasures. Instead, they are rendered memorialising spaces that are intim-ately tied to remembrances of the once-lived space and its subsequent ruination. The traces of the past are materialised in the places of erasure such as Afamia, the restaurants and coffee shops built on ground beneath which lay the rubble of al-Kilaniyya's razed homes and buildings.

The violence and destruction that befell Hama was not memorialised by the regime in the form of a physical, built memorial structure on or near the sites of the events. As such, there is not a permanent struc-ture linking the regime narration to the actual sites where the events took place. Instead, the regime opted for a politics of erasure by effacing remnants of the historical sites and by implementing urban plans that departed radically from the previous design and style. Thus, Hamawis were denied the ability to reclaim their memories in public. Yet through their journeys of remembrance and their spatialised counter-memory practices, they memorialise the events in the sites of their occurrence, even though the sites have been physically transformed to effect a rup-ture. Counter-memory practices also connect the narratives of the past – of what was, before the events – with the sites of the events, excavating the layers of history and life that lay beneath the work of erasure.

Subjects of Violence: Technologies of Memory in the Everyday

Among the victims, there could be found one merchant who cheats, and one who is honest and who did not cheat. Perhaps he was the kind who preferred sons to daughters. Among the victims, there could be found one who is conservative and who frowns in his home, but is joyful and humorous outside the home, and one who is arrogant and one who is kind, one who is courageous and truthful and one who is a coward and a liar, sometimes. One who is loving and generous and who is at times resentful. Many were planning for the hajj next year, and many were falsifying their taxes and hoarding capital. Among the victims there is one who spent money to show off his hospitality and one who spent in the way of good … It is said that many issued from good families and that many came from the rabble. Among them were those who did not pay their debts and those awaiting their dues … And, among them, there were teenagers who did not have the chance to be fathers, but their sin was great, their enthusiasm was their death, their death was because their parents taught them that hot blood is dignity and that chivalry is dignity and they acted as they were taught, and they were killed and buried … They were all like other people who live on earth. How many? It was said 30,000 and it was said 40,000. Although the difference between the two numbers is wide, the word thousands is small if compared to the humiliation and oppression that was engraved in the memories of the people and city. (al-Sarraj 2012, 150)

Al-Sarraj's latest novel '*Asi al-Dam*, published after the 2011 Uprising, returns to the period of the Hama events. This time, however, the work of remembering takes the form of a social documentary akin to an ethnography of life before, during and after violence that is life-shattering. '*Asi al-Dam* is a social-memory-making exercise, a narrative as practice of social memory, of living with the past or managing it, as discussed by Elizabeth Jelin (2003). '*Asi al-Dam* does not fall easily into only one genre such as historical novel or social history. For instance, it has elements of realist documentary with reference to actual places, events and real-life figures. Events are named. They are 'the Events' – the Hama Events. However, as a narrative, it is ethnographic in its telling of the everyday life of ordinary people, depicting alley and neighbourhood life, and families' quotidian interactions and relations. Life in the everyday is brought out vividly as different subjects are observed and as they self-reflect on their surroundings and social relations. The trail begins with Fouad's family, comprising Fouad – a merchant in the traditional *suq* – his wife Su'ad – a devout woman – and their eight children: five daughters, Fida', Samar, Bushra, Ghada and Lina, and three sons, Ayman, Mukhlis and Rabi'. The family's life, a social microcosm, allows a view of markets, schools, underground movements, fashionable dissidence and youth aspirations in a conservative religious environment. In a sense, there is life in both its fullness and its fragility. The ordinariness of life is shattered in the spectacular violence visited upon the city and the people. It is ordinariness that characterises the moment the city and its people were struck on 2 February 1982.

The power of the narrative is precisely in telling the history of small things, the horror of violence as it touches these small things and, to use Veena Das' (2009) words, as it folds into the everyday and descends into the ordinary. Al-Sarraj tells of this descent, of how the violence becomes inscribed in the mundane as, for example, when the residents of Hama name a type of bread 'the bread of the events' (*khubz al-ahdath*), because it was the only bread available when the city was assaulted and was put under curfew. Families learned how to store it and keep it for

a long period. The events become a marker of time and space in relation to which individual and collective lives are emplotted (narration of
life along a temporality defined by the events: life before and life after).
Emblematic discursive frames and references marked everyday speech.
For example, women who remained unmarried were described as having
lost their possible suitors during the events ('*adalha rah fi al-ahdath*);
family histories and kin relations were drawn around connections to
members who perished in the events.

The socialisation and the domestication of memories took shape
through everyday practices, in multiple ways of living them. In the
recollections of an exiled Hamawi:

> I did not witness the killing, slaughter and rape, though I am a witness to
> everything else. Who said that massacres are concluded with the end of killing,
> slaughter and rape? I witnessed Hama through my mother's daily prayer-
> bead supplication, 'O merciful One' ... as she spoke of my grandfather's
> love and kindness and of his death under torture ... I witnessed it in my
> grandmother's tears as she recalled her son who was killed in front of her eyes ...
> [I witnessed it] in my mother's avoidance of preparing rice *halwa* (sweet rice) so
> as not to remind my grandmother of her missing son for whom she had made the
> *halwa* on the day he departed. (Summayya 2012)

These recollections identify mundane activities as embodied practices
of memory: viscerally felt and shared sorrow, prayer-bead supplication
and abstaining from making a favoured sweet so as not to invite further
sorrow.

In his work on violence in Northern Ireland, Allen Feldman (2003)
notes the entanglement of violence with memory. Feldman observes that
violence serves as a reminder of power's injunctions. It inscribes itself on
the body and mind such that its object can forget neither the violence nor
the lessons to be derived from it. The bodily markings and inscriptions
of violence are formative of the subject, a form of disciplining and
subjectivation. Feldman's informant spoke of beatings and the breaking
of knees as practices intended to inscribe on the victims the lesson that
should never be forgotten. The social memories of Hama similarly point
to a pedagogy of violence. The practices of violence to which Hamawis
were subjected belong to a pedagogy of rule wherein bodily inscriptions
are used to teach lessons that would not be forgotten. In reflecting on the
subjectivities formed through violence, it is important to take note of how
bodily inscribed technologies of memories come to inhabit the everyday
through mundane practices and affective dispositions as captured in the
words of the Hamawi exile quoted above.

'*Asi al-Dam* illuminates for us, through characters such as Mukhlis
and Ghada, how embodied memories of humiliation are the key to

understanding the subjectivities formed through practices of violence and debasement. In the case of Mukhlis, he is left shattered and unhinged after personal encounters with the security services. Mukhlis is broken by the pain of humiliation during interrogation. He maintains silence about his experience of torture and about his degradation when, along-side other survivors of the massacre, he is forced to participate in a rally in support of Hafez al-Asad. After he goes into exile, he remains unable to reconstitute himself, ends up in a refugee compound in England and suffers mental breakdown.

In '*Asi al-Dam*, the subjects are transformed and remade by the violence and by their memories and shared experiences of humiliation. For one of the family's younger daughters, Ghada, the transformation culminates in her suicide. She takes her own life after being solicited by the security services to act as an informant. She commits suicide in a sleepwalking fashion as an ending in a cinematic reel of subjugation. The personal defeat and the societal defeat merge: Ghada's failure as a grown-up woman to find ground on which to stand in her search for friends and intimacy, connects with her early childhood defeat in the face of an abusive and authoritarian primary school teacher. Her Ba'thist schooling leaves her alienated and yearning for inclusion. Her inability to find anchor in her social surrounding is tied to her exposure to the workings of power at the micro level and the sense of abjectness that the encounters with regime agents elicit in her. Ghada's emotionality and silent volatility are not an instance of individual pathos intrinsic or unique to her. Rather, they are socially and politically induced by the manner in which violence permeates the mundane and quotidian and, at times, becomes inescapable. Thus, the absence of escape routes in Ghada's lived reality leads her to a final act of evasion. When she is recruited by the security forces to write reports on her university colleagues, she escapes in a journey to death.

In Mukhlis and Ghada, we encounter subjects who hide inside themselves and, in the process, their life comes to a standstill, halting at the traumatic moments, which they can no longer overcome or transcend. It may therefore be argued that Ghada's and Mukhlis' fate should be understood as symptomatic of severe trauma that was not treated and hence not overcome. However, for others who survived the afterlife of violence and seemingly cope with it, feelings of fear and humiliation are structuring their lives. These feelings orient a pact of silence among the city residents, within families, between neighbours and friends. This silence deepens the sense of isolation and marginality. One of my Hamawi interviewees stated that there was no trust in speech, and words and talk could not be trusted anymore: 'You do not talk so that the words would not come out. No one wanted to speak.' At the same time, there is a 'feeling of humiliation and of being broken, having to accept the power of the security services, to accept that this is fate (*iqrar bi ana hadha huwa al-qadar*)' (interview with a Hamawi in exile, December 2011). This forced resignation to the injustice suffered is experienced as humiliation and, indeed, the performance of this resignation entrenches this feeling. An aspect of this performance entails complicity with the official account of the violence in order to receive material reparation for the destroyed homes. The required display of loyalty through demonstrations and rallies in support of the president deepens the alienation and dissonance between the humiliated subject's public enactments and her silenced self.

Many Hamawis are inhabited by the memory of the beatings, humiliation and torture during detention and interrogation. Humiliation and abjection were aversive emotive terms used by Hamawis to describe how the experiences of violence shaped them. For the contemporaries of the massacres, the violence was a violation of all that is humanly sacred. The idea that the city was rendered an open space of violation (*istibahat al-madinat*) was most often articulated in reflections on the events and was closely linked with a sense of humiliation and abjection felt widely beyond Hama. Impunity for perpetrators during the assault and its aftermath had a profound impact on ordinary citizens throughout the country.

Humiliation and exposure to regime violence, as constitutive of selfhood and social memory, extend beyond Hama. The memory of the violence of the events has, in some sense, become a constitutive element of Syrian subjectivities in vague recollections and in the social imaginary writ large (as in statements such as 'they will do Hama again'). Indeed, during the Uprising, there was a strong feeling that Hama had been nationalised. Homs became Hama, as did Dar'a. Hama became the prototype event. Additionally, while in 1982 Hama experienced the most brutal massacres, other cities and towns were also subject to tremendous violence including massacres of smaller scale, but having deep and long-lasting impact.

At the beginning of the 2011 Uprising, when the city of Dar'a was under siege and the news filtered through of the unspeakable punishment meted out against the protesters, one of my interlocutors, originally from al-Suwayda, recalled an earlier incident of violence in her city. With much sorrow, she recounted a clampdown on a protest in al-Suwayda in 2000 in which twenty people were killed. She underlined how the incident was blotted out from public memory and only a few individuals outside al-Suwayda knew it took place. In her words, such experiences left 'pockets of open wounds' (*bu'ar jarh*) throughout the country. These wounds, caused by the acts of violence, remain open after the acts as illustrated in the comments made about al-Suwayda and as the narratives of Hama attest. If, in the making of social memory, '"history" is a register of concurrent claims' (McDougall 2010, 47), we need to pay attention to the differentiated grounds on which the practices of remembering take place (as noted at the beginning of the chapter). The recollections of those implicated in the violence or closely associated with the agents of violence, unfold in different modalities than the ones expressed by those engaged in remembering to recover a life by combating silence and mutedness.

Multiple Syrian Pasts in the Work of Memory

More than competing claims to legitimacy and truth, social memory opens a horizon of remembrances and recollections in which claims to recognition of different pasts and their interconnections are raised. I illustrate this point by discussing, briefly, the works of memory that narrate other pasts and their events of violence and that also, somehow, attempt to bind together their fragile threads. Other pasts of violence are recalled in narratives of the historical persecution of the Alawi community and of the massacres that are a constitutive element of the Alawi community's social imaginary. Works of recollection, such as Samar Yazbek's novel *In Her Mirrors* (*Laha Marayya*), show other pasts existing in tension with the present, competing with it, and defying chronological time. Against the backdrop of a love affair between a high-ranking officer and an actress, both Alawi from the Sahel region, Yazbek's narrative underscores how the past lives in the present. Leila, the actress, believes in the transmigration of souls and recounts stories of previous lives that she lived. One of her earlier lives was during the rule of the Ottoman Sultan, Selim, when a massacre against her community in Aleppo was committed. Leila's past selves seek a hearing and a presence. *In Her Mirrors* opens the gates of other histories. The multiple lives of Leila convey the synchronicity of historical times – parallel times running together and defying chronological time.

Yazbek's narration does not offer a history of Alawi persecution as a way of explaining or justifying the abuse of power by Alawi officers in government. The recollections, in some sense, open a dialogue between differing and competing social imaginaries and communities of memories within a national political community. In this respect, Yazbek's project is not one of competing victimhood unlike other writings on Alawi identity. For instance, Ubay Hassan's 2009 book offering meditations on his identity can be said to fall within the parameters of victim outbidding. Yet his work is nonetheless instructive of the lines of contest in the history-memory dyad. Hassan (2009, 7) treats the persecution of a group or an individual on the basis of religious or ethnic affiliation as a constitutive element of identity. Critical of what he considers as imposed silence about the history of Alawi persecution prior to the Baʻthist take-over in 1963, he stresses the impact of discrimination on the epistemic and psychological constitution of the group and on its identity forma-tion (Hassan 2009, 71). He bemoans Sunni recollections of the Hama massacres and the events of violence while the history of Alawi persecution remains unrecalled (Hassan 2009, 78). For Hassan, Alawi consciousness and imaginary retain discriminatory pronouncements and practices of previous ages, from the *fatwas* of Ibn Taymiyya in the fourteenth century, to massacres committed under Ottoman rule beginning in the fifteenth and sixteenth centuries, to forced conversion to Sunni Islam in the nine-teenth century. Hassan's recall of the history of persecution is, in part, undertaken as an outbidding of claims of suffering made in reference to the Hama massacre. He reviews a number of massacres of Alawis before asking why other groups, including the Muslim Brotherhood, com-memorate their massacres, but the Alawis do not commemorate theirs (Hassan 2009, 87). Hassan then advances the view that this may be the case because the Alawi community has transcended its wounds and that effecting a detachment from the history of violence is required of other groups (Hassan 2009, 87). Yet Hassan sets the violence suffered by the Alawis in the past as an element of community identity that necessitates recognition by others.

Hassan's claims for recognition arise against contestations of Alawi social and historical memory of persecution. Such contestations are undertaken by some Syrians in their denouncement of practices of vio-lence by the regime. A denial of Alawi memories is carried out in the pro-cess of delegitimising the regime. The mere mention of or referral to the Alawi experience of discrimination is construed as an attempt to excuse regime violence, as if admitting earlier historical injustice that befell the Alawi community would amount to accepting and justifying the atroci-ties committed by the regime. This problematic and, ultimately, hurtful judgement or verdict can be discerned in the reaction to writings that deny Alawi persecution. For example, Syrian writer Ibrahim al-Jabin's article entitled *The Myth of the Alawi Holocaust* (2011), refuting claims of Alawi massacres committed under Ottoman rule, was read by a number of my interlocutors as a mocking and belittling of Alawi selfhood.

In the making of community, multiple pasts compete for telling, for recognition and for understanding. In interviews on the memories of Hama, the narratives inevitably were about entangled histories and unsettled accounts of the past. One of the recurrent themes in the

recollections of the Hama events by Hamawis referred to an existing
Alawi vendetta against Hama (the city). One of my interviewees from
Hama referred to Alawi persecution in various historical periods. He
related an eighteenth-century historical episode of Alawi rebellion
against the Barazi family landlords who responded by beheading Alawi
men (interview with Ghiyath, Beirut, 2012). The more recent history of
relations between Alawis and Sunnis in Hama was often woven into the
recollections. Tareq recalled his grandmother saying that the rural Alawis
living in destitute conditions will take revenge on Sunnis in Hama. Yet
he questioned any claim to a special history of persecution by the Alawis
in reference to the oppression that they suffered at the hands of large
landowning Hamawi families. He said that his mother still remembered
that most Sunni families did not dare to walk by the homes of the rich
families. In other words, they too – Sunni-Hamawis – were subject to
oppression. Similarly, in her accounts, Manhal al-Sarraj notes Hamawis'
antipathy to the outsiders (al-barawiyya). She observes that Hamawis
were known to say that during the day Hama was unbearable because
it was full of outsiders. 'Outsiders' refers, here, to Alawi villagers who
originally came to the city to sell produce and, later, came to work as
government employees. Stories of separation and prejudice lay below
the tensions and fears. A common anecdote is that of Alawis coming
to the city and being mocked for their peasant attire and their dialect.
Although the history and memories of Alawi persecution are contested,
their experience of social and economic subordination is not denied.[11]

Conclusion

What do these struggles in social memory, in general, and the memories
of violence, in particular, tell us about the structuring of Syrian politics
and the fault lines of conflict and negotiation? In his study of communal
violence in India at the time of partition, Gyanendra Pandey (2001)
concludes that memories of violence enter into the making of community. In the same vein, memories of Hama are constitutive of a community of subjects of humiliation, whose lives were stifled or, in the words
of Manhal al-Sarraj, 'became still' (interview, Stockholm, 4 December
2011). The memories, muted as they have been, feed into sentiments of
grievance and a deep-rooted sense of discrimination – a sense that a historical wrong remains unrecognised and that no atonement or reparation
has been attempted.

---

[11] See Worren (2007) for an account of how narratives of Alawi history enter into the construction of contemporary Alawi identity.

The memories of the violence of Hama and the history/memory of Alawi persecution are not only memories in this drama of present pasts, living pasts, which are not lived with or 'inhabited comfortably', in McDougall's (2010) terms. I suggest that the tensions of memory practices and memory construction bring into question ideas of the nation and of belonging that were thought to have been settled with the establishment of the nation-state and the drawing of national territorial boundaries. During the Uprising, however, the question of the nation came acutely to the fore again. This is poignantly manifest when, in the face of the current violence, Manhal al-Sarraj asks: 'How is it that some sons of the nation do this to other sons of the nation?' This issue has pre-occupied Syrians prior to the Uprising, and since.

5   The Performativity of Violence and 'Emotionalities of Rule' in the Syrian Uprising

By most accounts, the March 2011 Uprising began as a series of peaceful protests against the persistence of authoritarian modes of government under the regime of Bashar al-Asad (see Ismail 2011; Leenders and Heydemann 2012). It is worth recalling here that the immediate catalyst for the nationwide protests were acts of body-centred cruelty and violence inflicted by the security services on a group of schoolchildren in the city of Dar 'a in southern Syria. The children were taken into custody for having written, on a wall of their school, the slogan of uprisings elsewhere in the region: '[T]he people want to bring down the regime.' It was reported that to punish and discipline the children, the security men of a local security branch pulled out the children's fingernails. The children were also detained for a period of time. Protests organised against the violation of the children's bodily integrity took place in Dar 'a and were immediately repressed by police and regime security forces using live ammunition. In solidarity with Dar 'a, protests and marches in other towns and cities were organised. These were also met with a violent response on the part of state security, including live gunfire. Although the regime and its supporters claimed that the Uprising was armed from its inception, the forms of protest that took place in the first six months were largely peaceful. In the face of the regime's use of extreme violence, the Uprising was gradually militarised and, subsequently, became increasingly violent. This militarisation of the opposition began with the formation of the Free Syrian Army – composed of defectors from the regular army – and the gradual taking up of arms by civilians.

My purpose in probing the Syrian Uprising in this chapter is not to chronicle events with a view to giving any kind of general account (for example, of the descent into war between the regime and segments of the population). Rather, I propose to use particular events of the Uprising to elucidate facets of the politics of violence in Syria that, while discussed in earlier chapters, are further crystallised in figurations of the violence enacted during and since the Uprising. One of the key arguments put forward in previous chapters is that violence and the memory of violence have been structuring factors in everyday politics in Syria, in the forms of rule and in the relations between rulers and ruled. In this chapter I argue that this politics is grounded in and expressive of a particular style of government that works through the affect and that elicits cognitive and affective states formative of Syrian political subjectivities. Specifically, I want to focus on the performative structure of violence. Relatedly, my aim is to show how the performativity of violence has elicited feelings and understandings mediated by the social and political configurations of rule. The sense of performativity used here underscores the artifice of acts of violence. In the first instance, violence *performs* by communicating political messages and producing meanings. Relatedly, it performs by acting on its victims and perpetrators. Performances of violence generate ways of thinking, feeling and relating to the world. Thus, the performativity of violence is materialised through its formative powers. At the same time, performativity derives meanings from the work consummated and from the narrative structure of performances, that is, from the emplotment of violent acts. As performances are imbricated in processes of subjectivation, their enactments and formative powers extend beyond their immediate outcome to the interpretative horizons they shape and to the manner in which they are lived and recalled.

Of the myriad forms of violence that have been enacted during the Uprising, the massacre and body-centred violations emerge as foremost among what may be termed affective technologies of government. These technologies are at work in the use of massacres to produce two particular effects: to enhance other forms of staging horror and to incite, in the subject, ways of feeling about and ways of understanding events, reality and her/his own positionality in the web of power. This chapter approaches the massacre as a spectacular instance of performative violence aimed at destroying an enemy group, targeting mostly unarmed members of the group but also, in some cases, fighters or armed personnel who are surrendering. By virtue of its targets and methods, the massacre often unfolds as an intimate practice of violence. My discussion of the massacre as a technique of government engages with theorisations of extreme violence, in particular of mass killings. These theorisations range from the socio-political dialectic framework advanced by Stathis Kalyvas (2003) and Jacques Sémelin (2003), among others, to the psychoanalytic explorations of Begoña Aretxaga (2000a, 2000b).

My analysis of the massacre and other acts of extreme violence offers certain analytics to grasp their nature and rationalities – analytics that would be useful for thinking about and theorising other cases of spectacular violence. I suggest 'horror' and 'the uncanny' represent analytical constructs for apprehending regime politics of extreme and spectacular violence and the affective and cognitive dispositions, which certain forms of body-centred violence engender, and how these underpin rationalities of rule. These constructs (horror and the uncanny) furnish us with analytic resources to interpret key events that capture what could be seen as a subtext of the form of rule that ordinary Syrians grasped but, perhaps, pushed to the margins of their everyday lives.

The chapter is organised along two axes. The first axis gives central focus to questions on the horror quality of violence. This refers to the staging and iteration of violence in a mode that engenders particular affective responses. As discussed in the Introduction, horror often entails a body-centred transgressive act that elicits affective and cognitive responses and dispositions, especially fear, dread, bewilderment and disorientation. To elucidate the affective and cognitive generative structure of horror, I examine an episode of political killing that took place during the early days of the Uprising. The episode serves to highlight the role of both the narrative and emplotment of events, and the affective states that are generated in the subject-citizens cum spectators. The second axis of enquiry addresses, specifically, the place of the massacre within the politics of horror. In this respect, I hone in on the performative and processual dimensions of massacres, paying attention to the aesthetics and semiotics of particular acts of violence carried out within the frame of massacres.

Horror in Regime–Citizen Relations: The Murder and Resurrection of Zaynab al-Hosni

Particular episodes of violence crystallise the workings of horror in the Syrian regime's management of violence and in Syrians' interpretative frames as witnesses and actors interpellated through specific performances of violence. These episodes reveal horror as an emotionality of government. By this, I refer to a form of government understood as an assemblage of techniques and ways of operation that are productive of horror affects. Relatedly, as discussed in the Introduction, I am concerned to develop the analytical import of the political uncanny as a category of affective experiences. To illustrate, I take the murder and resurrection of Zaynab al-Hosni as a paradigmatic case of an event whose circumstances became mired in uncertainty, ghoulishness and paradox to the extent that the real and unreal were no longer discernible or knowable. The violence of this case and the manner of its emplotment generated experiences of the uncanny – not as the return of the repressed at the subconscious level, but in the awareness and sensing of the dangers and unspeakable horror that lurk behind a circumstance of murder and resurrection.

In late September 2011, opposition websites and Facebook pages of Syrian dissidents carried a report of the murder, at the hands of regime security forces, of a young woman in her late teens or early twenties named Zaynab al-Hosni. From the details given in the report, the murder was violent, resulting from gruesome and shocking acts. Al-Hosni's dismembered body was found at a public hospital in the city of Homs. It was handed over to her mother when she went to the hospital morgue to identify the body of one of her sons, an anti-regime activist who was killed by security men. At the morgue, the mother was shown a body with severed limbs and a burnt face and was informed that the body belonged to her daughter Zaynab. She, and another son who was accompanying her, picked up the body parts, prepared the body for burial and subsequently buried it.

This case of body desecration and the violation of its integrity brought to the fore the production of body-centred horror as a dimension of the politics of horror. The dismemberment elicited widespread reactions of revulsion and condemnation. The images and narratives spoke to the worst suspicions and fears about regime violence. Out of sympathy and indignation, many dissidents and activists adopted the photo of al-Hosni as their Facebook moniker – an act that may have been intended to convey the message 'we are all Zaynab al-Hosni'. The straightforward narrative of the murder – nightmarish in various respects – went awry when, on 4 October 2011, state media challenged the account and 'produced' or 'conjured up', live on Syrian television, a living Zaynab al-Hosni in interview. The regime's objective in presenting the alternative account was, without doubt, to discredit the opposition. Yet, beyond that, it engendered uncertainty whereby, for many, the real and illusory became indistinguishable. Ambiguity, indeterminacy and shock are all characteristic elements of the horror template as identified, developed and deployed in films of the horror and film noir genre. The uncertainty and disorientation triggered through narratives of horror are caused by an epistemic deficit – a lack of knowledge needed to obtain or reach a coherent understanding of events and, in turn, a fear of what unknown, sinister forces lurk behind them (see Hills 2005).

In interview, Zaynab al-Hosni would deny that she had been arrested by the security forces and, instead, asserted that she left her family home because she was being bullied by her brothers. Al-Hosni's appearance on TV distorted the view for Syrians as both spectators of and actors in the unfolding conflict. It was no longer possible to get a clear picture of 'the real' or 'the truth' of events or to attain certainty about the occurrences being presented. Further, the episode incited feelings of the uncanny in the subject-citizens cum spectators, tapping into their familiarity with the repertoires of regime violence.

The Political Uncanny

The TV appearance or apparition of Zaynab al-Hosni prompted multiple questions: Who, in fact, was the person whose body had been dismembered? If it was not Zaynab's body, then whose was it? Was the woman who was interviewed on Syrian TV the real Zaynab or was she a lookalike? On Facebook pages and on internet blogs, members of the opposition as well as ordinary citizens were baffled and bewildered. Counter-narratives circulated, some asserting that the TV Zaynab was a fake or an imposter. As in a horror show or a film noir movie, the spectators – i.e. subject-citizens – gathered the visual and narrative clues to interpret the intrusion of the monstrous into the real. The TV Zaynab, some subject-spectators pointed out, had a different dialect than that of the real Zaynab (who spoke with a dialect typical of residents of Homs). For others, the TV Zaynab looked like the real Zaynab, but there were slight physiognomic differences. For example, it was said that the temples and forehead of the TV Zaynab were wider and her eyes more slanted than those of the 'real' Zaynab. The recourse to the idea of doubling to explain the staged resurrection of the publicly declared dead evokes one of Freud's instantiations of the uncanny, namely 'the double' or 'doppelganger'. The subject-spectators, disbelieving the case as confirming the return of a primitive belief – namely, the belief in the return of the dead – appear to have called upon another instance of the uncanny, that of the double, as a more plausible one. What I want to emphasise, here, is that the psychic frame for grasping the disturbing event arises out of a familiarity with the regime's register and repertoire of staging events to create incongruity and bewilderment. The real was fictionalised. There was a mystery murder and mystery resurrection surrounded by murky details.

The enigmatic tale of al-Hosni, in which the real and illusionary became difficult to distinguish, baffled Syrians whether as actors in the drama or as spectators and viewers of its unfolding. Significantly, Zaynab's mother gave an interview on an Al Jazeera news programme in which she conveyed her state of puzzlement and uncertainty (see Al Jazeera Satellite TV 2012). She expressed confusion over whether the young woman interviewed on Syrian state television as her daughter Zaynab was, indeed, her daughter. She asked, in bewilderment, if the living woman was her daughter, then whose dismembered body had she collected at the hospital morgue? The mother's concurrent statements that the girl was not her daughter, and that the girl may be the real Zaynab, and her uncertainty about the body that she believed to be that of her daughter, were imbued with a mixture of doubt and hope. At the same time, her own experience of horror reinforced the uncertainty in the minds of Syrians drawn in as spectators. The affective and cognitive conditions engendered by the murder and resurrection of al-Hosni presents what, in theorisations of horror, is referred to as 'object-directed horror' and 'objectless horror' (Hills 2005). On one hand, fear is provoked by an existing object that references body-transgressive acts of cruelty and brutality – the object, here, being the decapitated body handed over to the mother, and shown in YouTube videos. On the other hand, dread and anxiety are engendered by the narrative indeterminacy and uncertainty of the events – in this case, murder and then the undoing of murder through 'resurrection'.

The episode, in all of its details, was imprinted with surreal and nightmarish qualities: the 'accidental' handing over to the mother of body parts that she was led to believe belonged to her daughter Zaynab; Zaynab then appearing alive on TV; the murdered Zaynab in the figure of the dismembered body given to her family and shown on YouTube; the mother's inability to identify her daughter with certainty; the ambiguities in Zaynab's own account, on TV, of her disappearance. An added twist to this tale of horror was the circulation of a video, on YouTube, of an interview with Zaynab's brother speaking of how activists from the opposition had used his family in a bid to make political capital out of the murder of Zaynab and then abandoned the family, presumably as the regime took control of the narrative. Then the interview was seized upon by the pro-regime side as evidence of the fabrications of the opposition. With this last instalment, the circularity of the narrative was achieved.

The material and ideological structure of the political uncanny is manifest in a mode of operation that creates and leaves unresolved the bewilderment and disturbance experienced by subjects because of the blurring of lines between the real and the fictional. The denial of a resolution enabling subjects to establish the true nature of events is understood as a default style of governing. The mystery of the al-Hosni case requires information, accounting and explanation that would, by necessity, remain in abeyance. The questions raised by the regime-staged apparition of the real Zaynab could not be addressed within ordinary frames of explanation. The information required to answer these questions was out of reach and, in a sense, was in the purview of an omniscient power beyond the reach of the citizens. The horror in this episode pertains not only to the body-centred violence that befell the retrospectively unknown and unnamed victim. Rather, Zaynab's family and fellow citizens find themselves confronted with the threatening intrusion into their 'world of common reality' of implausible occurrences for which no narrative resolution can be achieved. The denial of resolution is mandated by the political order. The disconcerting feelings, bewilderment and fear that the citizens experience in this out-of-kilter universe are experiences of the political uncanny. The puzzles and mystery of the case are, in themselves, the work of mystifying powers that feel no compulsion to resolve incongruities.

The response to the 'resurrection' of al-Hosni illuminates facets of the Syrian polity, of the state and regime and of interaction among citizens. Along with the dismembered body and charred face and head, there were interpretative schemes and explanatory frames designed to render the horror decipherable. Important among the readings and interpretations was the idea that the entire event was staged by the regime: the severed body was delivered to the al-Hosni family with the anticipation that the opposition would adopt the story as an example of regime atrocity and thereby be tricked into publicising and decrying regime conduct only to have the story turned upside down, its circumstances disputed and falsified. In this tale of trickery, the regime aims at showing the opposition to be peddling a falsehood or at least to be incapable of telling and knowing the truth. The regime, as an auteur, is thereby engaged in a *mise-en-scène* of horror with a farcical subtext.

Proceeding on the basis of the idea of staging, an anti-regime blogger, known as 'the Syrian Infiltrator' (al-Mundasa al-Suriyya 2011), stated that the emplotment encountered in this murder-resurrection mystery was, indeed, anticipated. The blogger drew parallels with an earlier episode of political staging at the time of the assassination, in 2005, of Lebanese Prime Minister Rafiq al-Hariri and the subsequent Mehles Investigation into the assassination. The blogger reminded the readers that the surrealism of politics in Syria and the hallucinatory character of regime–citizen relations pre-date the Uprising. He referred, in particular, to the episode involving Houssam Houssam, a Syrian citizen who was called to testify as a witness in the Hariri assassination enquiry. Houssam had been enlisted by the Mehles investigators as a witness who had incontrovertible information implicating Syrian regime figures in the assassination. However, before he could give his testimony, he escaped from Lebanon back to Syria and declared that he had been coerced by the investigators. Following his return, Houssam gave hours of TV interviews narrating the foreign plot against Syria and his role in the collapse of the investigation – a role for which he was heralded as a national hero. Houssam's story was not only met with scepticism on the part of the political opposition, but was viewed with both suspicion and ridicule by many ordinary citizens (based on interviews with Syrians in Damascus in 2005). The televised interviews with Houssam and the tale spun around his role as witness and his escape were approached as a fantastical production by the regime and the state security agencies. On this occasion, the state is thought of as an auteur of a particular genre (see Aretxaga 2000a, 2000b). Subject-citizens, as spectators, are knowledgeable of the workings of the genre in the repertoire of regime staging and theatre. Yet they are nonetheless horrified even when they are cognisant of the farcical elements of the production. Like spectators of a horror film, they anticipate the horror acts but, when the acts happen, they are still horrified.

The ambiguity in horror lies in the effects of the unreal and surreal and in the suspense related to the unknown. Murkiness and elusiveness elicit fear and horror and, in the process, are constitutive of the polity and political subjectivities. The staging of horror contains farcical elements – occurrences are unbelievable, but still elicit a sense of the macabre and of being destabilised nonetheless. Ironic comments made in response to the televised interview with al-Hosni intimate recognition of the mix of the farcical and the horrifying. For example, following the interview dissidents called on the regime and security forces to bring back to life Hamza al-Khatib, and other youth killed by the security forces during the early period of the Uprising. While indicting the regime for murder, the episode was interpreted within the framework of a play of smoke and mirrors where the dead are resurrected.

The Politics of Massacre: Performative Violence

In my discussion in Chapter 1 of the place of the massacre in the structure of rule in Syria, I put forward the argument that the Asad regime, through the articulation of a discourse of patriotism, and through the deployment of technologies of violence, engendered a caesura – a break – in the body politic. The break that cut through society by means of the regime's articulations and violence instituted an 'us' and 'them' division into the domain of life, separating, along sometimes shifting ideological lines, 'those who must live and those who must die'. The violence of the late 1970s and early 1980s performed the fractioning of the population, with the 'us' identified as the pro-regime loyalists, and the 'them', or the enemy population, conceived and designated as the Muslim Brothers, their supporters and sympathisers, as well as all opponents of the regime.

The proposition that the massacre lay beneath the surface of political life was advanced by a number of Syrian intellectuals and activists and by ordinary citizens in reference to the political context in Syria.

As noted in an earlier chapter, during an interview in May 2011 a Damascene merchant commented to me that it was his conviction that, on his deathbed, Hafez al-Asad advised his sons 'to do Hama again' if their rule was ever challenged. Further, early in the Uprising at the end of March 2011, close observers of the regime spoke to me of the anticipation, among many, of the slaughter that the regime would unleash to end the protests. It may be said that such predictions, anticipations, fears and premonitions are limited to the conjuncture of the Uprising. Yet years earlier, in conversations I had with Syrians, they spoke of their anticipation of 'the massacre'. I recall filmmaker Ossama Mohammed's reflections on the ideas that animated the making of his 2002 film *Sacrifice* (*Sanduq al-Dunya*). In conversation, in April 2008, he stated to me that he was motivated by a desire to find an answer to the question: 'What is it that makes it possible that when the massacre needs you, you are always ready?' Mohammed looked for an answer in kin and patriarchal relations that cultivate dominance and hierarchy and that demand absolute loyalty from members of the group. He seemed to consider, as shown in his film, that there is an originary structure of violence that inheres in kin-type relations, which then forms the habitus of rule. Mohammed could be critiqued for postulating an ahistorical account of violence, but what is remarkable is the fact that he, like many other Syrians, lived in anticipation of the massacre.

A similar quest for understanding the permanent state of war that lay beneath the surface was evident in the words of writer Mundhir Badr Hallum, speaking at a public seminar on his literary work held at the IFPO in Damascus in January 2011. In his address, he spoke of the retrenchment, under the rule of the Ba'th and al-Asad, of culture as an edifying realm of life. This, in his view, caused a regression to a state of primitive monstrosity (*al-insilakh ila al-wahsh*) (Hallum, Damascus, 10 January 2011). Hallum's prognosis expresses a certain kind of idealism that arises out of a belief in the 'civilising' role of the cultural works of independent citizenry, particularly its writers and artists. This idealism notwithstanding, Hallum, like Ossama Mohammed, and a host of other artists and writers, undertook over the decade prior to the Uprising to explore, through cultural productions, the conditions that enabled the eruption of extreme violence in the past and that could foretell its possible eruption in the future. The imaginary of violence that these cultural figures represented through their work and reflections seems, in retrospect, to have been anticipating the gradual descent into war that occurred with the 2011 Uprising. Proceeding from the imaginary of 'a massacre foretold', I want to probe further the political fields of action expressed through and constituted by the massacre. I do so, first, by revisiting some of the explanatory frameworks developed in the literature on civil war and extreme violence wherein massacres structure the interaction between warring parties.

The search for causes and motivating factors and for facilitating conditions has come to represent an important preoccupation in writings on extreme violence and massacres. The approaches pursued in these writings have been classified according to the variables that they privilege in accounting for the causes driving social and political forces to participate in acts of mass killing. For instance, Jacques Sémelin (2003), in a discussion of the vocabularies of massacre, identified 'top-down' and 'bottom-up' explanatory frames: those that locate actors and motives as residing in the upper echelons of state and government and those that place perpetrators in their local contexts. Similarly, Stathis Kalyvas (2003) engages with the alignment of explanatory frames into two opposing camps: those upholding an abstract conception of political violence as unfolding along the lines of the Schmidtian dyad of the friend and enemy, and those adopting a Hobbesian outlook on mass killings as the expression of the intrinsic anarchic character of the social world. Both Sémelin and Kalyvas suggest that top-down and bottom-up variables interconnect and should be examined. They concur that local conflicts erupt when a given regime is challenged by armed insurrectionary groups. An abstract political conflict, involving a struggle for power between rulers and challengers at the top of the political structure, would give impetus to bottom-up violence for resuming localised collective disputes or for settling private accounts.[1] Criminal activities of looting find an outlet through killings and brutal acts at the time of such conflicts. Inversely, local-level conflicts may spur the eruption of generalised war drawing in the rulers. As will be discussed below, these broad outlines of how to account for extreme violence, and massacres in particular, illuminate aspects of the violence that broke out in Syria as the Uprising mutated. However, the interpretative frame I seek to develop here aims at getting at an analytic of massacre, as technique, in the governmentality of violence. In other words, I am particularly concerned with how the massacre is a *techne* in the emotionality of rule, operating on the affect and on cognition and productive of political fields of action and of languages of communication. Towards this end, I turn to explorations of the affective structure of extreme violence.

As discussed by Cavarero (2011) and Humphrey (2002), body-undoing violence is a core feature of horror. Additionally, however, the

[1] For a discussion of these dynamics, see Tilly (2003).

analysis of horror-type violence must take account of its performative structure and the terms of its narrativisation. Through signifying acts and emplotment of violence, horror addresses the affective and cognitive structures of subjects positioned as victims, as spectators or as potential victims. In other words, narrativisation and discursivity flesh out the communicative and rhetorical powers of violence. Communicative fields of violence extend beyond the acts of physical harm inflicted on victims. They also encompass the narratives that emplot the violence. Narrative work is undertaken by perpetrators, survivors, witnesses and bystanders, and by reporters and investigators. To understand the horror effects of violence we need to bring into the account the narrative acts and the emplotments of events undertaken by these diverse actors. In this respect, the distinction made between the horror genre of film or the novel (referred to as 'art-horror'), on one hand, and 'natural' horror, on the other, does not hold. This distinction is made on the basis that art horror is packaged and produced and that natural horror is experienced by victims in an unmediated fashion (see Hills 2005, 132–3). Yet the production of real horror involves staging, as well as a series of acts that are strung together and invested with significations and follow a plan or a plot with intended outcomes. Acts that are experienced by victim-subjects also have a narrative and discursive order that acquire meanings and interpretations through further narrativisation and discursive articulations in the accounts given by protagonists and observers alike.

Generalised War

In pursuing the objective of crushing the opposition and stifling protest in the very early days of the Uprising, the regime deployed military force on a large scale, moving armoured divisions to areas that witnessed widespread oppositional mobilisation. In Dar 'a, where the first large protests took place, the army's Fourth Division was moved into the city very soon after the large demonstrations began (see Human Rights Watch 2011). The army blockaded nearby villages and towns, laid siege to mosques, where people typically gathered before and after protests, blocked roads, and so on. Heavy firepower was used, resulting in many civilian deaths. The regime's justification for resorting to this militarised response rested on the claim that it was fighting armed gangs. However, witness accounts of the events of Dar 'a state that the security forces fired live ammunition, not on armed gang members or insurgents, but on unarmed protesters and civilians taking part in funeral processions.

The military and security forces' pursuit of counter-insurgency tactics, in their aim to effectively bring an end to public protest, produced an outright state of war. In line with such tactics, the security forces and army instituted 'clearance' and 'cordon and search' operations. The setting up of checkpoints and the closure of towns and villages was accompanied by the cutting off of services such as water and electricity. This happened, for instance, in Dar 'a in April 2011 to force the end of the sit-in at the central mosque. Soon after, large-scale military operations were conducted in protest areas throughout the Syrian territory. Army and security divisions were also charged with putting down the demonstrations in Homs, Hama, rural Damascus, rural Aleppo, Idlib, Latakiyya, Banyas and Deir al-Zour. The armed forces replicated the same tactics in most of these areas, establishing checkpoints, closing off city neighbourhoods and entire towns and villages. Meanwhile, security forces continued to fire on public demonstrations which, at times, resulted in mass killings (for example, security men opened fire on a large crowd of protesters at the Clock Tower in Homs in April 2011, killing sixty-eight according to press reports).

As noted above, under conditions of siege and a state of warfare led by regime forces, a gradual militarisation of the Uprising took place. As defections started within the ranks of both conscripts and officers of the Syrian national military, oppositional militias began forming and operating out of areas where civilian protests were intense. In some places, such as the neighbourhoods of Baba Amro and Khaldiyya in Homs, civilians took up arms and joined defectors in militia formation with the objective of defending the protesters and their families against the security forces and the paramilitary groups that worked in conjunction with the regime (interviews with activists from Homs, Beirut, October 2015). In some locales, civilians joined armed groups when the regime-sponsored clientelist networks fell and the rebels took control of resources and oversaw the running of municipalities and local governing bodies (Darwish 2015; Lund 2016). As has been widely noted, splintering and divisions occurred between and among armed opposition groups, including the breaking up and reconstitution of alliances, interfactional rivalries and factional infighting. The influx of foreign fighters aligning with the opposition (broadly defined) or independently engaging in armed conflict with state forces is undoubtedly a factor that contributed to the shifting alliances and infighting among the local armed groups.

Disentangling and identifying the groupings lined up, ostensibly, on either 'side' of the conflict is beyond the remit of this work. Yet it is relevant and of concern to acknowledge both the plurality of actors drawn into the performances of violence, and the labour invested in casting these actors in one form or another. The pro-Asad local actors are cast as 'patriots' by the regime and as *shabiha* by the opposition groups.

Meanwhile, the anti-regime groups have been homogenised under the labels of 'Islamists' and 'Jihadists' and castigated as 'traitors'. These labels and categories occlude the differing positionalities of agents of violence. Local factors and situational variables complicate this rendering of the conflict in binary terms. Rumours in various localities spurred 'pre-emptive' violence by one group or set of groups against others constructed as the enemy, often located in neighbouring or adjacent city quarters or villages (e.g. in Barzeh and Ish al-Warwar in Damascus or in Bab al-Siba' and 'Akrama in Homs).

Notwithstanding the ambiguity and murkiness that render the identification of perpetrators difficult and that create the conditions of interchangeability of victims and perpetrators, the protagonists in the violence do not simply align into the neat categories of two sides: the regime and the opposition. This is the case, in part, because there is fragmentation on the two purported sides. The camp of 'loyalists', in alignment with the regime, is fractioned along organisational, institutional and regional lines and does not constitute a homogeneous or unified bloc or entity.[2] Thus the 'loyalist' groupings comprise the military security forces, paramilitary units such as the National Defence Forces, and amorphously organised Ba'th militia composed of students and party members. These formations are reported to be fighting among themselves.

Security forces and certain military divisions were associated with particular regional affiliations. This facilitated a first-order topographical alignment, positioning villages and districts in the coastal region and Hama's interior against regions hosting the opposition and armed rebel groups. A second-order alignment arises through acts of violence drawing lines between warring factions. An element of the theatrical staging and narrativisation of violence entails a contest over representations of the actors. For example, Alawis are produced along a continuum of images, emerging out of the theatre of war, ranging from patriots to thugs. Needless to say, these characterisations occlude the Alawis' historical ensnarement as conscript communities and buffers for the regime. In addition, the shadow networks connected with the regime became recruiting grounds for militias. Through their historical, political and socio-economic positioning, Alawis were drawn, on the rulers' side, into the civil war regime long before the Uprising. This does not mean that they are either puppets of the regime or uniformly supportive

---

[2] See Kheder Khaddour's (2015) account of the social divisions among 'loyalists' of the Damascus neighbourhoods of Ish al-Warwar and Dahiya-t al-Asad. These divisions may explain the lack of involvement by Dahiya residents in the 'Ish al-Warwar conflict with anti-regime groups in Barzeh.

of it. Indeed, some youths from the Alawi community rejected military conscription and went into hiding in their villages or left the country (communication with Alawi dissidents from Jableh). Nonetheless, the implication of segments of the Alawi community in the apparatuses of violence supporting the regime stokes fears, and drives greater alignment of Alawis with the regime via the National Defence Forces (NDF) – a paramilitary force set up by the regime to supplement the Syrian army. The communal dimension is, however, mixed with appeal to national identity and to a sense of patriotism. In interviews, members of the NDF appeal to the idea of Syria as the homeland demanding sacrifices (Press TV 2013). In interviews, the NDF recruits' frames of reference and narratives are consonant with regime and loyalist media talk. However, the images of loyalist fighters, in pro-regime media, are managed. They aim to communicate absolute loyalty to the president and unquestioning willingness to sacrifice their lives for him. To this end, televised military funeral processions of fallen regime fighters are stamped with signs of loyalty, most notably the large photographs of the president looming over the burial ceremony setting. Pushed to the background, if not completely edited out from such televisuals, are the images of grieving families. Patriotic songs, played as the soundtrack of these ceremonies, drown out the voices of grief (drawing on Muhammad 2014).

Staging Slaughter

Horror was manifested fully in the outbreak of massacres mostly by regime forces, at first, then by an array of armed groups that formed with the militarisation of the Uprising. Using the term 'massacre' in its broad sense to mean all instances of large-scale killing, the Syrian Network for Human Rights (SNHR) has documented thousands of massacres committed by the regime and security agents, the pro-regime paramilitary groups, the armed opposition and the Islamist Jihadist militias and, at a later stage, by international actors, primarily the Russian military and the coalition led by the United States. The SNHR collated information on 516 massacres in 2015 alone and, for the period between March 2011 and December 2015, it reported that over 250,000 Syrians were murdered in massacre-type operations and incidents (SNHR 2015a, 2015b). The majority of the massacres are attributed to the regime and its armed supporters.

With a view to taking the method and the how of violence as key elements of the analysis and interpretation, I use 'massacre' in a restricted sense to refer to intimate killing that brings the perpetrators and victims into close proximity of one another, often face-to-face. Hence, instances of mass killings 'at a distance' using, for example, aerial bombardment or chemical weapons, are not included in my investigation and discussion, although aspects of their enactment are shared with the massacres examined. The exclusion of instances of killing 'at a distance' is due, largely, to the fact that they tend to be directed from the top down and, in accounting for their occurrence, it is less pertinent to analyse the microsocial dynamics on the ground. Nonetheless, they represent techniques of violence as a modality of government.

Thus, in this discussion, I approach the massacre as a performance and as an event through which the simulacrum of government and politics is produced. In this performance, staging develops as an important aspect of the production and communication of violence. Often, staging works to effect a play of mirrors and not necessarily to deliver a message about the actors and the causes they espouse or the motives behind their action. Rather, the play of mirrors serves to afford the subject-spectators a particular angle for viewing acts of violence and to incite in them ways of feeling about and understanding violence and thereby directing their positioning and engagement in relation to it.

In the early days of the Uprising, staging, as a discursive trope and practice, had been used by the regime and the opposition in the narrative representation of a video in which soldiers, in the town of al-Bayda in Banyas, were shown stepping on the bodies of men who were rounded up and made to lie face down on the ground. The soldiers are shown stomping on the backs of the civilians and kicking and pushing them with their boots. Pro-regime media claimed that the video was filmed in Iraq years previously. It was also asserted that the soldiers stomping on the backs of the civilians were members of the Kurdish Peshmerga forces (see Syrian and Arab media statements and interviews with regime supporters and unofficial spokespersons). This account was challenged when one of the arrested civilians who had appeared in the video, Ahmad al-Bayasi, confirmed that he himself had been stomped on by regime soldiers. In a video testimony, holding up his identity card to the camera, al-Bayasi gave a first-hand account of the incident. Al-Bayasi would later disappear and his fate would become subject to speculation. However, before his final disappearance, he appeared on Syrian state television and, in an interview, countered opposition claims that he had been imprisoned and killed by regime forces following his first testimony.

Al-Bayasi, an ordinary citizen, and an agent in events in his own right, was enlisted or conscripted in multiple acts of staging: as victim in the stomping incident; as truth-telling witness of the incident in the first video testimony; as victim of the authorities when he disappears and is assumed to have been abducted; as a witness on behalf of the regime when he appears again, this time on state TV, decrying opposition claims;

and finally as a figure of the unknown and the phantasmatic when he disappears without a trace. His story does not end there, however. He disappears from the stage but, in his absence, haunts it as the victim of multiple possible fates. His home village of al-Bayda becomes the site of a massacre wherein most, if not all, of his family members are said to have been murdered, along with many others. Additionally, the massacre at al-Bayda would be, like numerous other massacres, contested with reference to facts of the events and in relation to the identity of victims and perpetrators.

The trope of staging found in the accounts of the initial assault on the village of al-Bayda refers to one dimension of the performative structure of massacre. In the remainder of this section, I focus on how the massacre became a primary event for the articulation of a particular semiotics of violence. The massacres committed by different sides arose and developed as sites of communication and as theatres of power claimed and asserted over and through dead bodies. Further, massacres constituted frames for forming identities and redrawing boundaries between 'us' and 'them' where sectarian categories were superimposed over political divisions.

In this analysis, I am concerned with particular practices of violence and with the affective and cognitive dispositions that these practices provoke in the subjects of violence. Before proceeding further, it is necessary to highlight some general features of the massacres. As noted, massacres were committed by different sides of the conflict and, in a number of cases, the authorship remains contested and much ambiguity surrounds the events. Nonetheless, there are patterns and features that can be discerned through close examination. Regime-sponsored massacres are often preceded by shelling in preparation for a ground assault in which the massacre is part of preparing the terrain for establishing military and security control in a particular area. Agents/perpetrators comprise paramilitary forces that belong either to the groups referred to as *shabiha* or who are part of the Popular Army, National Defence Forces (*al-difa' al-watani*) or Ba'th brigades (formed in 2013). The security forces and military units appear to remain in the background during massacres that involve intimate killing. Intimacy here conveys the immediate physical contact between the killers and the victims, but also the pre-existing relations between them as, for example, having been neighbours or acquaintances. In many of the massacres, it has been difficult to determine whether the regime ordered them or was behind their planning. Yet regime agents, namely the military and security forces, and regime politics of instrumentalising particular groups, prepared the ground for the politics of massacre.

The massacre, as a technology of rule, is productive of horror. In what follows, I highlight particular aspects of the horror mode of violence: (1) its body-centred features and the power significations to which these give rise; (2) the mirror-play style of staging as an element of the performativity of massacres that generates uncertainty about the identity of both perpetrators and victims such that they become interchangeable; and (3) organised mimicry, wherein the semantics and semiotics of massacres are produced and reproduced by the opposing sides, thus reinforcing a different sense of interchangeability – that of the shared signature of violence whereby either side is willing and capable of committing it. To illustrate the workings of these three aspects of the horror mode, devised to read massacres, I sketch out the circumstances and contested claims of three massacres: those of al-Bayda, Houla and the Latakiyya Coast.

Body Horror   In his analysis of the politics of atrocity, Michael Humphrey (2002) hones in on key features of acts of face-to-face violence such as torture and massacre that are deployed as a political strategy. Importantly, he notes that these acts are defined by their excessive and transgressive character. They exceed any expectations of either victims or witnesses/spectators and transgress by producing 'body horror'. This body horror, as explained by Humphrey, is the core of atrocity conducted as a political strategy and a tactic of modern war. As a strategy, body horror possesses rhetorical power. It is on the body of the victims that the power of the dictator, or of the 'ethnic nation', is made real (Humphrey 2002, 2). Beyond this substantiation of power in a manner that harks back to expressions of medieval sovereignty, body horror speaks to what Cavarero identifies as the basic existential fear of violence that destroys the figural unity of the body. Spectacles of bodily violence, such as disfigurement and dismemberment, provoke affects of horror, primarily fear and disgust (see discussion of horror affects in Hills 2005 and Gelder 2000).

In connection with affective incitement, body horror often takes on particular significations that recall or establish political and social relations of power. The methods of killing, maiming and mutilating and the forms they take are not without signifying powers. The acts themselves and their representations should be approached as productive of meaning and of a language of communication. Some broad lines of regime representation of massacres committed by security forces and by loyalist militia could be detected in official and pro-regime coverage. In news reportage of regime operations, broadcast onsite where massacres took place, interviews with commanders and armed militia provide the pretext for propagating regime narratives advancing the view that the victims are all jihadist rebels. In addition to pushing the official line, the onsite videos inevitably show disfigured and mutilated bodies piled in public spaces with othering and dehumanising labels flashed onto the screen over them. For example, in a report containing footage taken immediately after the massacre in al-Bayda, security and National Defence Forces operatives and *shabiha* are shown gathered in the village square. The commanding officer speaks to the camera, pointing to slain bodies piled up nearby, declaring that he and his troops had cleared the area of the terrorists (Al Ekhbariya TV 2013). The privately owned Syrian television channel Al Ekhbariya, which broadcast the footage, showed the piled-up bodies overwritten with a caption reading 'bodies of terrorists' (see Al Ekhbariya TV 2013; see also report by Qanat al-'Alam TV 2013).[3]

The narrative of this Al Ekhbariya report coheres with regime framing of the violence as spearheaded by terrorists against whom it is conducting 'clean-up' operations. Yet the report is a televisual document, partial as it may be, of a massacre, showing its locale, perpetrators and victims. Some background information and further documentation would provide additional context to the body horror beamed on the TV screens and circulated on YouTube videos. Located in the coastal governorate of Tartous, residents of the town of al-Bayda joined in the Uprising in its early days, holding their first demonstration on 18 March 2011. This activism, and the security forces' determination to end it, positioned al-Bayda as an important and contested site of the staging and performance of scenes of humiliation and abjection. The security forces made their first entry into the town in April 2011 and performed the opening act of stomping on the bodies of the male residents made to lay face down in the town's public square. The intended pacification failed, and some of the men took up arms and the town received defectors and other insurgents. Against this background, the immediate trigger for the massacres was a clash on 2 May 2013 between the security forces and the pro-regime militias, on one hand, and a group of opposition fighters, on the other (Human Rights Watch 2013a).

The killings began when security forces and allied militia raided one of the homes hiding three defectors. Then, according to a Human Rights Watch report, the forces and militias 'entered homes, separated men from women, rounded up the men of each neighbourhood in one spot,

---

[3] In another onsite report following a massacre at Dayr al-Mawla in Homs, militiamen and uniformed soldiers played out the scripted account with its contradictory and incoherent parts. While one of the militiamen held up a photo of a preacher, naming him the terrorist leader of the local jihadist faction, other men held a banner of ISIS, presumably retrieved from the insurgents' hideout.

and executed them by shooting them at close range' (Human Rights Watch 2013a, 1). Besides the men, twenty-three women and fourteen children were reportedly killed. In one case, at least twenty-five bodies were piled up in a mobile-phone store and set on fire (Human Rights Watch 2013a, 1).

Witness testimonies, given to Human Rights Watch, describe indiscriminate shooting resulting in injury and death. This suggests that the aim was to execute village inhabitants thought to sympathise with and aid the rebels. There was also a pattern of shooting that targeted the eyes of victims in a significant number of cases (Human Rights Watch 2013a). The deliberate destruction of the eyes intimates an intended symbolism. In techniques of disciplining and taming used in prisons and in everyday life by the security services, the subjects are not allowed to look at their 'trainers' and, particularly, not to look them in the eye. In a similar manner, killing by shooting the victim in the eye(s) appears to be a figural message of breaking the body and the spirit (as in the figurative idiomatic description of 'kasr al-'ayn' used to denote taming). The manipulation of the victims' bodies was furthered with the use of knives and cleavers (Human Rights Watch 2013a, 26).

Um Mohammad, a survivor whose husband and sons were killed in the massacre, recounted stepping outside her home and seeing men and children being led to the square. She saw the son of her neighbour, a fourteen-year-old boy named Loqman al-Hirs, being slaughtered. In her account, the boy was held down by militiamen while one of them cut off his head. The description of the massacre scene and the state of the bodies in the aftermath indicates that methods of killing involved dismemberment and disfigurement. Um Mohammad observed: '[M]any had their body parts fall. We picked up afterwards. So many parts, we did not know which part belonged to whom (ma bin'araf had limin wa hada limin)' (Human Rights Watch 2013a, 26; see also Um Muhammad's testimony on Channel Four News 2013). She was only able to recognise her son among the killed from his finger, which had a distinctive scar from a childhood accident. Another survivor described the disfigurement of her murdered husband: '[T]here was nothing left on my husband's face apart from his mouth and nose. It was hideous' (Human Rights Watch 2013a, 26).

The excess violence used in al-Bayda is explained, in some commentaries and analyses, in terms of another strategic objective – that of displacing the civilian population with a view to establishing homogeneity among inhabitants of contiguous villages and neighbourhoods. Such objectives are commonly pursued in ethnic and sectarian conflicts and, in light of the sectarian narrative promoted by the regime and by some of the Islamist factions, a sectarian cleansing may have motivated the violence against the civilian population. Yet body horror goes beyond the drive to push out the inhabitants. Forms of violence targeting the body for disfigurement aim to undo the subject through intervention on the body such that its unity and integrity are denied. Such methods are consonant with the objectives of inciting the affective structure of horror not only in the opponents, but also in the wider population.

Accounts of the massacres at al-Bayda had their own twists, projecting the view of the interchangeability of victims and perpetrators. Although al-Bayda residents were identified in most accounts as supporters of the Uprising and as giving shelter to insurgents, among their numbers some were noted for being pro-regime. The fact that some of these loyalists were among the murdered in al-Bayda was part of a counter-narrative affirming that the insurgents were responsible for the massacres or, at least, for some of the killings. The murder of Omar al-Bayasi, the former mayor and loyalist figure, thus became corroborating evidence for an inverse account of the identity of the killers and their victims.

Play of Mirrors: Interchangeability of Victims and Perpetrators   As noted briefly above, in theatres of slaughter acts of violence often unfold as endless games of mirrors where the perpetrators and victims are interchangeable. The citizen-spectators are drawn into the theatre of violence to puzzle out the identity of the killers or their victims or, perhaps, to remain uncertain about both. Indeed, it is possible that the citizen-spectators would find themselves to be uncertain as to whether the staged slaughter ever took place at all. Such was the case with a widely reported massacre which, opposition activists claimed, was committed at the town of 'Aqrab in December 2012. Pro-regime media denied its occurrence.[4] As with the horror genre in film, feelings of the uncanny are generated, in part, by the uncertainty about the true identity of the killers and victims and more so by the open possibility that they are interchangeable. The mirror-play enactment of horror does not exhaust the entire repertoire of staged slaughter but, rather, constitutes a style of horror within the range of the performativity of massacres. To elucidate the mirror plays in this staging, we should review the events and competing narratives of the extensively publicised massacre in Houla.

---

[4] In the reported massacre at Aqrab, a town on the Homs-Misyaf Road, it is alleged by factions in the Syrian opposition that civilians from the Alawi community were killed by Alawi militiamen during a stand-off with insurgents (al-Hadid 2013). Though Russian media carried stories about a massacre in Aqrab, pro-regime news outlets in Syria did not.

The Houla massacre occurred during the early stages of the militar-isation of the Uprising. When it took place on 25 May 2012, Houla – a region in the northwest of the city of Homs, composed of a number of villages and towns – was increasingly aligned with the armed rebels oper-ating, then, under the banner of the Free Syrian Army (FSA). Although at the time Houla was surrounded by regime-managed checkpoints, it harboured insurgents, many of whom were defectors from the Syrian national army. In terms of the religious composition of the popula-tion, the majority of Houla residents were Sunni. The residents of the neighbouring towns, in majority, were Alawi. In Syrian documentary accounts of the massacre, inhabitants of Houla assert that prior to the Uprising there were no incidents of conflict between the neighbouring Alawi and Sunni villages and that their relations were harmonious (al-Hadid 2012). However, it is also noted that tensions in the area dated back to the early 1980s when the residents of the town of al-Qabou were mobilised against those suspected of Islamist sympathies in the region (al-Hadid 2012). As discussed in earlier chapters, sectarian differenti-ation and divisions had been superimposed on other distinctions, not-ably political positioning relative to the regime. Patterns of co-optation and incorporation into the apparatuses of violence instituted by the Asad regime took on a sectarian character that, in the course of the conflict, pitted regime loyalists against opposition forces and armed rebels. In this context, the communal identification of neighbourhoods, towns and villages became the marker of identity around which the pro- and anti-regime boundaries were drawn. Residents of Houla joined the Uprising, participating in demonstrations and other oppositional actions.

On the day of the massacre – a Friday – the residents of Teldow, a district of Houla, took part in a large demonstration. In the afternoon, military shelling was reported and so was heavy gunfire from one of the security checkpoints. Just before sunset, armed groups attacked a number of homes and their inhabitants were killed. By the end of the day, it was reported that over ninety civilians had been killed and that the victims included women and children. It would later emerge that most of the dead belonged to two families in Teldow, namely the al-Sayyid and Abdel Razzaq families.

The massacre was the subject of a UN-led international investiga-tion which did not reach a decisive conclusion. However, on the basis of patterns of violence involving the regime side and on the balance of probabilities, human rights groups that investigated the incident determined that there was a higher likelihood that the killings at Houla were committed by regime forces and by allied paramilitary units. In the meantime, some of the international media had provided a competing narrative, putting responsibility for the killings on the armed opposition/ rebels (see, for example, Hermann 2012).

In one account of the Houla massacre – based on testimonies collected by an anti-regime activist – men from the surrounding Alawi villages who were known in the local communities to be *shabiha* or thugs, were mobilised to lead the attack on Houla. The assault on Houla began with shelling originating, ostensibly, from regime checkpoints and the military college nearby (see Khawla al-Hadid's (2012) account). Testimonies collected by other activists and human rights organisations support the contention that the regime side was responsible for the massacre. The UN Commission of Inquiry identified patterns of government violations: shelling precedes entry of military and security forces into the town; snipers are positioned on rooftops throughout the area; and forces conduct house-to-house searches accompanied by militiamen (*shabiha*). Accounts of survivors and witnesses detail atrocities of the kind committed in other massacres, such as the murder of entire families in their homes. Of a total of 108 killed in the Houla massacre, thirty-two were children and many were women. Some were stabbed to death and others beaten to death (e.g. some of the dead were reported to have suffered severe head trauma). Some of the murdered children were chained together and had their hands and feet tied. A number of bodies were burnt. Homes and their adjacent fields were set on fire and a large number of cattle was killed (Human Rights Watch 2012).

Survivors identified the perpetrators as *shabiha* who came from nearby Alawi villages. Stories carry motifs of revenge on the part of some villages and of solidarity on the part of others. In the case of the nearby and predominately Alawi village of Maryamin, it is reported that villagers tried to stop *shabiha* from going to Houla (al-Hadid 2012; see also video testimony in Reuter 2012; Reuter and Adhun 2012; Spiegel Online 2012).

The regime's responsibility for the Houla massacre was contested in accounts provided by its affiliated media and by loyalists and known supporters. In these accounts, armed gangs committed the massacre ahead of the visit of a UN delegation to Syria – the purpose being to create a pretext for the invocation of the international community's 'Responsibility to Protect'. A Syrian TV report showed images purported to be from Houla and followed them with interviews with several people who claimed to be eyewitnesses to the rebels committing the killing. The same report interviewed citizens on the streets and in their cars who expressed the view that the perpetrators dressed up in army uniforms to implicate the Syrian army (Syria TV 2012). In pro-regime reports, the murdered families were designated as regime loyalists (see Syria

TV 2012). Further, investigative reports by some international media organisations cast doubt on the veracity of the consensus narrative that the *shabiha* and security forces carried out the slaughter (Hermann 2012). In the counter-narratives of foreign media, the communal identity of the victims was recast: they were said to be Shiʻa and, therefore, by extension the killings were acts of sectarian violence on the part of the rebels. According to this version of the massacre, the two extended families that suffered the greatest number of victims had converted to Shiʼi Islam. In effect, in pro-regime narratives, the perpetrators impersonate regime agents, and the victims are loyalists and not oppositionists.

As with a number of the massacres that have been committed in the war in Syria, the massacre at Houla was seized upon by the conflicting sides as evidence of the other side's brutality and monstrosity. The use of incidents of atrocity for political purposes, in particular to discredit opponents, is a common tactic in contexts of political violence. Paul Brass (1997, 63) teases out the dynamics at play when this tactic is deployed in a pluralist setting such as India. Brass highlights the proclivity in the rhetoric of atrocity to recite all the gory details about the attack in question and to show it to be more brutal and extreme than anything that had occurred on one's own side. Undoubtedly, this dimension could be found in the competing narratives of the warring sides in the Syrian conflict. However, there are structural differences between the political settings of India and Syria. While the contested claims in the Indian case could be examined and scrutinised by the local and international media, by the courts and by local and national institutions, the scope for access to victims and witnesses is much more limited in Syria. The regime, in many instances, continued to limit and deny access to outside observers. Further, by virtue of the political set up, an independent national judicial review of the atrocities was, and continues to be, ruled out. The rule of exception disallows the prospect of establishing responsibility and holding to account.

Brass (1997, 201) argues that, in the Indian case, 'a system of talk' about atrocities and horror stories of violence committed against 'Scheduled Castes' and poor Muslims obfuscated 'the truth' of the routinised violence against these categories of citizenry. He identifies different levels and circles within which narratives of violence are spun. The narratives are dialogic and embedded in the webs of power, in relations involving national and state offices and agents, in material antagonisms and more. He points out that the horror stories, as told by the various protagonists, are part of a system of talk about violence. This system of talk by necessity, if not by design, generates ambiguities. My proposition about the interchangeability of perpetrators and victims is somewhat different. The dynamics that render victims and perpetrators interchangeable do not arise simply because under these circumstances ascertaining facts is not possible or because the dominant rhetoric masks a particular 'truth'. Rather, these dynamics unfold within the performative structure of violence: staging, emplotted horror and shared signature. I would argue that this structure is not unique to the episodes of violence discussed here. Indeed, such patterns have also been discerned in enactments of violence in Colombia during the period of La Violencia (Uribe 2004a, 2004b). I also see the possibility of rereading and reinterpreting Brass' account along the lines developed in the analysis of violence here if the optic of analysis shifts emphasis to the performative structure of violence. In such a rereading, the bracketing or suspension of the truth about events is not merely the function of rhetoric, but also of the performative structure of violence. Within this structure, indeterminacy and uncertainty are the by-products of the emplotment and performance of violence and are upheld in the modes of apprehension and interpretative codes formed in citizens' interaction with the regime and with one another.

Organised Mimicry and Phantasmatic Violence   The accounts of the massacres attributed to the security forces, the army and pro-regime militias or to the armed opposition (primarily the Islamist camp), show that the assaults on towns and villages and the actions that unfold share some common features and resemblances. The affinities, in form and method, between massacres committed by the warring sides draw our attention to the imaginaries of violence that prefigure the acts and how these acts feed into these imaginaries. They also reveal the dialogic character of acts of extreme violence. The mimesis in methods and forms of killing does not arise simply from a desire for revenge so as to inflict damage in equal measure. Rather, theatricality and staging are of utmost importance.

The extreme violence of the massacres is, indeed, linked with such strategic objectives as clearing an area from its inhabitants to establish spatial and territorial pre-eminence or to secure transport roads for supplies. Yet the methods and forms of violence cannot be accounted for simply by reference to strategic objectives. The participation of paramilitary groups armed by the regime (e.g. the National Defence militia and the Ba'th militia) has drawn the civilian population into the conflict between the regime and the rebels (the latter, it should be recalled, being composed of defectors from the Syrian regular army as well as civilians who took up arms). This facet of the conflict brought civilian loyalists and the insurgent opposition into military conflict with one another. The intermeshing and intertwining of the state military with militia recruited from among civilians had the effect of implicating the entire civilian population in the conflict. Those fighting on the side of the regime were all cast as *shabiha*, while supporters of the opposition (actual or presumed), whether armed or unarmed, were all cast as 'terrorists'.

In accounts of violence, Begoña Aretxaga (2000a, 53) notes, with reference to the conflict between the Spanish state and Basque separatists, that events are narrated and imagined in a 'phantomatic mode', revealing 'a structure and modus operandi which produce both the state and terrorism as fetishes of each other, constructing reality as an endless play of mirror images'. In the Syrian case, it is not only the narratives that produce phantasmatic violence, it is also the performativity of violence – the methods and enactments of violence – that unfold in mimetic and hallucinatory manner. In the forms of violence enacted, organised mimesis dominates. The massacres' authorship could be attributed to either side of the conflict, investigations notwithstanding. This is not the same as saying that the perpetrators are not known. Rather, the contention here is that the patterns and enactments are reproductions of other acts committed by the opposing side. In some cases, each side produces an account that places the other in the role of perpetrator. The uncertainty that engulfs the massacres is not merely a problem of access to information which, if available or accessible, would permit the sifting through of the true from the false. Massacres, as technologies of death, are by definition cast in the horror mode wherein fog envelops the atmosphere and blurs vision, with multiple screens mediating the view and rendering the images askew.

The modus operandi of the actors produces the regime and the armed opposition as fetishes of each other: regime forces and *shabiha* enter an area, attack homes, ransack them, burn bodies, slit throats; armed opposition groups (jihadists and others) follow suit in an organised mimicry. For instance, in mimetic fashion, the massacres perpetrated during the 'jihadist operation' on the Latakiyya countryside, in August 2013, summon the images of the massacres committed by the security forces and *shabiha* during their 'operations' in al-Bayda as shown on Syrian television. The Latakiyya 'Operation', attributed to al-Farouq Battalion and Suqur al-'Iz, among others, as shown on the Ansar al-Deen television channel (as reported by Human Rights Watch 2013b), takes the form of mimetic violence, referencing a phantasmatic regime. The narratives and counter-narratives of these massacres follow the master narrative that the killings that take place are, on the whole, inevitably motivated by sectarian enmity and hatred. This interpretative frame, however, misses the processes through which subjects are constructed as superfluous and thereby slated for elimination. Equally important is the fact that the staging of the massacres, and the interpretative frames used by different sides, present both the victims and perpetrators as interchangeable.

The regime's violence conjures up a terrorist enemy – the armed gangs roaming throughout Syrian territory. This is not to say that there are no armed groups but, rather, that the regime called them forth through both the underlying imaginaries of civil conflict in the relations between rulers and ruled in Syria, and through a mode of operation that calls for the formation of such gangs. The regime interpellated the protesters and the opposition as foreigners, armed insurgents and the like, while official media discourse and propaganda cast them as marauding gangs roaming the territory from Dar 'a to Homs. Meanwhile, security forces, on the whole, are portrayed as guardians of the nation, killing traitors and foreign terrorists. In effect, the regime cast the opposition, whether partisan and organised or spontaneous and non-partisan, as an enemy population targeted for liquidation. The logic of the 'us versus them' appeared in slogans shouted and graffiti inscribed by regime loyalists declaring '*Asad aw la Ahad*' ('Asad or No One'), and '*Asad aw Nihraq al-Balad*' ('Asad or we Burn the Country').

In the meantime, armed opposition groups, in a play of mirror images, attack Alawi villages, call their populations '*shabiha*' and, in some cases, take women and children hostage. The gangs leave behind slogans and signs of a similar import to those that regime loyalists inscribe on the walls of opposition towns and villages. Jihadist propaganda video footage of their assaults on the villages of the Latakiyya coast show armed militiamen moving through the villages in broad daylight, engulfed by dust and smoke, forcing down the doors of homes (Human Rights Watch 2013b). In segments of one of the videos, bodies are shown on the ground with blood streaming from their heads. In another video, the armed men are shown walking around in the narrow, winding streets of the village of Barouda, shooting indiscriminately at homes, passing and stopping briefly by dead bodies on the streets (YouTube 2013). Transcribed over the recorded images of homes and bodies is the word '*shabiha*'.

The forms of violence enacted in the massacres suggest that there is a need to consider the performative dimension in its own right and not as a tag on other variables such as political economy or sectarian divisions. Undoubtedly, these variables inform and feed into the violence. Yet the performances have their own logic and processes. They generate and follow templates and scripts in which mimicry and parody are at work. The performances entail a dialogue of sorts: messages are communicated through graffiti slogans, video statements, signature killings, patterns of mutilation and disfigurement (see Human Rights Watch 2013a and 2013b reports).

The events of violence in the period known as La Violencia in Colombia provide a comparative perspective that helps crystallise our understanding of the practices and performativity of violence witnessed in the Syrian conflict. Extending between 1946 and 1964, La Violencia, a political conflict waged principally between opposing ideological camps at both elite and grassroots level, is an exemplar of political violence in the horror mode. During this period, it is estimated that between 200,000 and 300,000 people were killed (Roldan 2002). Massacres were perpetrated by government forces, by guerrilla groups and by members of peasant communities. The massacres by regime forces, paramilitaries and armed groups also appeared as mirror images of one another, with a strong mimetic dimension, though different groups applied different methods of mutilation to the bodies of their victims (Uribe 2004a). Similarly, in the Syrian case, paramilitary groups and popular and National Defence Forces draw a pattern of violence that is copied by some of the armed opposition groups. Similar steps are taken by both warring sides in insurgency battles: they start by shelling enemy areas, deploying snipers in strategic locations, setting up roadblocks, and proceeding to attack homes, dismember victims and burn bodies, property and land.

Further, in parallel with La Violencia in Colombia, the violence carried out in the massacres in Syria has its own semiotics: dismemberment, severing of hands and arms and decapitation and disembowelment (for comparison, see Uribe 2004a). In the case of La Violencia, the mutilation of bodies had specific signatures and aesthetics (Rojas and Tubb 2013; Uribe 2004a). In similar terms, the images taken of massacres in Syria indicate that bodies, in their arrangements and manner of display, are worked into the staging of horror: for example, bodies dragged from the square where the killing took place, piled up on each other and set afire, shirts pulled over heads, burning of faces, disfiguring all identifying features, slitting children's throats. As in surreal art works inspired by war, the aesthetics of massacres betray revelling in 'bodily fragmentation and disarticulation' through dismemberment and disembowelment (Lyford 2000, 45–7). As put forward by Arjun Appadurai (2006), intimate violence puts a premium on violation and degradation of the body. In mimetic violence, the mimesis expresses a style of inflicting harm and damage with a signature and an outbidding mimicry.

In their performative structure, and in the terms of their narrativisation, the massacres committed by the warring sides represent enactments of mimetic violence in the sense conceived by René Girard (1979), that is, as a non-differentiating violence. This refers to reciprocal violent performances, wherein there is no distinction between legitimate and illegitimate violence or between 'pure' and 'impure' violence.

As explained by Feldman (1991, 258): 'In Girard, unending mimetic exchange is polarized to a terminal, rarified, and singularized act of violence that encloses itself as ritual. The exchange values mobilized by mimetic reciprocity are in effect devaluing because they do not promote hierarchy and hegemony.' For Girard, the condition of stasis generated through mimetic violence could only be broken with the advent of sacrificial exchange, which reinstates symbolisation and differentiation in the cultural production of violence. However, there remains the possibility that sacrificial violence or ritual itself becomes subject to 'mimetic appropriation precisely because it establishes a ritualized form of violence and surrogate victimage as hegemonic' (Feldman 1991, 260).

The massacres, in 2013, in the coastal towns in the region of al-Haffa, located in the governorate of Latakiyya, are illustrative of the mimetic character of mass violence in the Uprising. The massacres were committed as part of a 'strategic operation' by armed rebel groups, most with declared Islamist affiliation (e.g. Jabhat al-Nusra, al-Farouq Battalion, the Islamic State), but with the participation of the Free Syrian Army. Having seized control of a number of villages in North Latakiyya, the armed groups sought to gain the upper hand over the military in the area. The operation began at dawn on 4 August 2013 with the rebels overtaking military posts positioned nearby the village of Barouda. The rebels then proceeded to run through Barouda and seven other neighbouring villages, shooting at residents while they were fleeing, and killing those who stayed behind either inside their homes or in the vicinity. The scope of the killing was extensive: in most cases, members from the same families were massacred as they stayed together indoors. Some of the victims were shot at close range in the head or the chest, and others were killed with knives. In some cases killing was done by slitting the throat (Human Rights Watch 2013b, 46–7). Residents of Barouda told Human Rights Watch that they witnessed executions and that they saw decapitated bodies (Human Rights Watch 2013b, 20). In the Human Rights Watch report on the massacre, it is noted: '[M]any of the bodies could not be identified because they were burned, badly disfigured or had decomposed significantly' (Human Rights Watch 2013b, 19).[5] In one of the villages, Sleibet al-Hamboushieh, some of the corpses had their heads and hands cut off (Human Rights Watch 2013b, 42).

---

[5] As part of their military attack on the villages, the rebels took 200 residents hostage – the majority of whom were women and children. The declared purpose of hostage-taking was to arrange a prisoner exchange. Beyond this objective, the hostage-taking was scripted into the performances of violence. A video was released showing one hostage explaining the terms and conditions of the prisoner exchange. The video also showed groups of hostages who would later be identified by family members.

There are various points to note about the performances of violence in the Latakiyya Coast Operation. Patterns and methods of killing and ideological proclamations resemble, in many respects, those observed in massacres committed by the security forces and *shabiha*. Common patterns include the conduct of raids on homes, the gatherings of families to separate men from women and children, and the execution of adult males. Although there appears to be a special targeting of men for execution, killings of women and children are recorded for the massacres committed by both regime forces and the rebels. The forms of body-centred violence that exceed the purposes of killing and aim at undermining the body's figural unity are produced by both sides. Mutilation, dismemberment and decapitation recorded for the Latakiyya Coast killings appear to mirror the slaughter methods used in massacres attributed to the regime as in al-Bayda and Houla.

Through mimicry, the violence enacted by the various protagonists becomes deeply intermingled and entwined. For the rebels, mimetic violence may be viewed as an expression of their drive to perform sovereignty, which is closely tied with the push to 'liberate' territory and install local government. However, mimetic violence should not be interpreted as the dissolution of governmental violence. The practices and performances of violence taken up and replayed by armed rebel groups reassert rather than undermine government through violence. In this political field, the regime and armed groups enact competing sovereignties through mutually imbricated performances of violence and shared repertoires of horror.

Conclusion

In the first part of this chapter, I discussed the case of the murder and resurrection of Zaynab al-Hosni to illustrate how episodes of violence are staged in a manner that creates ambiguity as to the actual events and actions. The ambiguity of excessive violence is achieved by positioning subjects as spectators who can only have askew views of the violence unfolding in front of them. By putting on public display the living Zaynab, the regime may have been able to discredit the claims of the opposition regarding a particular case of atrocity. Yet the case generated questions about the identity of the victim to whom the dismembered body belonged. The subject-citizens' experience of the political uncanny arises, in part, out of a deficit of knowledge and the persistent uncertainty regarding the events surrounding the murder and resurrection of Zaynab. At the same time, the interpretative frames mobilised by citizens, while not offering a resolution of the mystery, reveal their familiarity with the regime's modes of operation. The interpretative frames show recognition, on the part of citizens, that events are staged to generate indeterminacy and incite bewilderment. An important conclusion to make here is that, indeed, there is artifice in horror, and that this artifice is formative of the world of common reality.

In the context of generalised war, body horror produced in massacres and other face-to-face acts of violence engenders fear of a form of violence that transgresses against the body's integral unity. Further, through their performative structure – specifically staging, mirror play and mimicry – massacres generate affective and cognitive states formative of the subjects of violence (victims and spectators). This performative structure of violence is a key element of the stasis that has characterised the conflict in Syria over a number of years. This stasis is not a mere function of the retaliatory impulses driving the protagonists ('the tit for tat'). Rather, it is sustained by non-differentiating enactments of violence, wherein victims and perpetrators become interchangeable and the authorship of acts of horror is imprinted with the opposing sides' shared signature.

Conclusion: The Rule of Violence – Formations of Civil War

Under Hafez al-Asad's rule, commencing in 1970, and within the terms of the state of emergency declared in 1963, upon the Ba'th Party's takeover of political power a civil war regime developed as a form of government. By 'civil war regime', I mean a system of government that rests on and creates the conditions of a latent permanent war between rulers and ruled and between different components of society differentiated along various lines of division: sectarian, tribal, ethnic, regional, urban–rural and class. In Syria, these divisions align along an overarching political divide between two camps that, for simplicity, I refer to as loyalists and oppositionists. Through a constellation of practices and techniques, a division of the population into 'us' and 'them' was enacted: 'us' to be read as the Asad regime and its loyalists, and 'them' as opponents or as the political opposition constituted as expendable.

In different parts of this study, I attempted to show how this civil war regime developed, highlighting practices of polarisation and the entrenchment of divisions and foregrounding events that set the template of violence as a modality of government. A constellation of discursive and institutional practices served to produce 'loyalists' and 'oppositionists' (*muwalat* and *mu'arada*) as mortal enemies. This was achieved, in part, by producing the opposition as the subjects of banishment and death (as, for instance, in the categories of subjects charged with crimes of 'weakening the spirit of the nation' or 'acting against the goals of the Revolution') as designated in the Penal Code. The binary divisions introduced into the population are further articulated in a murderous discourse of elimination: for example, declarations of Rif'at al-Asad and speeches of Hafez al-Asad about the necessity of eliminating the enemy within. This will to kill is further communicated in announcements by army generals and governors, asserting a willingness and readiness to kill thousands (e.g. in a gruesome rhetorical flourish, General Ghazi Kan'an, a key figure of counter-insurgency against the Islamist opposition in the early 1980s, declared his readiness at that time to 'plant a thousand flowers' in the Homs desert). These announcements had much currency in citizens' interpretative frames for understanding and relating to the regime. Thus, during the 2011 Uprising, 'insider information' – attributed to high-ranking military sources – about the number of Syrians the regime was prepared to sacrifice to end the protests was in common circulation. The propagation of a discourse of war is taken up by the 'loyal' citizens themselves in, for instance, articulations and representations of the state of war and in slogans of civil war such as 'With spirit and blood we sacrifice for you [Hafez or Bashar]' or 'O Bashar do not worry, you have a people who drink blood' (i.e. the blood of their enemy). Other slogans perform exclusion or banishment as in 'Bashar or No One'; 'Bashar or We Burn the Country'. Such enunciations bear the marks of the eradicationist or liquidationist logic found in fascist regimes presiding over civil wars/permanent wars.

The civil war regime is also manifest in the organisational infrastructure of violence. Part of this infrastructure is militia formations such as the Defence Brigades, the Special Units and the army's Third Division. Under Hafez al-Asad, these latter were mobilised not only against the Islamist insurgency, but also against the civilian population and were responsible for committing large-scale massacres. In the current conflict, the same type of actors and forces are represented in the Republican Guards and the army's Fourth Division, in addition to the National Defence Forces, the Popular Defence Committees, the Ba'th militia and semi-independent units such as those that came to be known as the Tiger Forces (*quwwat al-nimr*) under Colonel Suhayl al-Hassan.

The civil war regime elevates 'enmity' to a war condition through the arming of loyalists and tasking them with the liquidation of oppositionists. This was evidenced, in the late 1970s and early 1980s, in the organisation of society in a civil war figuration through the arming of societal groups such as clans, Bedouin tribes, Ba'th Party members and party auxiliaries (in particular the Student Union, the Youth Federation and the Peasant Federation). It is telling that, in the context of the 2011 Uprising, accounts were given of the formation of militia among the civilian population during the late 1970s and early 1980s period of insurgency. It emerged that, at the time, these militia engaged in the liquidation of entire families suspected of supporting the Muslim Brothers (accounts from Ma'arat al-Nu'man in Idlib, and from Idlib city). Equally telling are the symbolic and material entanglements of old and new formations. Thus, the figure of Khaled Ghazala, in Idlib, projects continuity in bases of support and linkages with the regime. Yet the situation on the ground is more complex, as could be seen in the collapse of these bases and in shifts that occurred in places like Idlib city (see Lund 2016).

Sectarianisation of Institutions of Violence and of Space

An integral element of the civil war regime in Syria has been the sectarianisation of the apparatuses of coercion and of the political landscape, and the superimposition of sectarian affiliation on political contests. For instance, in terms of composition at both leadership and rank-and-file levels, the security services have been predominately Alawi. The absolute majority of the heads of the directorates and specialised branches and their governorate sections are drawn from the Alawi military officer corps. Moreover, a majority of military officers in command positions are Alawi and there are military units made up entirely of Alawi recruits. Thus, the political conflict between citizens and these institutions has been rendered in sectarian terms. The testimonies and prison diaries convey the identitarian investments of the institutions of violence. Prison guards, interrogators and wardens are recruited amongst Alawi members of the state military. Guards and political prisoners alike interpret the formula of rule positioning them in these roles along sectarian lines. In one prison diary, the diarist, a member of the Communist Action Party and an Alawi by descent, relates an incident of interrogation wherein his interrogator berates him for being seated at the front end of the interrogation desk (Sha'bo 2015). Reproachfully, the interrogator tells him that his place is behind the desk (as the interrogator) and not in front of it (as a suspect or prisoner). Other prisoners note how the dialect of prison interrogators and guards confirmed the sectarian character of rule. This was despite the fact that a large number of political prisoners issued from the Alawi community. Being Alawi became synonymous with being in a position of privilege even among prisoners.

Underpinning the civil war regime and its actualisation in the current conflict in Syria has been the sectarianisation of space. This spatial sectarianisation unfolded in the course of processes of internal migration and settlement and in patterns of employment and integration into state institutions, in particular the military and security services. Rural–urban migration and settlement along lines of sect affiliation was connected with terms of integration into the labour market and employment in state institutions. With the patterning of settlement on the basis of regional and sect affiliation, neighbourhoods emerged as appendages of the regime and as buffers against potential opposition and resistance. These latter were settled, in large part, by Alawi rural migrants who were integrated into the military and security services. This development must be situated in the context of wider labour trends wherein rural migrants of Sunni affiliation became engaged in the informal economy. In other words, the relationship to the state of these various migrant communities was different – some were co-opted as the arm of repression, others were excluded and constituted as the subjects of transgression.

Some Syrian observers and analysts argue that the regime intentionally implanted these urban settlements and neighbourhoods for protection and had planned for conflict all along. Indeed, this was an assertion made to me in 2005 by a former government minister who was in office during the period of Hafez al-Asad's rule. However, the extent to which the spatial sectarianisation was produced by design could be easily exaggerated. Economic and regional variables, as well as cultural divisions, certainly played an important role in the socio-spatial organisation of cities like Damascus, Homs, Latakiyya and Tartous, but their political investment by the regime entrenched their sectarianisation. The spatialised sect-based constellations of Alawi military neighbourhoods encircling Damascus, or of contiguous Alawi military quarters in central Homs, are exemplary features of the civil war regime. Earlier phases of resettlement in rural areas, dating back to the 1930s and 1940s, were marked by sectarian differentiation. However, under the Ba'th and Alawi security dominance, Alawi villagers were drawn into the politics of security by virtue of furnishing the regime with recruits into the army and security services. In the current conflict, villages with predominately Alawi populations, such as Drikish in Tartous and Rabi'a in the western region of Hama, have served as sources of fighter reserves for the regime.

The sectarianisation of institutions of violence and of space superimposed sectarian divisions on the 'us' and 'them' binaries drawn through practices of governmental violence. This, in effect, means that a sect-based account of the opposition to the regime does not offer a valid perspective on the conflict and violence that enmeshed the civilian population during the Uprising and its aftermath. The analysis of sectarianisation that is offered here differs from accounts that advance the view that the violence between the regime and its opponents expresses age-old sectarian hatreds between Sunnis, on one side, and Alawis and Shi'a, on the other. It may be the case that for some actors in the current conflict, symbols and frames of historical and doctrinal enmities animate their views and orient their action towards members of sects and religions differing from theirs. However, the sectarian divisions running through the population are grounded in the materiality of political and spatial processes of sectarianisation rather than being the expression of doctrinal discourses. Undoubtedly, sectarian discourses and charges of sectarianism have had their political uses historically and in the recent conflict. For example, during the late 1970s Islamist insurgency, the regime and the Muslim Brotherhood exchanged accusations of sectarianism. Propaganda writings attributed to the Muslim Brotherhood contained sectarian tropes, while figures tied to the regime sought to establish sect-based militia (e.g. Jamil al-Asad arming members of the Murtada group). With the militarisation of the Uprising, sectarian discourses and sect-based militia formed. Such developments extend the politicisation and functionalisation of sect within the civil war regime.

Political Economy of Subjectivation and Identitarian Politics

In a parallel manner to what Mbembe terms 'enclave economy', the 'shadow state' in Syria anchors the government of violence. The political economy of looting, smuggling and trafficking and the spatial fragmentation has been productive of socio-political divisions among the governed. Regime-supported patrons control networks of dependants, followers and appendages and are integrated into the system of rule. These networks are invested with the terms of the polarisation of the body politic and are productive elements of the conditions of civil war. For example, shadow networks were mobilised by the regime in its battle against the Islamists and the broader opposition in the late 1970s and 1980s. During the Uprising, some actors in the trafficking and smuggling networks were deployed against the protesters and, subsequently, formed loyalist, armed militia, while others joined or formed oppositional militia.

Practices of clientelisation and networks of the shadow state establish hierarchical social relations that structure interaction between citizens and government. Ordinary citizens cultivate discursive civilities that are integral to the formation of political subjectivities that apprehend the dangers and risks of political action. The ordinary citizen interprets his or her position as that of being exposed to risk and danger, making her or him *muwatin taht al-talab* ('wanted citizen'), someone who has potentially contravened a state regulation and could be hauled in by the agents of the security services. In the context of the politics of security and enframing, citizens identified threatening subjects such as *zalamat al-amn* (the security's man) – the one conjured up in conversations and anticipated in exchanges and dealings with others. The 'us' and 'them' could also be read in the categories of actors identified with the clientelist and shadow networks: *mahsub 'ala* (one who is on another's account) or *min jama'at fulan* (from the group of so and so) and *mad'um* (one who has the support of 'X'). Associated with the powerful, these political subjectivities stand in opposition to the 'wanted citizen'.

These subjectivities and their relations are expressive of a generalised war of sorts. All citizens are wanted, that is, they are all, in some sense, positioned as subjects who have contravened some regulation and could potentially be investigated and charged. In other words, they stand at the mercy of the apparatuses of violence. In mundane everyday exchanges, the war is also played out in the exercise of locating one's interlocutor in relation to the security services. That is, everyone is potentially *zalamat al-amn* – an indeterminate army of followers and watchers that required that one be on guard to avoid entrapment. Clientalisation and *istizlam* are thus both practices of incorporation and polarisation, drawing some citizens into the orbit of rule as beneficiaries, while excluding others. The enmeshment of these practices with the apparatus of security and the superimposition of identitarian divisions on them (read in sectarian terms) deepen the break into the body of the population.

Clientelism and favouritism facilitated and nurtured the organisation of various spheres of social interaction and exchange with reference to communal ties and connections. Clientelist networks created a sense of discrimination, which could be and was construed along sectarian lines, even though the networks entrenching differentiation are neither religious nor necessarily communitarian. Rather, the privileged position of the military in the structures of government meant that many Alawi families had better contacts and connections in the public administration, which facilitated the processing of paperwork and securing state employment. Thus, socio-economic antagonisms that arose because of differentiated relations to the regime and apparatuses of power came to be interpreted in identitarian terms.

Violence, Subjectivation and Affective Government

One of the central questions in this work concerns the role that violence plays in shaping Syrian political subjectivities and in governing Syrians as subject-citizens. I have approached this question by examining how particular institutions and practices of violence have been formative of citizens' understanding of the terms of rule. Relatedly, I have advanced the proposition that, in Syria, violence constitutes a modality of government. In this modality, the prison and the massacre are apparatuses of governing through the affect, eliciting feelings of abjection and horror in the subjects.

Approaching violence as governmental entails a rethinking of institutions and practices of violence beyond their repressive functions to their productive or formative effects. The political prison in Syria was, and continues to be, the apparatus of exclusion and of a pedagogy of rule wherein torture exceeds its conventional interrogational purposes and works to shape the subject and, in particular, to unmake dissident political subjectivities. In my discussion of the political prison, I draw attention to the assumptions that underlay practices of subjectivation. Key to these assumptions is the distinction between subjects categorised as nationally diseased and beyond 'unmaking' – as, for example, the Muslim Brothers – and other subjects held in abeyance for purposes of remaking. In Tadmur Prison, a paradigmatic site of the state of exception instituted by the Ba'th, rule was exercised by abjecting political dissidents. The seemingly capricious and random punishments meted out to political prisoners in Tadmur have their own rationalities. Physical punishment, soiling and contamination aim at negating the subject's capacity to dissent. These practices are part of the affectivity of rule. Imprisonment of political dissidents has as its objective the production of loyal and docile subjects as evidenced by the practice of *musawama* (negotiation) aimed at extracting the prisoners' renunciation of their political convictions and at securing their declaration of allegiance to the president. The practices and objectives of the political prison in Syria should not be considered as marginal to the body politic and to political life in that country. This is so, not only because incarceration of the political opposition was and continues to be far-reaching, but also because it has been formative of the citizenry's understanding of government and its affective relations with it. Tadmur, in this sense, is emblematic of this form of rule.

The accounts of brutalising and extreme physical violence found in the memoirs of former political prisoners may seem to confirm an understanding of physical violence as being solely repressive and harking back to medieval punitive systems lacking any objective beyond punishment. However, the memoirs open vistas of understanding on to the workings of governmental violence. Importantly, they invite us to question the posited disjuncture between body-centred penal practices and soul-oriented techniques (as conventionally understood from Foucault's work on the prison). This disjuncture does not hold here. Rather, body and soul are entwined in the extreme violence of the camp. It could, rightly, be argued that this violence does not reconstruct the soul in the manner that regimentation and observation in disciplinary-type modern prisons does. However, body-centred violence would be better viewed in the terms suggested by former political prisoner Ratib Sha'bo who explained the humiliating and degrading violence as soul-negating, and as intended to extinguish any spirit of resistance in the political dissident.

Yet despite the use of confinement on a massive scale and the widespread awareness, through socialisation, of the costs of imprisonment, political dissidence persisted with varying degrees of intensity. Subsequent to the period of heightened violence in the late 1970s and early 1980s, a war of attrition between the regime and politically active citizens ebbed and flowed. Episodic campaigns of arrest and imprisonment in the late 1980s and early 1990s targeted remaining pockets of political dissidence and extended to human-rights activists throughout the 1990s. How, then, should we account for what appeared as quiescence within the population at large? Addressing this question, or giving an account of self in terms of one's action or inaction, is a preoccupation of Syrians' recollections of everyday life under dictatorship. Their accounts of ordinary and routine violence offer explanations of what held them back and kept them in check.

Importantly, certain affinities, if not homologies, exist between practices of subjectivation in the prison, on one hand, and on the street and in everyday interaction, on the other. Integral to the politically formative role of violence are the processes of subjectivation in the everyday. These processes are traced through the memories of growing up in Ba'thist Syria. In recollections of school and family life, for instance, emblematic frames of everyday life experience of government emerge. Social memories of the everyday crystallise the terms in which precarity and abjection shaped citizens' senses of themselves and their interpretative horizons. Ordinary citizens' memories and accounts of quotidian encounters with security agents reveal resemblances with prison experiences, though the intensity of violent practices is lower. One of the recurrent motifs in remembrances of life under Hafez al-Asad was the sense of being the object of the security gaze – that of the security services or of a vast network of watchers in schools, at work and at home. Walls had ears and the regime had arms that could reach at any time into the places of mundane life, as depicted in Fadia Ladhiqani's account of an afternoon bus ride in the summer of 1980 (see Chapter 3). The unexplained slap that struck the bus passenger that day was not an exceptional occurrence, but part of a routine that had governmental effects.

The affectivity of the type of encounter described by Ladhiqani should not be viewed as belonging to isolated experiences or as resting on the idiosyncratic acts of individuals in positions of authority. Rather, the acts through which citizens are abjected belong to an order of government and a political environment. They may take forms and expressions bearing the imprint of their individual authors and may show improvisation, but they are undertaken in line with a modality of doing things, of casting down and of sapping the individual's spirit. The expression 'we lived abjection' (*ihna 'ishna al-dhul*) came to encapsulate what it feels like to be a subject of the Asad regime. It tells of patterned affective practices emergent in encounters with regime agents and embodied through the enactment of everyday routines and ways of relating to and inhabiting various spaces. 'Lived abjection' is a descriptor for the affectivity of ways of being and of doing within the political and social order. The terms of rule as laid down in the 'us' and 'them' divisions are given materialisation in countless encounters with the agents of rule and in the subjects' adopted postures and performances in relation to these agents: lowering one's gaze, 'walking by the wall', whispering or keeping silent. The feelings of abjection are thus called forth through the subject's surrender to the compulsion to conduct oneself in a manner that ultimately diminishes one's selfhood. During the Uprising, numerous videos showed the security forces, in their drive to restore 'order', labouring to force citizens to perform acts of self-debasement and degradation.[1] Lived abjection also conveys the terms in which the subjects experienced and related to their surroundings as instanced in their queues for basic food rations during the long periods of shortages in the 1980s. Within this context, a citizen's procurement on the black market of rice soiled with mouse excrement rendered him abject. Importantly, the experience is reflected upon and relayed for what it makes intelligible: a lived emotionality that accounts for the subject's withdrawal from political action and engagement.

The affective economy of citizen–regime relations draws on subsidiary exchanges in the school and the family. Formative experiences of discipline through the military training lessons and civics classes, and of being the object of monitoring by school inspectors and trainers, were all part of an order subsumed within the rule of violence. Stalking the halls and courtyards, the inspectors and trainers were relays and conduits of practices of subjectivation in tune with the system of rule. In a parallel manner to the depicted homology between the school and the regime, in recollections of everyday life under the Hafez al-Asad regime, some Syrians drew connecting lines between practices of government in the family and at regime level, starkly stating that they saw a direct line between the figure of Hafez al-Asad and their fathers. These observations are neither merely anecdotal nor exhaustive of citizens' experiences of government. Rather, they illuminate ways of thinking and feeling that develop in relation to practices of subjectivation (regimentation and securitisation). In turn, they are informative of the elements that shape the political positionality of citizens, not in fixed terms but in contingent and situational terms.

Syrians' recollections of everyday life under the Hafez al-Asad dictatorship speak of shared experiences of school and family that compelled

---

[1] For example, one video that circulated widely during the early days of the Uprising showed a young demonstrator forced to kneel and kiss an officer's boot, another showed protesters made to sit at pupils' desks in a school classroom while being slapped by security men.

performances of deference and subservience. Yet what their narratives underscore is that they felt a compulsion to enact docility as, for example, in their shouting slogans in school assemblies that they did not believe or understand. This compelled performance was a cause of discomfort and discordance for the youth who belonged to what is dubbed 'the Ba'th generation'. In some cases, their narratives affirm a desire for self-distancing from institutions and figures of authority. It is therefore important to consider the impact of the rancour and disquiet generated by enforced performances. In some instances, youths sought alternative spheres of action to the Ba'th-saturated spaces (Sufi orders, for example). More often, however, they found the alternatives – available because they were tolerated, if not co-opted, by the regime – to be unsatisfactory.

Ultimately, the party's monopoly over public space and discourse along with the securitisation and militarisation of mundane activities framed practices and routines that embodied abjection and precarity. Walking on the sidewalk, driving a car or taking a bus ride were activities that potentially put the subject at risk, exposing him or her to the disciplining violence of security services personnel. Passing by the security kiosks, ordinary citizens such as Hussam (see Chapter 3) experienced dread and had 'terrible feelings'. The emotionality evoked by Hussam alerts us to the kind of situated practices improvised in relation to the infrastructures of power. Hussam, like most other citizens, had to calibrate his moves so as to avoid encountering the security kiosks and the men occupying them. It is in such routines and relational practices that the affects of precarity and abjection are embedded. In part, negotiating a simple activity like traversing a sidewalk was infused with apprehension and dread. In his narrative of such a routine, Hussam also relayed his indignation at this predicament. In his account, the terrible feelings he had motivated his decision to leave Syria. This complex affectivity is underwritten by the extensive emergency powers that enable the petty sovereignty of the soldiers and policemen who would take offence at perceived slights such as a misplaced look or a posture conveying a hint of defiance.

Routine violence acquires its full import in conjunction with the spectacular violence enacted in Hama. Silenced, and communicated in silences and elided speech, the memories of the violence in Hama are embodied through affective practices that are constitutive of the subject. Embodied humiliation and violation is lived in a silence that is enjoined by the injunction 'not to speak so as not to let words out'. Still, the memories are lived in the everyday in visceral ways: in the feeling of the pain of interrupted life – the Hama survivor who could no longer make the sweet rice and who, on her prayer beads, called out in daily supplication

'*Ya latif-Ya latif*' ('O Merciful One'). The silenced memories of massacres haunted Hamawis and Syrians in a myriad of ways. Importantly, in line with the pedagogical objective of violence, the haunting referenced the fate that could befall them should they oppose the regime.

Syrians' silence about the violence of Hama signified not forgetting, but learnt lessons and lived memories. The silence was formative of Syrians as political subjects. It reminded them of their daily dissimulations and, for some, like novelist Manhal al-Sarraj, it elicited a feeling of betrayal of those killed and buried under the rubble of erased neighbourhoods such as al-Kilaniyya. Additionally, in Manhal al-Sarraj's narrative, silence entwined with acts of complicity with the regime in the pursuit of daily living, exemplified by Hamawis who, seeking compensation for their material losses, blamed the Muslim Brotherhood for the destruction of their homes and the death of their relatives and, in some cases, abandoned their quest for an account of the whereabouts of disappeared family members, settling instead for the issuance of a death certificate. Enforced complicity deepened feelings of humiliation as when Syrians, including Hamawis, were called upon to take part in rallies in support of the president. Subjects who joined in performances requiring dissimulation felt inevitably troubled, compromised and humiliated. Al-Sarraj notes that there was a deeply felt sentiment that this was fate and that it had to be accepted (*hadha huwa al-qadar*). Yet while self-enforced silence may express resignation to fate, the embodied memories of lived humiliation remain simultaneously constraining and demanding of action.

Against the imposed silencing on the Hama violence, Syrians both feared and anticipated the massacre. With the unfolding of the 2011 Uprising, the politics of the massacre rose to the surface. In this respect, the performative structure of the massacre is key to understanding its governmental objectives and effects. Massacres, as events and acts of extreme violence, are imprinted with the hallmarks of horror. At a basic level, there is the body horror resulting from gruesome acts causing disfigurement and undermining the figural unity of the body. Further, massacres unfold a narrative structure to be interpreted and understood within the discourses and practices of rule. The Syrian regime promoted sectarianism as a broad frame for interpreting the violence, positing the enemy as marauding jihadist gangs motivated by hatred toward religious minorities, Alawis and others. This interpretative frame was also adopted by segments of the opposition and ordinary citizens whereby the killings are invested with sectarian assignations by reference to the sect membership of the perpetrators and victims. This framing underpinned one dimension of the narrativisation of violence and its horror quality: the interchangeability of the identities of victims and perpetrators, while still preserving the 'us' and 'them' divide drawn around loyalists and the opposition. Although the discourse of sectarianism may be used to account for the contested claims of responsibilities and culpabilities, the ambiguities and inconsistencies that characterise acts of extreme violence arise through a particular narrative structure and emplotment of violent events.

Through emplotment and narrativisation, enactments of violence unfold as a play of mirrors wherein perpetrators and victims become interchangeable, hence creating ambiguities and uncertainties as to who is killing whom. The murkiness surrounding the al-Houla massacre was not solely or primarily the result of contested claims about the sect affiliation of the victims (whether they were Sunnis or converts to Shi'i Islam). Rather, in the theatre of loyalist and oppositionist confrontation, the tropes of impersonation and of staging are lenses through which the citizens view and interpret the events. In addition to the sectarian labels used as shorthand to identify the warring sides, culprits, in this particular case, are cast as impersonators of regime forces. In narratives of other cases of gruesome killings, regime forces were charged with impersonating victims by dressing them in national army uniforms. It is possible that fact-finding investigations and detective work could sift through information and evidence to determine the true identity of victims and culprits. However, the play of mirrors arises from a rationality of violence and from a mode of comprehending it. The regime, in its pursuit of a politics of annihilation of any and all opponents, calls forth a fantastical enemy that must be slain. Meanwhile, the conjured-up enemies mimic the all-powerful regime.

Indeterminacy and ambiguity appear to be key, perhaps inbuilt, qualities of extreme violence. It is such qualities that lend violence its uncanny effects. In this respect, the mystery case of Zaynab al-Hosni's 'murder' and resurrection is paradigmatic of a particular mode of governmental violence. The case involved gruesome acts of body horror, specifically decapitation and disfigurement. Further, the staged resurrection of Zaynab, the supposed victim, deepened this horror. The case is revealing in showing the patterning of affects, specifically the bewilderment and feelings of disconcert that are generated in the subject-citizens. Positioned as witnesses, spectators and prospective victims, these citizens were called upon to puzzle out the mystery, seek answers to questions about the true identity of the victim whose body was dismembered and handed to the al-Hosni family, and about the role that state agents played in the staging of the murder and resurrection of Zaynab: How was it possible for the state to issue a death certificate and authorise burial of a person and then bring the same person back to life? The suspense and the mystification with which such questions are met are elements of the conditions of rule and are understood as such by the subjects of rule. Citizens may attempt to reach a resolution to the mystification and uncertainties generated in the performances of violence, while still recognising that within the terms of rule, such resolution is unattainable. Therein lies the paradox of the political uncanny – a condition of domesticated horror.

Violence, both in its routine and spectacular manifestations, structured relations and interaction between citizens and the regime in Syria. Importantly, institutions, practices and relations of violence were formative of Syrians' political subjectivities, shaping their interpretative horizons and their shared understandings of the form of rule. The pedagogy of violence that developed within apparatuses such as the prison and the massacre, or that took expression in everyday encounters with agents of the security forces, worked through citizens' affect, infusing them and their lived environment with the senses of dread and precarity. There are no generalised and simple terms in which Syrians inhabited this environment and negotiated their relation to the terms of rule. Their withdrawal and retreat from public engagement as well as their political rising referenced conditions of lived abjection. That dissent and political opposition was never fully banished is attested to by the continued centrality of incarceration, torture and killing to the conduct of government over the entire history of the Asad regime. The politics of elimination and eradication, made visible with the Uprising, lay at the heart of the system of rule.

Postscript

In October 2015, I visited Lama, a thirty-eight-year-old Syrian woman from Qusayr, in her new home in Shtura, Lebanon. Lama had just moved home with her family. It was the third house move she had made in two years since she left Syria, displaced from her town and life. She was in Shtura with her husband, three young children and her elderly in-laws. The children were attending primary school run by a refugee support organisation. The dwelling the family occupied was on land owned by Bedouins. The husband rented it as 'bare structure' ('ala al-'azm, literally meaning a skeletal frame) without basic facilities. Lama's husband installed the makeshift windows, the cement flooring and the toilet. Still bare, the work as described by Lama nonetheless brought much improvement to the structure they rented.

Lama's narrative about how her family joined the Uprising and was then displaced was similar to accounts given by other refugees I interviewed in Beirut and in Shtura. Yet I was struck by a statement she made as she was talking about her life in Qusayr (her hometown in Syria), her work as a seamstress, her husband's municipality job and the comforts their jobs afforded them back then. Her narrative of loss and grief was offset by a heartfelt statement she made. In the course of conversation, she remarked to me: 'But our Revolution is beautiful.' From Lama's reflections, I gathered that the beauty of the Revolution was that she and other fellow citizens rose up in support of the people of Dar'a. She explained that had they not risen, they would not count as human beings.

Lama's comments speak to statements made by Syrian novelist Khaled Khalifa in a recent interview. Khalifa observed that Syrians lived in shame over what happened in the early 1980s in Aleppo, Hama and other places where massacres took place. The shame, according to Khalifa, was felt for having shied away from confronting the regime over the atrocities it committed. Khalifa used 'ar, the Arabic word for shame, to describe Syrians' affective relation to their history and to the regime. However, 'ar is not a word that had or has currency in Syrian writings and speech.

202

Instead, *dhul*, meaning humiliation and abjection, was commonly used to communicate how Syrians felt in relation to the regime, and to explain what drives their silences and motivates them to retreat, at times, and to act at others.

I interpret Lama's comments as signalling a profoundly felt responsiblity to act so as to defy the prospect of publicly lived humiliation which she and many other Syrians could foresee should the regime re-enact, in Darʿa, the Hama violence (that is, should the regime decide 'to do Hama again'). The spectacular violence of Hama stoked fears and horrified. Meanwhile, the imposed silence meant that Hama's horrors loomed large and the menace of more violence inhabited the landscape and its people. Thus, the people lived in anticipation of the massacre, pondering what would make one ready for it, or what could be done to avoid it or forestall it. The ghost of Hama lived on in embodied memories of humiliation – memories that were both constraining and demanding of action.

The question may be raised as to why Syrians would let their guard down, as they did in the 2011 Uprising, and enter into a domain of action premised on destruction and annihilation. Should the slogan 'death is better than abjection' (*al-mawt wala al-madhala*) be taken literally? I cannot claim that I have answered this question in my account of the terms of rule in Syria. It may be the case that practices of violence, whether routine or spectacular, kept Syrians in check and constrained their action for some time. Within the same terms of rule and practices of government, the material and symbolic possibilities for resistance, not only in small ways, but also in extraordinary and unexpected ways, existed. The number of Syrians arrested and subsequently incarcerated throughout the 1980s and 1990s gives a clear indication that political dissidence was constant, though the scale of activism varied. It is noteworthy that in the aftermath of Hama, human rights activists and Kurdish political actors pressed on with demands for greater civil rights and inevitably were subject to imprisonment. Activism persisted in the 2000s in the guise of the civil society forums and in dissident writings. I consider the artistic work of memory to have been part of Syrians' drive for a public accounting for the historical violence euphemistically named 'the events'.

I do not argue that the Uprising was inevitable. Nor do I argue that it was anticipated as an eruption of hidden tensions beneath the surface. It is the case that a great many Syrians aspired to the day the Asad regime would fall. In 2005, when the regime was faltering under the weight of international pressure linked to the Hariri investigation, there was a short-lived hope that international sanctions and the loss of support among its core constituencies would bring down the regime.

The scenarios at the time were that an inner circle member, possibly Asef Shawkat or Ghazi Kan'an, would remove Bashar al-Asad and (unrealistically) lead a transition. Among the regime's strongest critics, the hope was that an Alawi officer would carry out a coup d'état. But the moment of change, if there was one, came and passed.

In the 2000s civil activism focused on ending the state of emergency and the release of political prisoners, along with the removal of Article 8 from the Constitution. Civil activists spoke of lifting the ceiling of demands for reform. In dissident intellectual circles, the relative freedom of expression that the internet afforded in the early 2000s may have lulled the opposition into momentary hope. These hopes were quickly crushed with the entrenchment of security apparatuses, the rise in the number of prisoners and the emergence of Sednaya Prison as a substitute for Tadmur. The immobility of political life was thus confirmed. What has changed is that humiliation and abjection were now lived on the outside, more visibly. Visibility invited accounting. The Ba'th generation's exercises of self-authoring show a concern for giving account. Both cynicism and self-criticism characterised exercises of self-authoring prior to the Uprising. For ordinary Syrians, the moment of giving account came in 2011. The divisions and chasms separating them were expressed in their different positioning and narratives. For some within the Ba'th 'generation of small defeats', lived abjection was now fashioned in oppositional terms.

I return to Lama's aesthetics of Revolution. Amidst the destruction and ruins, it may be possible to still find the edifying force of the initial quest for affirming one's humanity and aspiration to live a life worth living. This does not mean that there are no regrets and there is no sorrow that the quest for a worthy life was subverted by the powers of death and destruction.

References

Abd-Allah, Omar F. (1983). *The Islamic Struggle in Syria*. Berkeley: Mizan Press.
Abu Lughod, Lila and Catherine A. Lutz (eds.). (1990). *Language and the Politics of Emotion*. Cambridge: Cambridge University Press.
Agamben, Giorgio. (1998). *Homo Sacer: Sovereign Power and Bare Life*. Stanford: Stanford University Press.
    (2005). *State of Exception*. Translated by Kevin Attell. Chicago: University of Chicago Press.
Anderson, Ben. (2016). *Encountering Affect: Capacities, Apparatuses, Conditions*. London and New York: Routledge.
Anker, Elisabeth. (2014). The Liberalism of Horror. *Social Research* 81, 4: 795–823.
Appadurai, Arjun. (2006). *Fear of Small Numbers: An Essay on the Geography of Anger*. Durham and London: Duke University Press.
Arendt, Hannah. (1968). *The Origins of Totalitarianism*. New York: Harcourt.
Aretxaga, Begoña. (1995). Dirty Protest: Symbolic Overdetermination and Gender in Northern Ireland Ethnic Violence. *Ethos* 23, 2: 123–48.
    (2000a). Playing Terrorist: Ghastly Plots and Ghostly State. *Journal of Spanish Cultural Studies* 1, 1: 43–58.
    (2000b). A Fictional Reality: Paramilitary Death Squads and the Construction of State Terror in Spain. In Jeffrey A. Sluka (ed.), *Death Squad: The Anthropology of State Violence*. Philadelphia: University of Pennsylvania Press, pp. 46–69.
Argenti, Nicolas and Katharina Schramm (eds.). (2010). *Remembering Violence: Anthropological Perspectives on Intergenerational Transmission*. New York and Oxford: Berghahn Books.
Asad, Talal. (2007). *On Suicide Bombing*. New York: Columbia University Press.
Asfour, Lana. (2006). Wheeling and Dealing. *New Statesman*, 5 June.
Balanche, Fabrice. (2000). Les Alaouites, l'Espace et le Pouvoir dans la Region Cotière Syrienne: Une integration nationale ambigue. PhD thesis, Department of Geography, Faculty of Law, Economics and Social Sciences, University of Tours.
    (2011). Géographie de la Révolte Syrienne. *Outre-Terre* 29, 3: 437–58.
Bargu, Banu. (2014). *Starve and Immolate: The Politics of Human Weapons*. New York: Columbia University Press.
Batatu, Hanna. (1982). Syria's Muslim Brethren. *Middle East Report* 110 (November–December): 12–20.

(1999). *Syria's Peasantry, the Descendants of Its Lesser Notables and their Politics.* Princeton: Princeton University Press.

Brass, Paul R. (1997). *Theft of an Idol: Text and Context in the Representation of Collective Violence.* Princeton: Princeton University Press.

Burkitt, Ian. (2014). *Emotions and Social Relations.* London: Sage.

Butler, Judith. (1997). *The Psychic Life of Power: Theories of Subjection.* Stanford: Stanford University Press.

Campbell, Elaine. (2010). The Emotional Life of Governmental Power. *Foucault Studies* 9: 35–53.

Cavarero, Adriana. (2011). *Horrorism: Naming Contemporary Violence.* Translated by William McCuaig. New York: Columbia University Press.

Cesereaunu, Alexandra. (2006). An Overview of Political Torture in the Twentieth Century. *Journal of Religions and Ideologies* 5, 14 (Summer): 120–43.

Chatterjee, Choi and Karen Petrone. (2008). Models of Selfhood and Subjectivity: The Soviet Case in Historical Perspective. *Slavic Studies* 67, 4 (Winter): 967–86.

Chatty, Dawn. (2010). The Bedouin in Contemporary Syria: The Persistence of Tribal Authority. *Middle East Journal* 64, 1: 29–49.

Connerton, Paul. (1988). *How Societies Remember.* Cambridge: Cambridge University Press.

Coronil, Fernando and Julie Skurski. (1991). Dismembering and Remembering the Nation: The Semantics of Political Violence in Venezuela. *Comparative Studies in Society and History* 33, 2: 288–337.

Das, Veena. (2009). *Life and Worlds: Violence and the Descent into the Ordinary.* Berkeley and Los Angeles: University of California Press.

Dean, Mitchell. (2004). Four Theses on the Powers of Life and Death. *Contretemps* 5: 16–29.

Debrix, François and Alexander Barder. (2012). *Beyond Biopolitics: Theory, Violence and Horror in World Politics.* London: Routledge.

Edele, Mark. (2007). Soviet Society, Social Structure and Everyday Life: Major Frameworks Reconsidered. *Kritika: Explorations in Russian and Eurasian History* 8, 2: 349–73.

Edkins, Jenny. (2003). *Trauma and the Memory of Politics.* Cambridge: Cambridge University Press.

Falasca-Zamponi, Simonetta. (1997). *Fascist Spectacle: The Aesthetics of Power in Mussolini's Italy.* Berkeley: University of California Press.

Fassin, Didier. (2009). Another Politics of Life is Possible. *Theory, Culture and Society* 26, 5: 44–60.

Fehérváry, Krisztina. (2009). Goods and States: The Political Logic of State-Socialist Material Culture. *Comparative Studies in Society and History* 51, 2: 426–59.

Feldman, Allen. (1991). *Formations of Violence: The Narrative of the Body and Political Terror in Northern Ireland.* Chicago: University of Chicago Press.

(2003). Political Terror and the Technologies of Memory: Sacrifice, Commodification, and Actuarial Moralities. *Radical History Review* 85: 58–73.

Fentress, James and Chris Wickham. (1992). *Social Memory.* Oxford: Blackwell.

Fitzpatrick, Sheila. (1999). *Everyday Stalinism: Ordinary Life in Extraordinary Times, Soviet Russia in the 1930s.* Oxford: Oxford University Press.

Foucault, Michel. (1977). *Discipline and Punish: The Birth of the Prison.* Translated by Alan Sheridan. New York: Vintage Books.

(2003). *Society Must Be Defended: Lectures at the Collège de France, 1975–1976.* Translated by David Macey. New York: Picador.

(2015). *The Punitive Society: Lectures at the Collège de France, 1972–1973.* Edited by Bernard Harcourt. Translated by Graham Burchell. New York: Palgrave MacMillan.

Freud, Sigmund. (2003 [1919]). The Uncanny. In *The Uncanny.* Translated by David McLintock. New York: Penguin Books, 121–62.

Frosh, Stephen. (2013). *Hauntings: Psychoanalysis and Ghostly Transmissions.* New York: Palgrave Macmillan.

Gelder, Ken (ed.). (2000). *The Horror Reader.* London: Routledge.

Gelvin, James. (1998). *Divided Loyalties: Nationalism and Mass Politics in Syria at the Close of Empire.* Berkeley: University of California Press.

Gentile, Emilio. (2000). The Sacralisation of Politics: Definitions, Interpretations and Reflections on the Question of Secular Religion and Totalitarianism. Translated by Robert Mallett. *Totalitarian Movements and Political Religions* 1, 1: 18–55.

Girard, René. (1979). *Violence and the Sacred.* Translated by Patrick Gregory. Baltimore: Johns Hopkins University Press.

Giroux, H. (2005). The Terror of Neo-Liberalism: Rethinking the Significance of Cultural Politics. *College Literature* 32, 1: 1–19.

Gordon, Avery F. (2008 [1997]). *Ghostly Matters: Haunting and the Sociological Imagination.* Minneapolis: University of Minnesota Press.

Halbwachs, Maurice. (1992). *On Collective Memory.* Edited and translated with an Introduction by Lewis Coser. Chicago: University of Chicago Press.

Haugbolle, Sune. (2008). Imprisonment, Truth Telling and Historical Memory in Syria. *Mediterranean Politics* 13, 2: 261–76.

Herbert, Matt. (2014). Partisans, Profiteers and Criminals: Syria's Illicit Economy. *The Fletcher Forum of World Affairs* 38, 1 (Winter): 69–85.

Hermann, Rainer. (2012). Neue Erkenntnisse zu Getöteten von Hula. Abermals Massaker in Syrien. (New insights into death in Houla). *Frankfurter Allgemeine,* 7 June. www.faz.net/aktuell/politik/neue-erkenntnisse-zu-getoeteten-von-hula-abermals-massaker-in-syrien-11776496.html

Hills, Matt. (2005). *The Pleasures of Horror.* London: Continuum.

Hinnebusch, Raymond. (1980). Political Recruitment and Socialisation in Syria: The Case of the Revolutionary Youth Federation. *International Journal of Middle East Studies* 11, 2: 143–74.

(1989). *Peasant and Bureaucracy in Ba'thist Syria: The Political Economy of Rural Development.* Boulder: Westview Press.

(1990). *Authoritarian Power and State Formation in Syria: Army, Party and Peasant.* Boulder: Westview Press.

(2001). *Syria: Revolution from Above.* London: Routledge.

Humphrey, Michael. (2002). *The Politics of Atrocity and Reconciliation: From Terror to Trauma.* London and New York: Routledge.

Ismail, Salwa. (2009). Changing Social Structure, Shifting Alliances and Authoritarianism in Syria. In Fred H. Lawson (ed.), *Demystifying Syria.* London: Saqi Books, pp. 13–28.

(2011).The Syrian Uprising: Imagining and Performing the Nation. *Studies in Ethnicity and Nationalism* 11, 3: 538–49.

(2013). Urban Subalterns in the Arab Revolutions: Cairo and Damascus in Comparative Perspective. *Comparative Studies in Society and History* 55, 4: 865–94.

Jelin, Elizabeth. (2003). *State Repression and the Labors of Memory*. Minneapolis: University of Minnesota Press.

Kahf, Mohja. (2001). The Silences of Contemporary Syrian Literature. *World Literature Today* 75, 2: 224–36.

Kalyvas, Stathis N. (2003). The Ontology of 'Political Violence': Action and Identity in Civil Wars. *Perspectives on Politics* 1, 3: 475–94.

Kang, Jin Woong. (2011). Understanding the Dynamics of State Power in North Korea: Militant Nationalism and People's Everyday Lives. A Dissertation Submitted to the Faculty of the Graduate School of the University of Minnesota.

Khaddour, Kheder. (2015). Assad's Ghetto: Why the Syrian Army Remains Loyal. *Carnegie Middle East*, 4 November. http://carnegie-mec.org/2015/11/04/assad-s-officer-ghetto-why-syrian-army-remains-loyal-pub-61449

Khalaf, Sulayman. (1981). Family, Village and the Political Party: Articulation of Social Change in Contemporary Rural Syria. Unpublished PhD Dissertation, Department of Anthropology, University of California, Los Angeles.

(1987). Shaykhs, Peasants and Party Comrades in Northern Syria. In M. Mundy and B. Mussalam (eds.), *The Transformation of Nomadic Society in the Arab East*. Cambridge: Cambridge University Press, pp. 110–22.

Khalili, Laleh. (2008). Commemorating Battles and Massacres in the Palestinian Refugee Camps of Lebanon. *American Behavioral Scientist* 51, 11: 1562–74.

Kristeva, Julia. (1982). *Powers of Horror: An Essay on Abjection*. Translated by Leon S. Roudiez. New York: Columbia University Press.

Krylova, Anna. (2000). The Tenacious Liberal Subject in Soviet Studies. *Kritika: Explorations in Russian and Eurasian History* 1, 1: 119–46.

Lambek, Michael. (1996). Past Imperfect: Remembering as Moral Practice. In Paul Antze and Michael Lambek (eds.), *Tense Past: Cultural Essays in Trauma and Memory*. New York: Routledge, pp. 235–54.

Langer, Lawrence. (1991). *Holocaust Testimonies: The Ruins of Memory*. New Haven: Yale University Press.

Lawson, Fred. (1982). Social Bases for the Hama Revolt. *MERIP Reports* 110: 24–8.

Lazreg, Marnia. (2008). *Torture and the Twilight of Empire: From Algiers to Baghdad*. Princeton: Princeton University Press.

Leavitt, John. (1996). Meaning and Feeling in the Anthropology of Emotions. *American Ethnologist* 23, 3: 514–39.

Leenders, Reinoud and Steven Heydemann. (2012). Popular Mobilisation in the Syrian Uprising: Opportunity and Threat, and the Networks of the Early Rises. *Mediterranean Politics* 17, 2: 139–59.

Lefèvre, Raphael. (2013). *Ashes of Hama: The Muslim Brotherhood in Syria*. Oxford: Oxford University Press.

Li, Tania Murray. (2007). *The Will to Improve: Governmentality, Development and the Practice of Politics*. Durham and London: Duke University Press.

Lund, Aron. (2016). Asad's Broken Base: The Case of Idlib. *The Century Foundation*. https://tcf.org/content/report/assads-broken-base-case-idlib/

Lyford, Amy. (2000). The Aesthetics of Dismemberment: Surrealism and the Musée du Val-de-Grace in 1917. *Cultural Critique* 46: 45–79.

McDougall, James. (2010). Social Memories 'in the Flesh': War and Exile in Algerian Self-Writing. *Alif: Journal of Comparative Poetics* 30: 34–56.

Malkki, Liisa. (1995). *Purity and Exile: Violence, Memory and National Cosmology among Hutu Refugees in Tanzania*. Chicago: University of Chicago Press.

Mbembe, Achille. (2001). *On the Postcolony*. Berkeley: University of California Press.

    (2003). Necropolitics. Translated by Libby Meintjes. *Public Culture* 15, 1: 11–40.

Mbembe, Achille and Janet Roitman. (1995). Figures of the Subject in Times of Crisis. *Public Culture* 7: 323–52.

Michaud, Gerard. (1982). The Importance of Bodyguards. *MERIP Reports* 110 (November–December): 29–31.

Mistzal, Barbara A. (2003). *Theories of Social Remembering*. Maidenhead: Open University, McGraw Hill Professional Publishing.

Nakkash, Aziz. (2013). *The Alawite Dilemma in Homs: Survival, Solidarity and the Making of Community*. Berlin: Friedrich Ebert Stiftung.

Nash, David and Anne-Marie Kilday. (2010). *Cultures of Shame: Exploring Crime and Morality in Britain, 1600–1900*. New York: Palgrave Macmillan.

Navaro-Yashin, Yael. (2009). Affective Spaces, Melancholic Objects: Ruination and the Production of Anthropological Knowledge. *Journal of the Royal Anthropological Society* 15: 1–18.

    (2012). *The Make Believe Space: Affective Geography in a Post War Polity*. Durham: Duke University Press.

Nelson, J. S. (2003). Four Forms of Terrorism: Horror, Dystopia, Thriller and Noir. *Poroi: An Interdisciplinary Journal of Rhetorical Analysis and Invention* 2, 1: 79–107.

Oksala, Johanna. (2012). *Foucault, Politics and Violence*. Evanston: Northwestern University Press.

Olick, Jeffrey K. and Joyce Robbins. (1998). Social Memory Studies: From Collective Memory to the Historical Sociology of Mnemonic Practices. *Annual Review of Sociology* 24: 105–40.

Palmer, Bryan D. (1997). Night in the Capitalist Cold War City: Noir and the Cultural Politics of Darkness. *Left History* 5, 2: 57–76.

Pandey, Gyanendra. (2001). *Remembering Partition*. Cambridge: Cambridge University Press.

Perthes, Volker. (1997). *The Political Economy of Syria under Asad*. London: I. B. Tauris.

Pierret, Thomas. (2013). *Religion and State in Syria: The Sunni Ulama from Coup to Revolution*. Cambridge: Cambridge University Press.

Pierret, Thomas and Kjetil Selvik. (2009). Limits of Authoritarian Upgrading: Private Welfare, Islamic Charities, and the Rise of the Zayd Movement in Syria. *International Journal of Middle East Studies* 41, 4: 595–614.

Pinto, Paulo G. (2006). Sufism, Moral Performance and the Public Sphere in Syria. *Revue des mondes Musulmans et de la Méditerranée* 115–116: 155–71.

Poole, Ross. (2008). Memory, History and the Claims of the Past. *Memory Studies* 1, 2: 149–66.

Rabo, Anika. (1985). Great Expectations: Perceptions on Development in Northeast Syria. *Ethnos: Journal of Anthropology* 40, 3–4: 221–5.

Rejali, Darius. (2007). *Torture and Democracy*. Princeton: Princeton University Press.

Reno, William. (2008 [1995]). *Corruption and State Politics in Sierra Leone*. Cambridge: Cambridge University Press.

Reuter, Christopher. (2012). Increasing Barbarity: Gaining a Clear View of the Syrian War. *Spiegel International Online*, 31 December. www.spiegel.de/international/world/gaining-a-clearer-view-of-the-increasing-barbarity-in-syrian-civil-war-a-874027-2.html

Reuter, Christopher and Adhun Abd al-Khader. (2012). A Syrian Bloodbath Revisited: Searching for the Truth behind the Houla Massacre. *Spiegel International Online*, 23 July. www.spiegel.de/international/world/a-look-back-at-the-houla-massacre-in-syria-a-845854.html

Richardson, Michael. (2016). *Gestures of Testimony: Torture, Trauma, and Affect in Literature*. London: Bloomsbury Academy.

Ricoeur, Paul. (2004). *Memory, History, Forgetting*. Translated by Kathleen Blamey and David Pellauer. Chicago: University of Chicago Press.

Rivkin-Fish, Michele. (2009). Tracing Landscapes of the Past in Class Subjectivity: Practices of Memory and Distinction in Marketising Russia. *American Ethnologist* 36, 1: 79–95.

Robben, Antonius. (2000). State Terror in the Netherworld: Disappearance and Reburial in Argentina. In Jeffrey A. Sluka (ed.), *Death Squad: The Anthropology of State Violence*. Philadelphia: University of Pennsylvania Press, pp. 91–113.

Rojas, Cristina and Daniel Tubb. (2013). La Violencia in Colombia, through Stories of the Body. *Bulletin of Latin American Research* 32, 1: 126–50.

Roldan, Mary. (2002). *Blood and Fire: La Violencia in Antioquia, Colombia 1946–1953*. Durham: Duke University Press.

Rose, Nikolas. (1999 [1990]). *Governing the Soul: The Shaping of the Private Self*. London and New York: Free Association Books.

Royle, Nicholas. (2003). *The Uncanny*. Manchester: Manchester University Press.

Sadowski, Yahya M. (1985). Guns and Cadres: The Eighth Regional Congress of the Syrian Ba'th. *MERIP Reports* 134: 3–8.

Salamandra, Christa. (2004). *A New Old Damascus: Authenticity and Distinction in Urban Syria*. Bloomington: Indiana University Press.

Scarry, Elaine. (1985). *The Body in Pain: The Making and Unmaking of the World*. Oxford: Oxford University Press.

Seale, Patrick. (1988). *Asad of Syria: The Struggle for the Middle East*. London: I. B. Tauris.

Sémelin, Jacques. (2003). Toward a Vocabulary of Massacre and Genocide. *Journal of Genocide Research* 5, 2: 193–210.

Sidel, John. (1999). *Capital, Coercion and Bossism in the Philippines*. Stanford: Stanford University Press.

Stern, Steve J. (2006). *Remembering Pinochet's Chile: On the Eve of London 1998* (Book One in the Trilogy: The Memory Box of Pinochet's Chile). Durham and London: Duke University Press.

Strozier, Robert M. (2002). *Foucault, Subjectivity and Identity: Historical Constructions of Subject and Self*. Detroit: Wayne State University Press.

Suarez-Orozco, Marcelo M. (1990). Speaking the Unspeakable: Towards a Psychosocial Understanding of Responses to Terror. *Ethos* 18, 3: 353–83.

(2003). The Treatment of Children in the 'Dirty War': Ideology, State Terrorism, and the Abuse of Children in Argentina. In Scheper Hughes and Philippe Bourgois (eds.), *Violence in War and Peace: An Anthology*. Hoboken: Wiley-Blackwell, pp. 378–88.

Thompson, Elizabeth. (2000). *Colonial Citizens: Republican Rights, Paternal Privilege, and Gender in French Syria and Lebanon*. New York: Columbia University Press.

Tilly, Charles. (2003). *The Politics of Collective Violence*. Cambridge: Cambridge University Press.

Trouillot, Michel-Rolph. (1995). *Silencing the Past: Power and the Production of History*. Boston: Beacon Press.

Tyler, Imogen. (2009). Against Abjection. *Feminist Theory* 10, 1: 77–98.

(2013). *Revolting Subjects: Social Abjection and Resistance in Neoliberal Britain*. London: Zed Books.

Uribe, Maria Victoria. (2004a). Dismembering and Expelling: Semantics of Political Terror in Columbia. *Public Culture* 16, 1: 79–95.

(2004b). *Anthropologie de l'inhumanité: Essai sur la terreur en Colombie*. Translated from Spanish by Line Koslowski. Paris: Calmann-levy.

Van Dam, Nikolas. (1996). *The Struggle for Power in Syria: Politics and Society under Asad and the Ba'th Party*. New York: Palgrave Macmillan.

Warwick, Tie. (2004). The Psychic Life of Governmentality. *Culture, Theory and Critique* 45, 2: 161–76.

Wedeen, Lisa. (1999). *Ambiguities of Domination: Politics, Rhetoric, and Symbols in Contemporary Syria*. Chicago: University of Chicago Press.

Wetherell, Margaret. (2012). *Affect and Emotion: A New Social Science Understanding*. London: Sage.

Wisnewski, Jeremy J. (2010). *Understanding Torture*. Edinburgh: Edinburgh University Press.

Worren, Torstein Schiotz. (2007). Fear and Resistance: The Construction of Alawi Identity in Syria. Unpublished Master Thesis in Human Geography, Department of Sociology and Human Geography, University of Oslo.

Zeydanlıoğlu, Welat. (2009). Torture and Turkification in the Diyarbakir Military Prison. In Welat Zeydanlıoğlu and John T. Parry (eds.), *Rights, Citizenship and Torture: Perspectives on Evil, Law and the State*. Oxford: Inter-Disciplinary Press, pp. 73–92.

Žižek, Slavoj. (1991). *Looking Awry: An Introduction to Jacques Lacan Through Popular Culture*. Cambridge: MIT Press.

ARABIC LANGUAGE REFERENCES

Abbas, Kamil. (2006). Ihtiraf Thawri 'ala Tariqat Ma al-'Amal fi Madinat Hamah 'Am 1977 (Revolutionary Apprenticeship Taking the Path of *What Is to Be Done* in Hama City 1977). *Al-Hiwar al-Mutamadan*, 9 May. www.m.ahewar .org/s.asp?aid=64351&r=0

Abd al-Hakim, Omar. (1991). *Al-Thawra al-Islamiyya al-Jihadiyya fi Surriyya (the Jihadist Islamic Revolution in Syria)*. NP.

Abi Samra, Muhammad. (2012a). *Mawt al-Abad al-Suri: Shihadat Jil al-Samt wal-Thawra (The Death of the Syrian Eternal: Testimonies of the Generation of Silence and Revolution)*. Beirut: Riyyad al-Rayyis Books.

(2012b). Shabihat Halab (Shabiha of Aleppo). *Al-Nahar Supplement*, 15 September. https://mhamadabisamra.wordpress.com/2012/09/15/شبّيحة-حلب//

Abu Nijm. (2017). Arb'un 'Aman 'ala al-Wilada (Forty Years Since Birth). *Al-Aan* 84. https://facebook.com/pacsyria/posts/1480945861917823

Al-Mundasa al-Suriyya. (2011). Zaynab al-Hosni … Shu Mshan al-Jusah? (Zaynab al-Hosni: What about the Corpse?). 28 September. http://the-syrian.com/archives/42478

Amiralay, Omar. (1970). *Muhawala 'An Sad al-Furat* (An Essay on the Euphrates Dam). Documentary film.

(1997). *Wa Hunak Ashya' Kathira Kana Yumkin An Yatahadath 'Anha al-Mar'* (And There Are Many Other Things One Could Have Talked About). Documentary film.

(2003). *Tufan fi Bilad al-Ba'th* (Flood in the Country of the Ba'th). Documentary film.

Attasi, Mohammed Ali al-. (2003). 'An Mushkilat al-Shabab (On the Problems of the Youth). In *Fa'iliyyat al-Muntada: al-Sana al Ula, 2001 (Activities of the Forum, First Year-2001)*. Damascus: Muntada Jamal al-Din al-Attasi lil-Hiwar al-Watani, pp. 320–32.

Badawiyya, Nahid. (2014). Shihada 'An al-I'tiqal al-Siyasi fi Suriyya (A Testimony About Political Internment in Syria). *Al Hiwar al-Mutamadin*, 21 October. www.m.ahewar.org/s.asp?aid=438053&r=0&cid=0&u=&i=338&q=

Barout, Mohammed Jamal. (2012). *Al-'Aqd al-Akhir fi Tarikh Surriya: Jadaliyya al-Islah wal-Jumud (The Last Decade of Syria's History: The Dialectics of Stagnation and Reform)*. Doha: Centre for Research and Policy Studies.

Bassam, 'Abir (ed.). (2005). Surriyya min Awasit al-Thamaninat hata Awasit al-Tis'inat (Syria from the Mid 80s to the Mid 90s). *Sada al-Balad al-Lubnaniyya*. Republished in *Elaph*, 10 December. http://elaph.com/Web/NewsPapers/25/12/111795.htm?sectionarchive=NewsPapers

Berro, Muhammad. (2015). Sijn Tadmor … Dhakira min al-Jahim (Tadmur Prison … Memory from Hell). *Al-'Arabi al Jadid*, 1 July. www.alaraby.co.uk/politics/2015/6/1/ةركاذ-لقتعم-يف-رمدت

Biraqdar, Faraj al-. (2006). *Khiyanat al-Samt wa al-Lugha: Taghribati fi al-Sujun al-Suriyya (Betrayals of Silence and of Language: My Exile in Syrian Prisons)*. Beirut: Al-Jadid.

Bishara, Azmi. (2013). *Surriyya: Darb al Alaam Nahw al-Hurriyya, Muhawala fi al-Ta'rikh al-Rahin (Syria: The Path of Pain Towards Freedom, An Attempt for a Historiography of the Present)*. Doha: Arab Centre for Research and Policy Studies.

Dabbagh, Hiba al-. (ND). *Khams Daqa'iq wa Hasb: Tis' Sanawat fi al-Sijun al-Suriyya (Just Five Minutes: Nine Years in Syrian Prisons)*. NP.

Dahamsha, 'Abdallah al-. (2009 [1982]). *'Adhra' Hama (Hama Virgin)*. Beirut: Dar al-Nawa'ir.

Dalila, 'Aref. (2002). Al-Batala wal-Faqr: Asbabahuma wa 'Ilajahuma (Unemployment and Poverty: Their Causes and their Cure). *Al-Hiwar al-Mutamadin*, 5 August. http://m.ahewar.org/s.asp?aid=2411&r

Darwish, Sabir (ed.). (2015). *Suriyya: Tajrubat al-Mudun al-Muharrara (The Experience of Liberated Cities)*. Beirut: Riyyad al-Rayyis Books.

Deeb, Kamal. (2011). *Tarikh Suriyya al-Mu'asir min al-Intidab al-Firansi ila Sayf 2011 (The History of Modern Syria: From the French Mandate Until the Summer of 2011)*. Beirut: Dar al-Nahar.

Doghaym, Mahmud al-Sayyid al-. (2005). Na'm l-Hizb Kuluna Shurka' fi al-Watan, La l-kul al-Qam'iyyin wa al-Mutasalitin wa al-Zalama al-Murtashin (Yes to the Partisans of We Are All Partners in the Nation and No to the Partisans of Repression, and to the Unjust Bribe-Takers). 9 May. www.oroom.org/forum/threads/المحجتلة-سوري/3872

Eid, Abd al-Razzaq. (2005). Thaqafat al-Khawf (The Culture of Fear). In *Yas'alunak 'an al-Mujtama' al-Madani: Rabi' Dimishq al-Maw'ud (They Ask you about Civil Society: The Stifled Damascus Spring)*. Cairo: Center for Development and Civilization, pp. 55–67.

Faysal, Yusuf al-. (2007). *Dhikrayat wa Mawaqif (Memories and Stances)*. Damascus: al-Takwin.

Habib, Matanyous. (2004). Mudakhala fi Mushkilat al-Batala (An Intervention on the Problem of Unemployment). Syrian Economic Society. www.mafhoum.com/syr/articles_04/habib.htm

Haddad, Reda. (2004). Excerpts from the Testimony of the Journalist Reda Haddad. The Syrian Human Rights Committee, 11 January. www.shrc.org/?p=6891

Hadid, Khawla al-. (2012). Tawthiq Majzara al-Houla (Documenting the Houla Massacre). Al-Hadarah Blog. Posted 29 May. www.alhadarah.com/documents-وثائق/توثيق-مجزرة-الحولة-مجزرة-الحولة-وتح/

(2013). Majzarat 'Aqrab: Ta'addat al-Riwayat wa al-Qatil Wahid (The 'Aqrab Massacre: Narratives Are Plural, the Murder Is Singular). Al-Hadarah Blog. Posted 27 January. www.alhadarah.com/documents-وثائق/مجزرة-عقرب-تعدد-الروايات-و-القاتل-واحد/

Hallum, Mundhir Badr. (2009a). *Awlad Sakiba (Children of Shakiba)*. Algiers: Arab Scientific.

(2009b). *Saqat al-Azraq min al-Sama' (Blue Fell from the Sky)*. Beirut: Riyad El-Rayyes Books.

Hamidi, Ibrahim. (2005). Al-Asad Yasbih al-Amin al-'Am wa 'Ilgha al-Qiyada al-Qutriyya … Mu'tmar al Ba'th: Taghyyir fi 'al-Haras al-Qadim' … Tahat Saqf Baqa'uh al-Hizb al-Hakim (Asad Becomes General Secretary … The Ba'th Congress: Change of the 'Old Guard' for the Preservation of the Ruling Party). *Al-Hayat* 1539, 22 May, 15.

Hammad, Muhammad Salim. (1998). *Tadmur Shahid wa Mashhud (Palmyra: A Witness and a Testimony)*. Centre for Syrian Studies.

Hassan, Rosa Yassin. (2007). *Negative: Riwaya Tawthiqiyya (Negative: A Documentary Novel)*. Damascus: NP.

(2011a). *Abanos (Ebony)*. Damascus: al-Naya and Muhaka.

(2011b). Al-Khawf wal-Taraqub wal-Shabiha: fi Tahdim Bina Dhawakirna (Fear, Anticipation and Shabiha: On the Felling of the Architecture of our

Memories). *Safahat Surriyya*, 21 August. http://syria.alsafahat.net/
‏ذ-بنى-تهديم-في-و الشبيحة-ألترقب،-الخوف،/

Hassan, Ubay. (2009). *Hawiyyati Man Akun: Fi al-Ta'ifiyya wal Ithniyya al-Suriyyatayn (My Identity: Who Am I? On Syrian Sectarianism and Ethnicism)*. Beirut: Bisan.

Hassoun, Ali. (2004). Jil Kamil La Ya'rif min al-Hayat ila al-Tahrib: Madinat al-Qusayr Tadfa' Thaman Dhanb Lam Tartakibah!! (An Entire Generation that Knows in Life only Trafficking: Qusayr Pays the Price of a Crime it did not Commit). *Abyad Wa Aswad* 64, 12 January, 39–42.

Hayan, Salman. (2007). *Iqtisad al-Zil aw al-Iqtisad al-Khafi (Shadow Economy or Hidden Economy)*. Syrian Economic Society. www.mafhoum.com/syr/articles_07/suleiman.pdf

Hebo, Majed. (2001). Al-Mu'taqal al-Siyasi, Shihada: al-Halaqa al-Ula (The Political Detention Centre, Testimony: Part One). *Moqarabat* 2/3: 176–82.

(2002). Shihada 2 (Testimony 2). *Moqarabat* 6/7. www.mokarabat.com/m17.6-7.htm

Hourani, Akram al-. (2000). *Mudhakarat Akram al-Hourani (Memoirs of Akram al-Hourani)*. Cairo: Madbouli.

'Issa, Mahmoud. (2016). *Matar al-Ghiyab (The Rain of Absence)*. Beirut: Dar al-Khayal.

Jabin, Ibrahim al-. (2011). Khurafat al-Holocaust al-'Alawi (The Myth of the Alawi Holocaust). *Al-Hiwar al-Mutamadan*, 30 October. www.ahewar.org/debat/show.art.asp?aid=281657

Karabit, Aram. (2010). *Rihlat ila al-Majhul: Yawmiyati fi al-Sujun al-Suriyya (A Journey to the Unknown: My Diaries of Syrian Prisons)*. Dar Mada lil-Nashr.

Khalifa, Khaled. (2008). *Madih al-Karahiyya (In Praise of Hatred)*. Beirut: Dar al-Adab.

Khalifa, Mustafa. (2008) *Al-Qawqa'ah (The Shell)*. Beirut: Dar al-Adab.

Khani, Khaled al-. (2013). 'Isht l-arwi lakum Tufulati, wa 'Ayna Abi wa Majzarat Hama (I Lived to Narrate to You about My Childhood, My Father's Eyes, and the Massacre of Hama). *Orient*, 27 January. www.orient-news.net/ar/news_show/1723

Kuluna Shurka' fi al-Watan. (2012a). Khaled Ghazal Yushakil fi Idlib Katiba min al-Ba'thiyyin l-tasfiyat al-Nashitin (Khaled Ghazal Forms a Ba'thist Militia to Liquidate the Activists). 3 June. http://all4syria.info/Archive/43711

(2012b). Fadi Zaydan wa 'Omar al-Abdallah Yadliyan b-shihadathuma l-kuluna Shurka (Fadi Zaydan and Omar al-Adbadallah Give their Testimonies to Kuluna Shurka). 24 June. www.all4syria.info/Archive/45821

Ladhiqani, Fadia. (2013). Dimishq: Saba' Bahrat, wa Sijn wa Hariqa (Damascus: Seven Fountains, Prison and Hariqa). *Safahat Surriyya*, 1 September. http://syria.alsafahat.net/%D8%AF%D9%85%D8%B4%D9%82% D8%8C- %D8%B3%D8%A8%D8%B9- %D8%A8%D8%AD% D8%B1%D8%A7%D8%AA-%D9%88%D8%B3%D8%AC%D9%86- %D9%88%D8%AD%D8%B1%D9%8A%D9%82%D 8%A9- %D9%81%D8%A7%D8%AF%D9%8A%D8%A7- %D9%84%D8%A7%D8%B0%D9%82/

Majmu'a min al-Bahithin fi al-Maktab al-I'lami lil-Ikhwan al-Muslimin (A Research Collective in the Media Bureau of the Muslim Brothers). (2003). *Hama: Ma'sat al-'Asr (Hama: The Tragedy of the Age)*. Beirut: Dar al-Yaqadha.

Malas, Mohammad. (1994). *Al-Layl* (The Night). Drama.

Mohammed, Ossama. (1979). *Khutwa Khutwa* (Step by Step). Documentary film. (2002). *Sanduq al-Dunya* (Sacrifice). Drama.

Muhammad, Yamin. (2014). 'Adasat al-Sulta ... 'Ayn al-Nidham 'ala Muwalah (Power's Camera Lens ... The Regime's Eye on Its Loyalists). *Bidayyat*, 6 January.

Mustafa, Muhannad. (2014). I'raf Adwak: 'Kata'ib al-Ba'th' (Know Your Enemy: The Ba'th Militia). *Al-Maktab al-'I'lami fi Banyas*, 17 May.

Naji, Abdallah al-. (ND). *Hamammat al-Dam fi-Sijn Tadmur (Bloodbaths in Tadmur Prison)*. NP.

Sa'd al-Din, 'Adnan. (2010). *Al-Ikhwan al-Muslimun fi Suriya Mudhakkirat wa-Dhikrayat: Sanawat al-Majazir al-Mur'iba min 'Am 1977 hatta 'Am 1982 (The Muslim Brothers in Syria, Memoirs and Remembrances: The Years of the Horrifying Massacres from 1977 until 1982)*. Cairo: Madbouli Bookshop.

Sadeq, Mahmud. (1992). *Hiwar Hawla Suriyya (A Dialogue about Syria)*. NP.

Saleh, Yassin al-Haj. (2003). Tariq ila Tadmur (Road to Tadmur). *al-Hiwar al-Mutamadin* 692, 24 December. www.m.ahewar.org/s.asp?aid=12903&R=0

(2005a). 'Ala Sharaf Halat al-Tawari': Hafla li Sayad al-Khawna bayna al-Qasr al-'Adli wa Sahat al-Shuhada' (In Honour of the State of Emergency: A Celebration to Catch the Traitors between the Palace of Justice and the Martyrs Square). *Al-Hiwar al-Mutamadin* 1146, 20 March. www.m.ahewar .org/s.asp?aid=34097&r=0

(2005b). Shi'arat Harb fi al-Madina (War Slogans in the City). *Al-Ra'y*, 12 June.

(2011a). Al-Tughyan wal-Akhlaq fi-Suriyya al-Asad (Tyranny and Ethics in Asad's Syria). *Al-Hiwar al-Mutamadan*, 9 December. www.m.ahewar.org/ s.asp?aid=286775&r=0

(2011b). Aya Nihayya l-Nizam al-Harb al-Ahliyya? (What End for the Civil War Regime?). *al-Hayat*, 11 September. http://international.daralhayat.com/ internationalarticle/306005

(2012a). *Bil Khalas Ya Shabab: 16 'Ama fi al-Sijun al-Surriyya (May We Be Freed, O'Young Men: Sixteen Years in Syrian Prisons)*. Beirut: Saqi Books.

(2012b). Fi al-Shabiha wal-Tashbih wa Dawlatahum (About the Shabiha (Thugs), Thuggery and Their State). https://souriahouria.com/ في-الشبّيحة-والتشبيح-ودولتهما-وياسين/

Sarraj, Bara' al-. (2011). *Min Tadmur Ila Harvard: Rihlat Sajin 'Adim al-Ray' (From Tadmur to Harvard: A Journey of a Prisoner With No Point of View)*. Chicago: NP.

Sarraj, Manhal al-. (2007a). *Kama Yanbaghi li-Nahr (As Should a River Be)*. Algiers: Arab Scientific.

(2007b). *'Ala Sadri (On My Chest)*. Beirut: Qadmus.

(2011). 'An Istirkhas Ruh al-Muwatin fi Surriyya (On the Devaluing of the Citizen's Life in Syria). *Safhat Surriya*. Syria.alsafahat.net

(2012). *'Asi al-Dam*. Beirut: Dar al-Adab.

Sha'bo, Ratib. (2015). *Madha Wara' hadhi al-Judran? (What Lies Behind These Walls?)*. Beirut: Dar al-Adab.

Shantut, Khaled Ahmad al-. (ND). Mudhakarat Mudaris Falsafa (Diaries of a Philosophy Teacher). Personal Website of Dr Kahled Ahmad al-Shantut. http://dr-khaled.net/index.php?option=com_content&view=article&id=178:-1&catid=36:2010-09-05-20-57-46&Itemid=59

Sharaf al-Din, Maher. (2007). *Abi al-Ba'thi (My Father, the Ba'thist)*. Beirut: al-Jadid.

Sharbaji, Ayman al-. (ND). *Mudhakrat al-Tali'a al-Mujahida fi Suriyya* (Memoirs of the Combatant Vanguard in Syira). www.sooryoon.net

Shilash, Asaad. (ND). Hawla Saraqib (About Saraqib). Zaytoun. www.zaitonmag.com/?p-627

Shmayt, Ghassan. (1993). *Shay' ma Yahtariq* (Something Burns). Drama.

Sliman, Nabil. (2005). *Daraj al-Layl … Daraj al-Nahar*. Latakiyya: Dar al-Hiwar lil-Nashr.

   (2011). Zaman al-Shabiha wa al-Baltajiyya (The Era of Shabiha and Thugs). *Al-Safir*, 17 June.

Summayya. (2012). Jirah al- Dhakira … fi Dhikra Hama (The Wounds of Memory – In Commemoration of Hama), 2 February. *Qisas min-al-Thawra al-Suriyya* (Stories from the Syrian Revolution). http://syrstories.wordpress.com/2012/02/02/جراح-الذاكرة-في-ذكرى-حماة/

Tamer, Zakariyya. (2002 [1974]). *Al-Numur fi al-Yawm al-'Ashir (Tigers on the Tenth Day, Collected Short Stories)*, 5th edition. London: Riyad al-Rayyes Books.

Tawfiq, Rami. (2016). Qariyat al-Mashi: Fantaziya Suriyya al-Asad Bayna Intihari Da'ish wa al-PKK (Al-Mashi Village: The Fantasy of Syria al-Asad between Da'ish Suicidals and the PKK). *Al-Ghorab*, 17 October. http://alghorab.com/?p=5195

Tayyara, Hazem. (2011). Halab bayna al-Thamaninat wal-Yawm (Aleppo Between the Eighties and Today). *Al Jazeera Talk*, 28 June.

Tizzini, Tayyib. (2002). *Min Thulathiyat al-Fasad Ila Qadaya al-Mujtam' al-Madani (From the Trinity of Corruption to the Questions of Civil Society)*. Damascus: Jafra House for Research and Publication.

'Udwan, Mamdouh. (2003). *Haywanat al-Insan (Bestialisation of the Human)*. Damascus: NP.

Wannous, Dima. (2009). *Kursi (Chair)*. Beirut: Dar al-Adab.

Yazbek, Samar. (2010). *Laha Marayya (In Her Mirrors)*. Beirut: Dar al-Adab.

Ziadeh, Radwan. (2010). *Sanawat al-Khawf: Al-Haqiqa wa al-'Adala fi Qadiyyat al-Mukhtafin fi Suriyya (Years of Fear: Truth and Justice for the Enforced Disappearances in Syria)*. Washington: Freedom House.

ONLINE AUDIOVISUAL SOURCES

Al Ekhbariya TV. (2013). Tathir Qariyat al-Bayda min al-Irhabiyyin (Cleansing al-Bayda Village from the Terrorists). https://m.youtube.com/watch?v=9r9BWYWAKXo

Al Jazeera Satellite TV. (2012). Liqa' Hasri ma'a Walidat Zaynab al-Hosni (Exclusive Meeting with Zaynab al-Hosni's Mother). www.youtube.com/watch?v=8Jixh0PAAMw

(2015). *Al-Sunduq al-Aswad: Majzarat Hama 1982* (The Black Box: The Hama Massacre 1982). https://m.youtube.com/watch?v=CC-iP8iNXI

Channel 4 News. (2013). Al-Bayda: Anatomy of a War Crime. www.youtube.com/watch?time_continue=29&v=sp22U837O5g

Press TV (2013). Syrian National Defense Force. Documentary. www.youtube.com/watch?v=l3bN0n3m-VY

Qanat al-'Alam TV. (2013). Taqrir Qanat al-'Alam fi al-Bayda b-rif Banyas (Al-'Alam Station Report from al-Bayda in Banyas' Countryside). www.youtube.com/watch?v=trZPu3Ctv70

Spiegel Online. (2012). The Houla Massacre Video Special. www.spiegel.de/flash/flash-29263.html

Syria TV. (2012). Syria News, 27 May 2012. www.youtube.com/watch?v=HX7n0U5hvWQ

YouTube. (2013). Barouda Village Battle, Rural Lattakiyya. www.youtube.com/watch?v=ttV8jPGYsp4

DOCUMENTARY SOURCES

Amnesty International. (1983). *Report from Amnesty International to the Government of the Syrian Arab Republic*. Amnesty International.

(2001). *Syria: Torture, Despair and Dehumanization in Tadmur Military Prison*. AI Index 24/014/2001.

Asad, Bashar al-. (2011). President Bashar al-Asad Speech at Damascus University. 20 June.

Asad, Hafez al-. (1980a). Kalimat al-Sayyid al-Ra'is Hafez al-Asad fi al-Dhikra al-Sabi'at 'Ashr l-Thawra al Thamin min Adhar (Speech of Mr President Hafez al-Asad at the Seventeeth Commemoration of the Eighth of March Revolution). 8 March.

(1980b). Kalimat al-Sayyid al-Ra'is Hafez al-Asad fi al-Jalsa al-Khitamiyya lil-Mu'tamar al-Qawmi al Thalith 'Ashr (Speech of Mr President Hafez al-Asad to the Closing Session of the Thirteenth National Congress). 2 August.

(1982). Kalimat al-Sayyid al-Ra'is Hafez al-Asad fi al-Dhikra al-Tasi'at 'Ashr l-Thawra al Thamin min Adhar (Speech of Mr President Hafez al-Asad at the Nineteenth Commemoration of the Eighth of March Revolution). 7 March.

Asad, Rif'at al-. (1980). Khitab al-Rafiq al-Doctor Rif'at al-Asad fi al-Mu'tamar al-Qutri al-Sabi' l-hizb al-Ba'th al-'Arabi al-Ishtraki (Speech of Comrade Dr Rif'at al-Asad to the Seventh Regional Congress). January.

Human Rights Watch. (1991). *Syria Unmasked: The Supression of Human Rights by the Asad Regime*. New Haven: Yale University Press.

(2011). *We have Never Seen Such Horrors: Crimes against Humanity by Syrian Security Forces*. Human Rights Watch. June.

(2012). *In Cold Blood: Summary Execution by Syrian Security Forces and Pro-Government Militia*. Human Rights Watch. April.

(2013a). *No One Is Left Human Rights Watch: Summary Executions by Syrian Security Forces in al-Bayda and Baniyas*. Human Rights Watch. September.

(2013b). *You Can Still See their Blood: Executions, Indiscriminate Shootings, and Hostage Taking by Opposition Forces in Latakia Countryside*. Human Rights Watch. October.

SHRC (Syrian Human Rights Committee). (2001). *Report on the Human Rights Situation in Syria over a Twenty-Year Period, 1979–1999*. London: Syrian Human Rights Committee.

(ND). Qa'imat al-Mafqudin (List of the Disappeared). www.shrc.org/?page_id=15623

SNHR (Syrian Network for Human Rights). (2015a). *Ma la Yaqil 'an 516 Majzara fir 'am 2015 wa 55 Majzara fi Kanun al-Awal* (Not Less than 516 Massacres in 2015 and 55 Massacres in December). www.sn4hr.org.

(2015b). *Hasad Arba' Sanawat l-Abraz al-Majazir fi Suriyya* (Four-Year Census of the Most Notable Massacres in Syria). www.sn4hr.org.

NEWSPAPERS AND MAGAZINES

Abyad wa Aswad
Al-Ba'th
al-Munadil
Al-Thawra
Middle East Mirror, 14/145, 31 July 2000
Middle East Monitor, 24 November 2000
Syria Today
Tishrin

Index

Entries which refer exclusively to footnotes are indicated in *italics*

Other Books in the Series